AF477888

*New Perspectives in Policy & Politics*
Edited by Sarah Ayres, Steve Martin and Felicity Matthews

# MEDIA AND GOVERNANCE

## Exploring the role of news media in complex systems of governance

Edited by Thomas Schillemans and Jon Pierre

First published in Great Britain in 2019 by

Policy Press
University of Bristol
1-9 Old Park Hill
Bristol
BS2 8BB
UK
t: +44 (0)117 954 5940
pp-info@bristol.ac.uk
www.policypress.co.uk

North America office:
Policy Press
c/o The University of Chicago Press
1427 East 60th Street
Chicago, IL 60637, USA
t: +1 773 702 7700
f: +1 773 702 9756
sales@press.uchicago.edu
www.press.uchicago.edu



*Policy & Politics* is a leading international journal in the field of public and social policy, published by Policy Press. Spanning the boundaries between theory and practice and linking macro-scale debates with micro-scale issues, it seeks to analyse new trends and advance knowledge by publishing research at the forefront of academic debates. It is published four times a year, and is ranked on the Thomson Reuters Social Science Citation Index. Please visit the website for more information: http://policypress.co.uk/journals/policy-and-politics

British Library Cataloguing in Publication Data
A catalogue record for this book is available from the British Library

Library of Congress Cataloging-in-Publication Data
A catalog record for this book has been requested

ISBN 978-1-4473-4143-7 hardcover
ISBN 978-1-4473-4145-1 ePub
ISBN 978-1-4473-4146-8 Mobi
ISBN 978-1-4473-4144-4 epdf

The right of Thomas Schillemans and Jon Pierre to be identified as editors of this work has been asserted by them in accordance with the Copyright, Designs and Patents Act 1988.



The statements and opinions contained within this publication are solely those of the editors and contributors and not of the University of Bristol or Policy Press. The University of Bristol and Policy Press disclaim responsibility for any injury to persons or property resulting from any material published in this publication.

Policy Press works to counter discrimination on grounds of gender, race, disability, age and sexuality.

Cover design by Policy Press
Front cover image: kindly supplied by Asif Akbar

# Contents

# List of figures and tables

## Figures



## Tables

# Notes on contributors

**Saar Alon-Barkat** is a postdoctoral researcher at the Institute of Public Administration at Leiden University. His main research interest is in the interrelations between bureaucracies and their external audiences, and their implications for democracy. His doctoral research project focused on bureaucracies' use of symbolic elements in their communication with citizens and their effect on citizens' perceptions of government organisations.

**Anna Christmann** was a postdoctoral fellow at the Centre for Democracy Studies at the University of Zurich until 2013, when she started working for the science ministry in Stuttgart. Since 2017, Anna Christmann has been an elected member of the German Bundestag.

**Monika Djerf-Pierre** is professor of journalism, media and communication at the University of Gothenburg, and adjunct professor of journalism at Monash University. Her research areas include journalism studies, risk- and crisis-communication, political communication, and gender studies.

**Andres Friedrichsmeier** is consultant at the Ministry of Education, Youth and Sports, at the Free State of Thuringia, Germany.

**Sharon Gilad** is associate professor at the Federmann School of Public Policy and Government and the Political Science Department, at the Hebrew University of Jerusalem. Her research focuses on public agencies and civil servants' responses to external pressures and societal concerns. Methodologically, she specialises in mixed-methods designs, combining quantitative and qualitative tools within the same projects.

**Karin Hasler** was a doctoral student at the Centre for Democracy Studies at the University of Zurich, and is now a freelance consultant.

**Erik Hans Klijn** is professor in the Department of Public Administration at the Erasmus University Rotterdam and visiting professor at the University of Birmingham (School of Government and Society). His research focuses on the impact of network management on network performance, the role of trust in complex decision-making, public private partnerships, the influence of media attention on complex decision-making, and public sector branding.

**Daniel Kübler** is a professor in the Department of Political Science, and the co-director of the Centre for Democracy Studies at the University of Zurich. His research focuses on multi-level governance, urban politics and democracy, as well as representative democracy.

**Sandra Jacobs** is an assistant professor in Corporate Communication at the Department of Communication Science and the Amsterdam School of Communication Research (ASCoR) at the University of Amsterdam. In her research, she focuses on strategic communication of public sector organisations, mediatisation, and the construction of public debates.

**Frank Marcinkowski** holds a chair in communications at the Department for Social Sciences at Heinrich-Heine-University Duesseldorf, Germany.

**B. Guy Peters** is Maurice Falk Professor of American Government at the University of Pittsburgh. His research focuses on new models of governance, on comparative public policy and administration, and more specifically on American public administration.

**Jon Pierre** is professor in political science at the University of Gothenburg. His research focuses on contemporary governance and the changing role of political institutions. Key issues are political responsiveness and democratic accountability.

**Thomas Schillemans** is professor in public governance, accountability, behavior and institutions at the Utrecht University School of Governance. His research focuses on public accountability, behavioural knowledge for public policy and the role of the media.

# Entangling and disentangling governance and the media

Thomas Schillemans and Jon Pierre

## The book

Over the past decades, governments in most developed countries have for a variety of reasons reformed the ways in which public policy is designed and delivered (Pollitt and Bouckaert, 2004; Levi-Faur, 2012). Although the trajectories of change diverge across countries and over time, one recurring element is that many governments have systematically, although generally not programmatically, shifted executive powers and responsibilities away from the congested political-administrative centres of the state toward a host of third parties: nonprofit organisations, privatised state enterprises, networks, transnational and international organisations, semi-autonomous agencies and local governments. This strategy has enabled governments to increase their points of contact with societal actors and stakeholders and to develop networks for service delivery and governance (Peters and Pierre, 1998; Torfing and Sørensen, 2014). It has also meant that more actors – and different kinds of actors – now bear at least some responsibility for public policies. This endows them with a strategic interest in the news media as an arena where their interests can be served and where the credit for success and the blame for failures are distributed (Schillemans, 2012; Hood, 2002).

Alongside these developments in democratic governance, the media sector has undergone at least as significant changes as governance. The 24-hour news cycle, the rise of social media, and a more competitive and more vulnerable economy of news production and delivery have changed the landscape of journalism (Krause, 2011; Djerf-Pierre, 2000). In addition, the practice of journalism has increasingly emphasised critical scrutiny and the imposition of a mediatised format on politics (Mazzoleni and Schulz, 1999; Esser and Strömbäck, 2014). Meanwhile, the need – or the perceived need – to spin political messages and the ability to manage the blame game has added a new dimension to governing. On the one hand, the role of classical journalistic media has come under pressure, with the rise of social media, the furore surrounding fake news and direct challenges by populist politicians. On the other hand, however, the new social media reality offers opportunities for the traditional media, for instance as new sources of information (Brands et al, 2018) or for the verification of the credibility of sources (Fletcher et al, 2017). These parallel but, at least in their early stages, not closely integrated processes have had the joint outcome of producing a new hybrid media system where public actors engage, and are engaged by, the media (Chadwick, 2013).

Thus, the past few decades have seen rather profound changes in the sphere of government, in the media, and in how these two fields engage each other. Yet we know surprisingly little about the nature of this interaction and how it shapes government, public policy, governance or the media industry and social media. We only have scattered accounts of bureaucracies' strategies to deal with the news media or the increasing number of communications experts in government (Thorbjørnsrud et al, 2014; Maggetti, 2012). For example, it appears clear that changes in publicity laws have provided the media with new avenues into government (Roberts, 2005), and we 'know' a fair amount about how the rise of social media affects the work of politicians, civil servants and public officials (Ross et al, 2015; Meijer and Torenvlied, 2014). A stream of new literature further explores the intersections between media and governance. Researchers dissect how strategic communication has become integrated in the daily routines of civil servants (Salomonsen et al, 2016) who are found to 'serve the media minister' (Figenschou et al, 2017). Public, private and nonprofit organisations are often found to be highly media-oriented (Wonneberger and Jacobs, 2016) and reputational concerns, related to the media, may have a strong impact on the policies and outputs of public agencies (Rimkuté, 2018). This leads to profound changes within the machinery of governance and claims of a mediatisation of politics (Landerer, 2014) and governments (Garland et al, 2018).

This volume aims to further our understanding of both governance and media behaviour. We investigate the effects of media on governance, which has not been done before. It is highly relevant: research suggests that unelected political actors occupy a substantial niche in the daily news (30–40%) (Schillemans, 2012), and unelected and elected policy actors alike claim that the media are a highly important external contingency in their daily work (Cook, 2005). Yet, despite the fact that practitioners and observers seem to agree that the media is indeed a critical arena and actor in contemporary governance, systematic empirical research is scarce, scattered and hard to come by.

This book is an extremely rare, if not unique, collection of empirically based studies on the impact of media-related factors on political actors and processes in contemporary distributed systems of governance. Our research is situated at the intersection of academic disciplines which allows us to fill in blind spots and to address intersectional concerns. From a governance perspective, many have said that the media are 'important'; this book opens up this black box of media importance. We also open up the black box of unelected politics (Vibert, 2007), by looking at how new types of organisations, governance networks and disaggregated public bodies inform governance. In addition, we look at different elected and unelected officials within those bodies and organisations. And, inevitably, we address the many non-linear and, to be sure, often normatively ambiguous, effects of media on governance.

One apparent reason why the governance–media juncture has been so relatively ignored is that it falls between the stools of academic disciplines. Governance scholars acknowledge that the media is a powerful and uncontrollable actor imposing its format on politics and administration but their field lacks the analytical instruments to conceptualise its significance. At the same time, media and journalism experts observe the process of mediatisation but are, for the most part, not concerned with unelected policy actors as an object of study.

This book puts that field of research on the social science agenda. There are any number of approaches into this set of issues which should be of interest to both governance and journalism and media experts. The shift of executive governance from the centre of the state towards more peripheral local, bureaucratic, quasi-nongovernmental or proto-political institutions raises a number of questions that relate to the role of the media. Governance reforms basically rearrange the politico–strategic environment in which public policies are delivered. In this environment, public sector organisations and quangos may become more exposed to the media, may become more dependent on media for their vulnerable reputations and may make more investments in media management, as they (are supposed to be) more independent from central government (Fredriksson et al, 2015; Maggetti, 2012).


## Commonalities and questions

There are several commonalities among the chapters in this book. First, they all focus on *unelected actors* in governance (although a couple of them also include elected officials in their analyses). Previous research on the relationship between politics and the media has often focused on elected officials and election campaigns. Our objective is to avoid the extraordinary, spectacular nature of election campaigns and instead explore the everyday, routinised interactions between public actors and the media sector.

Second, all the chapters display the role of the media in *governance reform*, that is, the emergence of new fields of interactive and reflective behaviour between public actors and the media. One of the many paradoxes surrounding the media's role in governance is that although there appears to be consensus that the media are indeed influential, they do not have access to the processes where governance objectives and means are defined. Therefore, other fields of interaction – virtual or real, ad hoc or institutionalised, formal or informal – have evolved. These fields of interaction do not replace other arenas of governance but they do provide the media with a gateway into the sphere of politics and administration.

Third, all the chapters focus on the *effects of media* on some governance issue such as accountability, media management, organisational performance and organisational structure. The role of the media in governance can only be understood with regard to specific aspects of such governance or to specific governance issues. Again, the media is not a player in conventional governance processes and there is no general, conventional role of the media from which our studies can depart. Our research has therefore, by necessity, been designed so that it concentrates on some specific issue. Finally, all chapters focus on different *levels of governance*: central state, national policies, the local level, networks, unspecified sets of organisations, or some specific type of organisation such as universities. The book provides a comprehensive overview of different levels and aspects of contemporary systems of governance and the role of the media in that governance.

The 'governance and the media' theme invokes at least two sets of questions. The first set of questions focuses on the meso-level of unelected political entities and their connections to the media. Important questions relate to the 'uses' and 'practices' of media for public sector organisations. The issues here are largely descriptive and comparative, are aimed to gauge just how unelected organisations incorporate the media in their general strategies, and the barriers and risks involved in the process.

On the aggregated level of public sector governance, important questions arise on the role of the media as agents of public sector accountability and public sector change. Issues here are both empirical and theoretical. Empirical and comparative analyses have been made of the role of the media in holding executive powers accountable, both in routine cases as for misconduct and in crises. The theoretical questions emanating from this approach focus on the role of the media in democratic governance, relating the critical scrutiny by the media to the role of formal institutions of accountability (parliaments, the courts, independent regulators) and the citizenry in democracies.

## The themes

The book is organised in four groups of two connected chapters. It starts with two more generic, theoretical chapters and then proceeds to discuss three spheres of governance: the state, policy implementation and governance networks.

### *Media, governance and accountability*

The book starts with two chapters exploring the theoretical connections between media and governance. The first chapter, 'Governance and the media: exploring the linkages' by B. Guy Peters, links the governance debate to the role of the media and analyses how the media have evolved into powerful but academically somewhat neglected agents in the governance debate over the past couple of decades. Peters disentangles the governance process in four consecutive phases and discusses how the media affects those processes in a variety of ways.

Among the many theoretical issues involved, 'accountability' may be the most important, as both governance reforms and the expansion of the role of the media strongly affect accountability (Djerf-Pierre et al, 2013). The second chapter, 'Media and public accountability: typology and exploration' by Sandra Jacobs and Thomas Schillemans develops a typology of the various roles news media may fulfil in public accountability. The chapter is based on content analyses of media reporting and parliamentary questions in the Netherlands. It develops four roles of the media in public accountability and concludes that the indirect roles of the media – where they trigger responses in organisations and from parliament – is empirically more important than the direct role of media as critical scrutinisers of public organisations.

### *The state, change and the media*

The second theme focuses on the level of the state and gauges state interactions with the media in two highly disparate time frames: a momentous and unprecedented event (Chapter Three) and a 30-year time span (Chapter Four).

The third chapter 'Political control or legitimacy deficit? Bureaucracies' symbolic responses to bottom–up public pressure' by Saar Alon Barkat and Sharon Gilad, explores how some 30 Israeli bureaucracies responded to the 2011 mass protests (related to 'Occupy'). More specifically, it analyses changes in expenditures on advertising and campaigns for the various bureaucracies. The analysis suggests that more tightly politically controlled bureaucracies are more responsive to the social protests, that is, that those bureaucracies are more inclined to advertise themselves in response to the social protests. In that sense, the traditional bureaucracies (directly managed and financed by politically elected leaders) respond more readily and strongly to bottom-up public pressure than their more autonomous cousins. The fourth chapter, 'Mediatised local government: social media activity and media strategies among local government officials 1989–2010' by Monika Djerf-Pierre and Jon Pierre, adopts a radically different temporal perspective. It reports a study on how elected and unelected local officials in Sweden attune to the media over time; how they use the media, rate the media and cooperate (or not) with the media. Their study draws on a survey with an almost unique longitudinal comparison of over 31 years, which allows the authors to assess how social media feed into existing patterns of media relations. The results clearly show that social media are presently not a game-changer. Social media intensify the mediatisation of local governance rather than replace conventional patterns of media communication.

## Policy implementation, NPM and mediatisation

New public management (NPM) has been the somewhat ambiguous name of the game in policy implementation in the past decades (Pollitt and Bouckaert, 2004). Proponents of NPM have taught us to disaggregate policy implementation from policy design and to use incentives, transparency and competition in order to increase the value for money. These four key NPM themes – disaggregation, incentives, transparency and competition – have immediate consequences for strategic media management and media impacts in organisations implementing public policies. These consequences are explored in a comparative discussion of government agencies (Chapter Five) and an explorative discussion of public universities (Chapter Six). In the fifth chapter, 'Fighting or fumbling with the beast? The mediatisation of public sector agencies in Australia and the Netherlands', Thomas Schillemans compares how agencies in both countries have adapted to their media environments. The study is based on a small-$N$ survey distributed among executives and senior strategic staff in public agencies in the Netherlands and Australia. The empirical material also includes interviews and focus group meetings. The point of the chapter is alluded to in its title: in both countries government agencies have made substantial changes to their internal organisation that allow them to get along with the 'media beast' (Mathis, 2005). The Australian agencies have done so more proactively, almost aggressively ('fighting the beast') than their more hesitant Dutch counterparts ('fumbling with the beast'). Irrespective of these differences, however, everyday policy practices within these agencies have come to be directly and fundamentally affected by the news.

The sixth chapter, 'The mediatisation of university governance: a theoretical and empirical exploration of some side effects' by Andres Friedrichsmeier and Frank Marcinkowski, pierces more methodically into some of the negative side effects of the media on public organisations. It relates the role of the media to the typically NPM performance-oriented policy changes in German higher education and some of the negative effects of these changes to core functions of universities. The chapter thus assesses some negative effects of the role of the media in governance. The analysis draws on content analyses of media reporting and some case studies. The results bear testimony to the supposition that NPM recipes such as transparency, league tables, competition and performance management may be hazardous for professional public services (for example, Bevan and Hamblin, 2009).

### Networks, media and attribution

The last set of two chapters focuses on one of the more prevalent, promising and problematic features of modern governance, particularly in Europe: governance networks (Peters and Pierre, 1998; Klijn, 2008). The first analyses how perceptions of media negativity affect the performance of governance networks (Chapter Seven) while the second analyses how the media attribute responsibility and blame for policy outcomes to the various participants in complex governance networks (Chapter Eight).

Erik Hans Klijn's chapter, 'Managing commercialised media attention in complex governance networks: positive and negative effects on network performance', analyses how managers of complex governance networks 'manage' the media, that is, how they influence the media, but also, conversely, how the media affect their policies. The study draws on a survey of managers of large governance networks, mainly in complex infrastructure projects. It finds evidence that perceptions of media negativity (or 'commercialised media attention', as it is operationalised in the chapter) negatively affect network performance. Network management, however, can be helpful to alleviate some of the pressure and to enhance the cohesion, trust and, ultimately, the performance of the network.

Karin Hasler, Daniel Kübler, Anna Christmann and Frank Marcinkowski contribute the last chapter of the book, entitled: 'Over-responsibilised and over-blamed: elected actors in media reporting on network governance. A comparative analysis in eight European metropolitan areas'. They explore whether the media manage to keep track of the effects of governance reforms in which responsibilities are shared with unelected actors. They studied the distribution of responsibilities in eight cities in four countries (Germany, Switzerland, the UK and France) among network participants and subsequently analysed the extent to which all participants are attributed responsibility and blame for policy outcomes by the media. They show that 'elected actors are clearly in the focus of the media when it comes to attributing responsibility for policy success or failure'.

## To conclude

It would be impossible, and probably somewhat deflating, to summarise the findings from the various chapters. The book clarifies and describes, compares and explains how governance and media connect and interact. All the chapters suggest that the impact of media on governance is substantial indeed, and that all policy actors, each in their own ways, now need to 'govern with the news' (Cook, 2005). As a consequence, it is fair to say that contemporary governance has become thoroughly, although not necessarily fundamentally, mediatised. Mediatisation is the process in which organisations and institutions adapt themselves to some extent to the rules, norms and values of the media (Hjarvard, 2013). Actors in modern governance respond to media pressure and have altered their routines and practices in order to be able to operate effectively.

Mediatisation has profound effects on governance, as this book documents. Those effects are, however, often normatively ambiguous. On the one hand it is found that the media environment may have negative effects on performance (Chapter Seven) and may also induce perverse side effects (Chapter Six). Simultaneously, however, do the media also help sort out complex issues of responsibility in governance settings (Chapter Eight) and do the media also assist the traditional democratic power centres, such as parliament (Chapter Two)? The effects are thus manifold and do not fit easily in a simple black-and-white normative framework.

Furthermore, this book is set in a governance context of transformation, where all sorts of unelected agents have become integrated in policy processes. The book is set in a media context of profound change, with shifting economies, professional styles, news formats and types of media. It documents and describes many of those changes, and they go in many directions. However, perhaps somewhat surprisingly, a common thread running through most chapters is that those changes in governance and media also confirm and reconfigure traditional patterns and roles. It is, for example, found that the traditionally most media-attuned local government officials are also those who take up social media most readily (Chapter

Four). Bureaucracies operating closer to the political power centre are more responsive to public pressure than those with more autonomy (Chapter Three).

All in all, then, the undercurrents in this book are confirmatory. At the surface level, the chapters sketch a vivid empirical portrait of media and governance in nine western democracies. They connect the somewhat disconnected academic worlds of media and governance studies and produce a rare collection of comparative studies at the intersection of academic communities. The undercurrent confirms the relevance of the transformations of media and governance and, thus, the mediatisation of governance. But the undercurrent is also confirmatory in the sense that while traditional forms of governance and media are indeed changing, traditional power centres, relationships and practices are reconstituted and reconfirmed.

## References

Bevan, G, Hamblin, R, 2009, Hitting and missing targets by ambulance services for emergency calls: Effects of different systems of performance measurement within the UK, *Journal of the Royal Statistical Society: Series A* (Statistics in Society) 172, 1, 161–90.

Brands, B, Graham, T, Broersma, M, 2018, Social media sourcing practices: How Dutch newspapers use tweets in political news coverage, in J Schwanholz, T Graham, P Stoll (eds) *Managing democracy in the digital age*, pp 159-78, Berlin: Springer.

Chadwick, A, 2013, *The hybrid media system: Politics and power*, Oxford: Oxford University Press.

Cook, T, 2005, *Governing with the news: The news media as a political institution*, Chicago, IL: University of Chicago Press.

Djerf-Pierre, M, 2000, Squaring the circle: News in public service and commercial television in Sweden 1956–1999, *Journalism Studies* 1, 2, 239–60.

Djerf-Pierre, M, Ekström, M, Johansson, B, 2013, Policy failure or moral scandal? Political accountability, journalism and new public management, *Media, Culture and Society* 35, 8, 960–76.

Esser, F, Strömbäck, J, 2014, *Mediatization of politics: Understanding the transformation of Western democracies*, London: Palgrave Macmillan.

Figenschou, T, Karlsen, R, Kolltveit, K, Thorbjørnsrud, K, 2017, Serving the media ministers: A mixed methods study on the personalization of ministerial communication, *The International Journal of Press/Politics* 22, 4, 411-30.

Fletcher, R, Schifferes, S, Thurman, N, 2017, Building the 'Truthmeter'. Training algorithms to help journalists assess the credibility of social media sources, *Convergence*, https://doi.org/10.1177/1354856517714955

Fredriksson, M, Schillemans, T, Pallas, J, 2015, Determinants of organizational mediatization: An analysis of the adaption of Swedish government agencies to news media, *Public Administration*, https://doi.org/10.1111/padm.12184

Garland, R, Tambini, D, Couldry, N, 2018, Has government been mediatized? A UK perspective, *Media, Culture & Society* 40, 4, 496–513. Hjarvard, S, 2013, The *mediatization of culture and society*, Oxford: Routledge.

Hood, C, 2002, The risk game and the blame game, *Government and Opposition* 37, 1, 15–37.

Klijn, EH, 2008, Governance and governance networks in Europe: An assessment of ten years of research on the theme, *Public Management Review* 10, 4, 505–25.

Krause, M, 2011, Reporting and the transformations of the journalistic field: US news media, 1890–2000, *Media, Culture and Society* 33, 1, 89–104.

Landerer, N, 2014, Opposing the government but governing the audience? Exploring the differential mediatization of parliamentary actors in Switzerland, *Journalism Studies* 15, 3, 304-20.

Levi-Faur, D (ed), 2012, *The Oxford handbook of governance*, Oxford: Oxford University Press. Maggetti, M, 2012, The media accountability of independent regulatory agencies, *European Political Science Review* 4, 3, 385–408.

Maggetti, M, 2012, 'The media accountability of independent regulatory agencies', *European Political Science Review*, 4, 3, 385–408.

Mathis, M, 2005, *Feeding the media beast: An easy recipe for great publicity*, West Lafayette, IN: Purdue University Press.

Mazzoleni, G, Schulz, W, 1999, 'Mediatization' of politics: A challenge for democracy?, *Political Communication* 16, 3, 247–61.

Meijer, AJ, Torenvlied, R, 2014, Social media and the new organization of government communications: An empirical analysis of Twitter usage by the Dutch police, *The American Review of Public Administration*, https://doi.org/10.1177/0275074014551381

Peters, BG, Pierre, J, 1998, Governance without government? Rethinking public administration, *Journal of Public Administration Research and Theory* 8, 2, 223–43.

Pollitt, C, Bouckaert, G, 2004, *Public management reform: A comparative analysis*, Oxford: Oxford University Press.

Rimkutė, D, 2018, Organizational reputation and risk regulation: The effect of reputational threats on agency scientific outputs, *Public Administration* 96, 1, 70-83.

Roberts, AS, 2005, Spin control and freedom of information: Lessons for the United Kingdom from Canada, *Public Administration* 83, 1, 1–23.

Ross, K, Fountaine, S, Comrie, M, 2015, Facing up to Facebook: Politicians, publics and the social media(ted) turn in New Zealand, *Media, Culture and Society* 37, 2, 251–69.

Schillemans, T, 2012, *Mediatization of public services: How organizations adapt to news media*, Frankfurt: Peter Lang.

Salomonsen, H, Frandsen, F, Johansen, W, 2016, Civil servant involvement in the strategic communication of central government organizations: mediatization and functional politicization, *International Journal of Strategic Communication* 10, 3, 207-21.

Thorbjørnsrud, K, Ustad Figenschou, T, Ihlen, Ø, 2014, Mediatization in public bureaucracies: A typology, *Communications – The European Journal of Communication Research* 39, 1, 3–22.

Torfing, J, Sørensen, E, 2014, The European debate on governance networks: Towards a new and viable paradigm?, *Policy and Society* 33, 4, 329–44.

Vibert, F, 2007, *The rise of the unelected: democracy and the new separation of powers*, Cambridge: Cambridge University Press.

Wonneberger, A, Jacobs, S, 2016, Mass media orientation and external communication strategies: exploring organisational differences, *International Journal of Strategic Communication* 10, 5, 368-86.

# CHAPTER ONE

# Governance and the media: exploring the linkages

## B. Guy Peters

Anyone who has been at least half awake for the past several decades would find it difficult to deny that the media has a significant impact on the capacity to govern and the style in which governance is produced. This influence can be seen most readily in electoral politics, but it is also pervasive in other aspects of governing. Presidents and prime ministers have news conferences, and they and other ministers invest substantial energy in 'spin' and in attempting to shape the coverage of public affairs to suit their own political and policy objectives. And even further down in public organisations seemingly lowly public servants may find themselves the subject of media attention if there appears to be a good story (see Schillemans, 2012).[1]

To understand contemporary governance one needs to be cognisant of the manner in which media, and perhaps more generally information, is used as a component of the process. The fundamental contention of the mediatisation literature is that institutions and organisations adapt to the pervasive role of the media (Pallas et al, 2014), and this chapter argues that the same is true for the processes of governance. Thus, contemporary governance reflects the extent to which the formal and informal actors in governance have adapted their behaviours to the media environment within which they function. Whatever the goals of a government, they must pursue those goals within the environment shaped (in part) by mediatisation.

At the same time that the media do appear to be a pervasive component of governance, there are also some pressures to 'demediatise' governing. This reflects something of a populist urge of leaders to connect directly to the people. This pattern may involve social media, but may denigrate most broadcast media. The most obvious exponent of this attack on the conventional media is President Donald Trump, but other populist leaders are having their own skirmishes with the media (Frej, 2018). For these politicians the task is not so much to adapt to the role of the media as to undermine the central place of media in governance.

The political pressures undermining the media, and especially mainstream media, have been described as 'post-truth' politics (Suiter, 2016). Claims of 'fake news' have been a mainstay of presidential tweets in the United States, mostly directed at the principal news organisations in the country, such as the *New York Times* and the *Washington Post* that have been less than supportive of President Trump. However, it is not just in the United States that questions about the existence of 'truth' in politics and policy have become important (Speed and Manion, 2017). There have been more general attacks on the role of expertise, including that of the media, and a rejection of established science in areas such as climate change and vaccination. And simply lying has apparently become acceptable political behaviour – President Trump has by one count made over 3,000 false statements since becoming president, and done so with impunity (Kessler et al, 2018).

The established, and establishment, media are thus in a somewhat paradoxical position. For many members of the elite the media are crucial sources of information, and crucial sources of accountability for government. For other elements of society, including other members of the political elite, the established media are conceptualised as 'fake' or 'corrupt' because they disagree with the messages being carried within the media. In contemporary politics this rejection of the media has, for some, gone beyond usual disagreements on politics and ideology. There are attempts, at least implicitly, to undermine the institution of a free press and to undermine any sense of objectivity in news, science or the universities.

## Governance in a media age

We have argued that governance is most fundamentally about steering the economy and society through some means of collective choice (Pierre and Peters, 2000, 2016). While much of the discussion about governance has focused on alternative candidates for the central actor in the process – a debate typically between the state and social actors – we have adopted a more functionalist position attempting to understand what has to occur for governance to be produced. To the extent that we are concerned about actors, we tend to assume that there is ample space for involvement of any number of actors from both state and society, and that the interactions among these actors produce governance, with different mixes producing different styles of governing.

Just as information, or 'nodality' in Hood's (1986) term, can be used as an instrument for policy making, information is crucial for governance. Indeed, governance can be conceptualised as a cybernetic process in which the governance system is heavily dependent upon information flows to and from its environment (Peters, 2013). This flow of information is used both to detect the conditions of the environment – meaning the society and economy – and to produce changes within that environment. In such a conception of governance the speed and accuracy of information flows become crucial to successful governance, and the increasing role of media of all sorts in society affects that flow of information. The question then becomes the extent to which mediatisation is facilitating the capacity to govern, and the quality of governing, or if it is skewing the process in any manner. All information flows involve a certain amount of noise and distortion, and the role of media in governance will be no different. Further, we need to differentiate the upward and the downward flows of information, and consider the differential effects of mediatisation on those aspects of governance, as well as the processing of information among decision-makers.

As I develop some points concerning the effects of media on steering capacities of governance systems there will be an implicit, and at times explicit, contrast with some 'Golden Age' of information utilisation and policy analysis within the public sector. The emergence of the Reagan, Thatcher and Mulroney administrations signalled a return to a more ideological style of governing at the expense of performing proper evaluation research (Vedung, 2013), and a greater emphasis on the short-term rather than longer-term consequences of policy choices (Jacobs, 2011). This meant that although information was still being utilised, the selection of that information was done more on ideological and strategic grounds than on substantive grounds.

The question then becomes the extent to which greater availability of media can substitute for some of these losses in policy analysis and evaluation, and enable governance arrangements to utilise large volumes of available information effectively. There is an apparent paradox in these interactions between governance systems and their publics. Never has there been more information available for those who would govern; and never has there been more information available for the public to utilise in challenging their would-be governors. But numerous critiques of media and its effects of governance appear to argue that this information is not being used effectively to create open and effective governance (see for example Helms, 2012; Hajer, 2009). These problems with decision-making are prime examples of mediatisation; the pressure for immediacy rather than deliberation that reflects the style of the media rather than good governance (see Klijn et al, 2014). The logic of the media becomes the logic of governing. The generic value of information qua information is secondary to its instrumental use of the media in either critiquing or embarrassing political authority or to ensure the media's continuing control of the agenda.

While governing has never been easy, contemporary governance is perhaps more difficult simply because of the complexity of the issues involved. Arguably most societies are also more complex, with ethnic, gender and other social differences having to be considered more actively when making policy decisions. As will be argued below, that complexity may be reflected in a fragmentation of political and social life that can be sustained, if not encouraged, by the availability of multiple media sources. That said, some politicians may attempt to simplify that inherent complexity and create simple narratives pitting 'us' versus 'them', and use media and social media to spread that vision of politics. Again, the post-truth era in politics makes constructing alternative views of reality easier, and almost expected. Indeed, it could even be argued that this fragmentation and complexity of society and the complex issues confronting policy makers have created an opportunity for the media to reassert its position vis-à-vis the political and administrative elites.

## Mediatisation and steering

I will now proceed to develop a set of points concerning the influences of an increasing media role in society on governance. The difficulty that arises in making these arguments is to differentiate the impact of media from the impact of the individuals who utilise the media in governance. Are there specific technical effects from the media being used, or are the effects primarily a function of the individual actors involved in the production and dissemination of information and those who attempt to utilise the media for governance purposes (and often their own political purposes)? The relationships among these sets of variables are almost certainly complex interactions, but it is important to attempt to sort out how much of the observed issues in governance are merely extensions of the 'normal' behaviour of political and social actors.

### Agendas: more open, but potentially skewed

For governance systems to be able to steer they need to receive information from their environment concerning the conditions within that environment. Further, in Eastonian terms, the system must be open to the wants and demands from citizens in the surrounding polity. Expressed in other ways, what impact does the increasing media role in society have on the pattern of agenda setting for contemporary governance (Baumgartner and Jones, 2010), and what effects, if any, does changing agenda setting have on governance?

The conventional description of agenda-setting patterns for the 'advanced democracies' has become punctuated equilibrium. The evidence from an extensive corpus of research points out that agenda items come and go rather quickly, with one item flashing onto the political scene, but then being supplanted equally quickly by another, and then another. This vision of agenda setting can be contrasted with other views that stress the role of political elites in setting and managing agendas (Cobb and Elder, 1972; see also Rose and Mellon, 2011). This contrast in perspectives can, for example, be seen in Chapter Eight.

The dominance of formal political institutions and leaders over the policy agenda has almost certainly been overstated, and more open models, such as the several versions of the multiple streams approach (Zahariadis, 2007), have provided a more open perspective on this crucial stage of the governance, and policy, process. The increase in the mediatisation of policy making and governance more generally has had the positive effect of opening the policy agenda. To the extent that the agenda for public sector action can be made more inclusive then more segments of society have some opportunity to influence the actions of their governments.

With widespread media penetration into all aspects of our lives, the public agenda should be more open, but the question may be: open to what? Some issues are easier to frame than are others for a mass political audience, and different audiences will understand issues differently (for a brief review see Scheufele and Tewksbury, 2007). In general, issues that can be encapsulated in relatively simple statements, or even better in pictures, can be more effective than more complex issues. Further, the immediacy of media coverage may again deflect attention from longer-term and less obvious issues toward apparently simpler issues. If we consider agenda setting as processing information about wants and demands, then the system will be seen as having a strong bias toward certain types of issues.

At least some of the bias built into the flow of information for governance results from transformation of the media itself. The time available for the delivery of information and opinion in the broadcast media is generally restricted to short 'sound bites' (see below). The tendency to depend upon short snippets of information also tends to emphasise the existence of problems rather than the nature of solutions. Discussing alternative solutions to complex public problems requires time and detail that may not be possible in the contemporary format for the news. And emphasising problems can also be seen as means of using the media for enforcing accountability (see Chapter Three), albeit again without much detail and without much focus on ameliorating the observed problems.

Social media may be better at moving information upward to decision-makers, but even here attempting to cope with complex policy issues is difficult. If one barrier to effective governance is the complexity of problems such as climate change and poverty, attempting to encapsulate any meaningful statement in a limited number of characters would be difficult. Citizens may be able to express general sentiments, but not convey much in terms of substantive contributions to informed debate. As with the general mediatisation argument, the nature of the media here is influencing the conduct of governance. Mediatisation, we need to remind ourselves, is not so much about the media providing an arena for deliberation and debate between the public and their political leaders as it is about imposing and enforcing the media logic on the conduct of policy making and governance.

### Knowledge: the things we think we know for making policy

The spread of media coverage and the dissemination of information may create a false sense of confidence among citizens, and even among the political and administrative elites who attempt to control the flow of information. Donald Rumsfeld's famous rant about the knowledge of policy makers (Rumsfeld, 2011; Pawson et al, 2011) points to the dangers of making decisions without understanding the limits of the knowledge that constitutes the foundation of decisions. In particular his observations that there are things that we think we know but do not are especially dangerous for governance.

The Rumsfeld observations were about the use of knowledge within formal governance structures based on excessive confidence about our knowledge. The same may be even more true for individual citizens. To the extent that we are making evaluations of our governments based on unfounded confidence about our knowledge base we may be equally incorrect, although perhaps with less obvious consequences. Still, to the extent that holding governments accountable depends upon the level of information of citizens then in democratic terms this unwilful ignorance is indeed significant.

For both politicians and ordinary citizens information has to some extent been replaced by ideology and unmediated 'information' based as much on ideology as on management and analysis of information. An example is the spread of disinformation about Obamacare in the United States, and the claims about function.[2] As noted below, the segmentation of media and information may reduce the probability of self- correcting mechanisms providing citizens with a less biased perspective on the news.

1.  *Sound bites, tabloidisation and trivialisation* The first and more obvious problem that mediatisation has created for the knowledge of participants in the policy process, as well as ordinary citizens, is that the time available for the delivery of information and opinion in the broadcast media increasingly is restricted to short 'sound bites'. The evening news, regardless of the network or even the country, tends to be a mosaic of those 30-second reports and the two- or three-sentence interviews of policy makers or analysts. Again, somewhat paradoxically, in an era with a continuous news cycle and large amounts of time and energy devoted to 'news', very little analysis or evaluation of information actually reaches the public on a consistent basis.

    Associated with hard news being given in drips and snippets, 'soft news' tends to be pervasive on broadcast news and on the internet. Although these tendencies are exacerbated in commercial media they are far from absent in publicly funded media (see Plasser, 2005). Thus, the burgeoning time available for media coverage appears increasingly consumed by trivia and soft news. Indeed, some scholars argue that it is becoming difficult to distinguish soft news from entertainment programming (Baum, 2003).

2.  *Narrowcasting* A second dimension of the role of the media in generating less than adequate information for citizens, and even for policy makers, is the movement away from broadcasting toward 'narrowcasting' of policy and political information. In fairness, this transformation of information use is largely the result of consumer behaviour rather than the producers of information. There are any number of sources of information available to the viewer or reader who wants them, but most citizens attend to only a few.

    The proliferation of information sources addressing politics and policy issues has produced a number of news channels, websites, blogs and other sources that provide the consumer with information tailored to their preferences.[3] Furthermore, the print media in many political systems is also highly differentiated by political party or ideology (see Powers and Benson, 2014), so that readers as much as viewers may be able to select media that reinforces their views. Thus, paradoxically, in an era with so much information available citizens may actually be less well informed than in the past, or may be exposed to more but increasingly biased information. That having been said, as several other chapters show (see the chapters by Djerf-Pierre and Pierre; and by Schillemans, in this volume), government agencies and local authorities, too, use the internet to provide the public with information about public service performance, thus helping them to make informed choices, for example, when choosing schools or hospital services.

Few of us are so broad-minded about politics and policy that we enjoy reading or listening to opinions with which we disagree. Likewise political elites and policy analysts look for information that supports their own positions and preferences. Whether wittingly or unwittingly we gravitate toward those media sources with which we are more likely to agree. And thus our information and our knowledge of the world of governing is segmented, making it difficult for citizens and elites to even agree on facts, much less values, as we attempt to govern ourselves (Baum and Kernell, 1999). Whereas once the public consumed more or less the same information, leaving alternative realities to conspiracy theorists, several alternative realities now populate the political universe.

The tendency to consume a very limited range of information and opinion in a world brimming over with information represents a serious paradox concerning contemporary governance. The revived interest in policy advice in the political science community is important but to some extent may mis-specify the issue at hand. That is, rather than being a problem of inadequate advice, the problem may be an excess of advice and limitations on the consumers of that advice (Feldman, 1989; Peters, 2012). Those limitations include the tendency to attend only to sources that reinforce biases but also the simple inability to process and evaluate information with ambiguity and uncertainty, that is, almost all genuinely useful information about policy.

From the perspective of steering through information, this segmentation of media implies that any governor (whether government or social actor) will not be reaching, or at least will not be credible to, a significant portion of the population. Likewise, to the extent that political leaders also attend to a limited range of sources, the information on which they make decisions may also be biased. If governance is about the capacity to steer a society then this goal becomes transformed into steering various segments, or perhaps even more, reinforcing their movements in the directions in which they were already going.[4]

Steering through information points to the potential importance of the media in implementation. Although most implementation is done through financial or legal instruments, information, or 'sermons', can be effective and very inexpensive. With the development of 'nudge' and other information and psychology-based instruments the dispersion of signals to the public becomes even more important for governance (Thaler and Sunstein, 2008).

## Presidentialisation, leadership and control of the media

Although the term is almost certainly a misnomer, there has been extensive discussion of the 'presidentialisation' of politics in parliamentary systems (Poguntke and Webb, 2007).[5] As used in this literature, presidentialisation refers to the increasing domination of cabinet and parliament by the prime minister and the accretion of powers into the person and the office of the PM. Stated most simply, parliamentary governments became cabinet governments and then became prime ministerial governments. The role of the media in governance has been a defining aspect of 'presidentialisation', as well as one of the consequences. In the first place, the media, and especially the pervasive focus of the media on presidents and prime ministers at international events, has tended to place these executives at the centre of politics even more than they might otherwise be. When at a European summit or an Asia-Pacific Economic Cooperation (APEC) meeting these executives have little competition for attention, even if the opposition might wish to press their own agendas. Even in domestic politics campaigns increasingly focus around the candidates for the top position, even if the race may actually be defined in hundreds of individual seats (McAllister, 2005).

The presidentialisation of politics and the central positions assigned to, or assumed by, the prime minister has also been characterised by those chief executives attempting to control more directly the image of their government presented by the media (see Bevir and Rhodes, 2006). Governments have always hoped to control their images with the public but the increasing penetration of the media into governing has made that control more of an imperative. The difficulty, however, may be that with both narrowcasting and the expansion of social media the capacity of executives to control their own image among the public has perhaps lessened.

The difficulties faced in controlling media, and of course especially social media, does not prevent executives from trying. One extreme example of this attempt to control the media by a presidential-style parliamentary system comes from Canada. Donald Savoie (2008) referred to the style of Chretien government as 'court government', likening the governing style to a monarch. Research on the media management of that and subsequent governments has demonstrated even more pervasive efforts to control the media. Paul Thomas (2011; see also Glenn, 2014), for example, documents the extent to which the Harper government has controlled the manner in which the entire government, including their own ministers, communicates with and through the media (see Barns, 2005, for a very similar account from Australia). In this case, changes in the central political institutions are producing efforts to undo some of the openness in governing that has contributed, at least in part, to a more informed public. In some ways, this is a logical response of the political elite to mediatisation. In order to counter this development, the core executive perceives information increasingly as a strategic asset to be managed and used accordingly. Governments in most countries employ a growing number of people to manage their diffusion of information at the right time to the right recipients and forums in order to ensure that government controls the flow of information (see Dahlström et al, 2011). Similarly, senior politicians assess media appearances more carefully than before and may decline to comment or appear unless they have full control of the media format within which they are to appear. Again, while logical, this strategy is not conducive to what Mark Bovens (2007) describes as 'answerability' and accountability, a fundamental aspect of media scrutiny of government.

Although the presidentialisation literature focuses on changes in prime ministers, some of the same changes have occurred for real presidents. There has been an extensive discussion of the manner in which US presidents have used the media to enhance their capacity to govern, beginning perhaps with Theodore Roosevelt's discussion of the presidency as a 'bully pulpit' when print media were the only option.[6] For example, Kernell (2007; but see Edwards, 2003) has emphasised the importance of the president 'going public' and appealing to the voters over the head of Congress and other opponents by using the broadcast media.

There are several paradoxical elements in the relationship between the media and political executives. The usual assumption about going public is that this is a means of focusing agendas on issues about which the president is vitally concerned. There is, however, some evidence that presidents also focus attention away from issues that might be damaging (Miles, 2013). The bully pulpit then becomes a means of blame avoidance as well as a means for promoting active policy making (Hood, 2011). In either case, however, the central role of the president, and of other chief executives, provides them the capacity to shape the public agenda in ways that other political leaders would not find possible.

In other presidential systems, such as those of Latin America, the impact of media may have not dissimilar effects, taking into account the differing politics of these systems. For example, the media have been contributed to the capacity of neo-populist politicians to appeal to the public and to maintain their power once in office (Boas, 2005). The media focus on the president as the central political actor in these systems enables them to overcome the fragmenting effects of clientelism and neo-patrimonialism (Waisbord, 2013).

---

While there have been significant changes in the structural elements of the role of prime ministers and presidents, there also have been more subtle changes in behavioural elements, perhaps the most important of which is leadership. The notions above of the 'bully pulpit' and 'going public' by American presidents, and by inference also other political leaders, appear to have been replaced somewhat paradoxically by more timid forms of executives, responding to public opinion and emphasising damage control much more than exercising leadership from the front.

This analysis of the effects of media on executive leadership focuses on several constraints on effective leadership arising from mediatisation (see Helms, 2012). Perhaps the most obvious of these constraints is governing in a goldfish bowl, knowing that every action will be subjected to close inspection and media coverage. While that openness might be considered highly desirable from the perspective of accountability, it is also likely to result in safe decisions that may not produce the type of policy change required. Somewhat paradoxically, in an age of wicked problems and complex policy challenges political 'leaders' appear to offer modest attempts to policy reform at best. The pervasiveness of polling and their dissemination through the media is another, related, constraint on executive leadership. As has been argued popularly, as well as in scholarly analyses, politicians often appear to be following the polls rather than attempting to shape those perspectives (Canes-Wrone, 2010). The polls are not, of course, media per se but the rapid dissemination of the polling results tends to drive the behaviour of politicians, whether chief executives or not. Further, that information may make citizens wonder why their leaders are not following the views of the followers. Finally, although the development of media has influenced the manner in which the political executive functions, the public bureaucracy has also been influenced by the pervasiveness of the media. Bureaucracies have always been information-processing institutions but the growth of media influence in governing has accentuated their need to manage information and to interact with the media. On the one hand, public organisations, like the rest of the governance system, have had to develop the means of coping with demands for information under freedom of information legislation. On the other hand, these organisations have had to find means of protecting the confidentiality of sensitive information in the face of those demands, leaks and even hacking. And finally, they have had to find ways of using the media to improve their capacity to govern. 'Spin doctors' are usually considered to reside in the entourage of politicians, but they reside in the halls of government bureaucracies.

### Decisions: transparency, and the dangers of transparency

Finally, governance requires making decisions. The flow of information to and from society is crucial guidance, but this information must be processed and decisions made. The assumed virtue, and to some extent the real virtue, of mediatisation in the public sector is that it makes the processes of governing more transparent. A standard critique of policy making and governance more generally is that it is opaque and that ordinary citizens, and even other components of government, may not know how the decisions are being made, and why.

Any number of constitutional and legislative initiatives have been launched to try to open government to the sunshine, and to make the internal processes of government more knowable. A spate of legislation on the freedom of information during the 1970s has been followed by attempts to make the electronic communications of government more open to the public and to the media. This strategy does not square with the current philosophy to only disseminate information when it is strategically advantageous to do so. What is more important is that the emphasis on openness has more recently come into conflict with perceived needs to maintain greater secrecy for national security reasons in the face of terrorism. Those tensions have played out in day-to-day debates over access as well as more extreme cases such as WikiLeaks and the Edward Snowden revelations. The obvious intended benefit of these reforms has been greater accountability in government.

The media play an obvious role in promoting that openness within the public sector. That role for the media is, however, somewhat more complex than might be assumed. On the one hand, the media have been a major source of information about the actions of government through investigative reporting and more general coverage of political news. On the other hand, the generally enhanced climate of transparency has tended to feed back into facilitating a more influential role for the media in governance. Even if they would want to, it becomes more difficult for people in the public sector to avoid cooperation with media actors. This almost symbiotic arrangement may again deflect the agendas of governments as well as to some degree muting the role of the media.

While there are obvious virtues arising from transparency, we should not be unequivocal in our praise (Fung et al, 2007; Fox, 2007). The most obvious issue is that certain forms of transparency may inhibit effective decision-making, and particularly may make it more difficult for politicians to make difficult decisions. If they know the public will be aware of every vote and every argument, they will generally pick the popular if perhaps suboptimal route for action. Thus, increased transparency may actually reduce the quality of the decisions made by governments (Coglianese, 2009). Further, the interaction of an emphasis on relatively brief presentations of news and an emphasis on openness may lead to relatively simplistic conceptions of accountability. Indeed, although in many ways accountability within government is becoming more evidence based, if only through the rather weak format of performance management, the style of the broadcast media becomes more like old-fashioned embarrassment rather than a more evaluative approach.

Although in general negative news appears to capture public interest more readily than do more positive stories, these also may depend upon the ability to encapsulate them in relatively simple narratives about cause and effect and culpability. The current furore about care in Veterans Affairs (VA) hospitals in the United States makes this point rather well. The focus in this discussion has been primarily about the malfeasance, or nonfeasance, of officials in local hospitals. That may be true but the media have largely ignored the massive underfunding of the VA health system for years, a problem exacerbated by the ageing of the Vietnam War generation now coming into the system in large numbers. In this discussion the role of the media in transparency should perhaps distinguish between airing the decision process and airing the outcome of that process. That is, it is easy to argue that citizens need to understand what decisions governments have made and the basic logic of those decisions. It is less clear, however, that direct involvement in the process as it occurs can serve the same public function. Indeed, some crucial aspects of governance, such as the formation and implementation of elite pacts in post-conflict and transitional societies (Slater and Simmons, 2013), appear to work effectively only under the veil of secrecy.

Finally, one potential issue with the mediatisation of policy discussions is that there may be too much information rather than not enough. That is, if there are large volumes of unmediated information then citizens and even elites may not be able to process that information and may instead rely on simple partisan cues. Indeed, one strategy for public sector actors to avoid accountability may be to overload the media with unprocessed information and make them find the issues on their own (see Davis and Meckel, 2012).

## Summary and conclusions

This chapter has discussed a number of issues concerning the relationship between the media and the public sector in contemporary governments. These relationships between the institutions are complex and perhaps this chapter has excessively emphasised the negative consequences of mediatisation. Whether the changes being produced are positive or negative, there is little doubt that there are changes being generated by the continuing expansion of the role of media in the public sector, and by the ways in which those changes feed back into changes in the media structures themselves.

I have attempted to stress throughout that in spite of this chapter's focus on the media, there are also a set of broader issues about the use of information within the public sector, and within society as its members consider public issues. There are a number of paradoxes involved in the use of information and the role of the media. Perhaps the most important of these is that despite the range of information available, and the increased openness of the public sector, the participants in the process may in fact be less well informed than in the past.

Implied in this discussion is the assumption that these changes have made a fundamental difference in the manner in which governance is conducted. There is a substantial literature on the digital divide existing in many countries, even the most affluent with highly developed infrastructures for the internet and other Information and Communications Technologies (ICTs) (Voltmer, 2013). This divide is argued to be largely one based on class and geographical region, with some segments of the population being effectively excluded from participating in the economic and social benefits of these media. The same divide exists, to an ever greater extent, between the affluent and less affluent countries in the world.

This discussion of the role of mediatisation in governance points to the possible existence of yet another version of that divide. Arguably there are two versions of governance occurring simultaneously, but perhaps without the close connections that might be desirable – especially in democratic regimes. One of these systems of governance is rich in information and analysis, involving political and administrative elites. Its most recent developments have included an emphasis on 'evidence-based policy' (Pawson, 2006) and increasingly data mining. While perhaps not as rich in analysis as some periods in the past, the availability of large volumes of information can overcome some of those challenges.

The other version of governance is dominated by sound bites, tweets, soft news and other relatively trivial forms of processing information. This version of governance involves the large majority of the mass public, even in societies with well-developed broadcast media. This version of governance may also be highly segmented, with different opinions and even different facts dominating the discourse based upon ideology or religion or other social variables. There is information flowing within this version of the governance system but it tends to be relatively useless for those involved in governance who may actually be making decisions.

The apparent existence of these two versions of governance highlights a point made by Samuel Huntington (1974) some four decades ago. He commented on the emerging paradox of societies that were better educated and had much greater access to information than in the past, but yet would be largely excluded from effective involvement in decision-making. Huntington places the blame for this separation of the public from decision-making primarily on the nature of the issues being processed. It appears, however, that if this separation has indeed occurred (and it does appear that it has) then some of the opprobrium might also be directed toward mediatisation. This is true both for the broadcast media that emphasises soft news and social media that emphasises immediacy rather than content.

There are obvious implications for democratic governance in this divide. As Huntington pointed out, there is a clear paradox of populations who should be more capable of effective political participation being marginalised in the political process. While we may blame the media, there is of course the confounding factor that much of the population likes soft news and does not want to be bothered with more difficult policy issues; the media may merely be responding to demand. But this is hardly the type of participatory democracy that might be imagined for the twenty-first century.

**Notes**

[1] For example, mid-level managers in hospitals run by the Department of Veterans Affairs in the United States have been the subject of substantial media, and congressional, attention because of their alleged culpability for long delays in treating veterans (Greenwood, 2014). It is not clear, however, to what extent they are really responsible for the problems that have been identified.

[2] See http://mediamatters.org/research/2013/10/01/15-myths-the-media-should-ignore-during-obamaca/196181. The political right converted a proposal that physicians should discuss end-of-life issues with their patients to a scare campaign that Obamacare would somehow lead to mass euthanasia.

[3] This may be a particularly American perspective, given the presence of sources such as Fox News and MSNBC, not to mention the blogosphere, that provide very different accounts of politics, policy and governing (see Feldman et al, 2010). Even without the extremes of Fox News, the wide availability of social media and internet sources permits anyone to attend to only a limited range of ideas.

[4] In his cybernetic model of governing Karl Deutsch (1967) developed a concept of 'gain', meaning the extent to which any signal was amplified and produced disproportionate responses. The segmentation and reinforcement

through media can produce substantial gain, albeit in differentiated segments of the polity.

[5] The term is at least in part a misnomer because although presidents do tend to have larger personal offices and entourages than prime ministers, they are generally less powerful figures within government than is the average PM, facing an independent legislature that may be controlled by the opposition party or parties. Of course, there are significant variations in the roles and powers of both offices.

[6] Even earlier Thomas Jefferson said he would prefer to live in a country without political parties to one without newspapers.

## References

Barns, G, 2005, *Selling the Australian government: Politics and propaganda from Whitlam to Howard*, Sydney: University of New South Wales Press.

Baum, MA, 2003, *Soft news goes to war: Public opinion and American foreign policy in the New Media Age*, Princeton, NJ: Princeton University Press.

Baum, MA, Kernell, S, 1999, Has cable ended the golden age of presidential television?, *American Political Science Review* 93, 99–114.

Baumgartner, FR, Jones, BD, 2010, *Agendas and instability in American politics* (2nd edn), Chicago, IL: University of Chicago Press.

Bevir, M, Rhodes, RAW, 2006, Prime ministers, presidentialism and Westminster smokescreens, *Political Studies* 54, 671–90.

Boas, TC, 2005, Television and neo-populism in Latin America: Media effects in Brazil and Peru, *Latin American Research Review* 40, 27–49.

Bovens, M, 2007, Analysing and assessing accountability: A conceptual framework, *European Law Journal* 13, 447–68.

Canes-Wrone, B, 2010, *Who leads whom? Presidents, policy and the public*, Chicago, IL: University of Chicago Press.

Cobb, RW, Elder, CD, 1972, *Participation in American politics: The dynamics of agenda-building*, Baltimore, MD: Johns Hopkins University Press.

Coglianese, C, 2009, The transparency president? The Obama administration and open government, *Governance* 22, 529–44.

Dahlström, C, Peters, BG, Pierre, J (eds), 2011, *Steering from the centre: Strengthening political control in Western democracies*, Toronto: University of Toronto Press.

Davis, JW, Meckel, M, 2012, Political power and the requirements of accountability in the age of WikiLeaks, *Zeitschrift für Politikwissenschaft* 22, 463–91.

Deutsch, KW, 1967, *The nerves of government*, New York: Free Press.

Edwards, GC, 2003, *On deaf ears: The limits of the bully pulpit*, New Haven, CT: Yale University Press.

Feldman, M, 1989, *Order without design: Information production and policymaking*, Stanford, CA: Stanford University Press.

Feldman, L, Mahlbach, EW, Roser-Renouf, C, Leiserowitz, A, 2010, Climate on cable: The nature and impact of global warming coverage on Fox News, CNN and MSNBC, *International Journal of Press Politics* 17, 13–31.

Fox, J, 2007, Government transparency and policymaking, *Public Choice* 131, 23–44.

Frej, W., 2018, Trump named no. 1 oppressor of press freedom, *Huffpost*, 19 January.

Fung, A, Graham, M, Weil, D, 2007, *Full disclosure: The perils and promise of transparency*, Cambridge: Cambridge University Press.

Glenn, T, 2014, The management and administration of government communications in Canada, *Canadian Public Administration* 57, 3–25.

Greenwood, M, 2014, 40 US veterans die while on Phoenix VA waiting list, *New York Daily News*, 24 April, www.nydailynews.com/life-style/health/40-veterans- die-va-hospital-secret-wait-list-report-article-1.1767284

Hajer, M, 2009, *Authoritative governance: Policy-making in an age of mediatization*, Oxford: Oxford University Press.

Helms, L, 2012, Democratic political leadership in the New Media Age: A farewell to excellence, *British Journal of Politics and International Relations* 14, 651–70.

Hood, C, 1986, *The tools of government*, Chatham, NJ: Chatham House Publishers.Hood, C, 2011, *The blame game: Spin, bureaucracy and self-preservation in government*, Princeton, NJ: Princeton University Press.

Huntington, SP, 1974, Post-industrial politics: How benign will it be?, *Comparative Politics* 6, 163–91.

Jacobs, A, 2011, *Governing for the long term: The politics of investment*, Cambridge: Cambridge University Press.

Kernell, S, 2007, *Going public: New strategies of presidential leadership*, Washington, DC: CQ Press

Kessler, G, Rizzo, S, and Kelly, M, 2018, President Trump has made 3,001 false or misleading claims so far, *The Washington Post*, 1 May.

Klijn, E-H, Van Twist, M, Van der Steen, M, Jeffares, S, 2014, Public managers, media influence, and governance: Three research traditions empirically explored, *Administration and Society*, https://doi.org/10.1177/0095399714527752

McAllister, I, 2005, The personalization of politics, in RL Dalton, H-D Klingemann (eds) Oxford handbook of political behavior, pp 571–88, Oxford: Oxford University Press.Miles, M, 2013, The bully pulpit and media coverage: Power without persuasion, *International Journal of Press Politics* 19, 68–84.

Pallas, J, Strannegard, L, Jonsson, S, 2014, *Organizations and the media: Organizing in a mediatized world*, London: Routledge.

Pawson, R, 2006, *Evidence-based policy: A realist perspective*, London: Sage.

Pawson, RG, Wong, G, Owen, L, 2011, Known knowns, known unknowns, unknown unknowns: Dilemmas of evidence-based policymaking, *American Journal of Evaluation* 32, 518–46.

Peters, BG, 2012, On leading horses to water: Developing the information capacity of governments, *Halduskultuur: Administrative Culture* 13, 1, 10–19.

Peters, BG, 2013, Information and governing: Cybernetic models of governance, in D Levi-Faur (ed) *The Oxford handbook of governance*, pp 113–28, Oxford: Oxford University Press.

Pierre, J, Peters, BG, 2000, *Politics, governance and the state*, Basingstoke: Macmillan.

Pierre, J, Peters, BG, forthcoming, Governance and comparative politics, Cambridge: Cambridge University Press.

Plasser, F, 2005, From hard to soft news standards: How political journalists in different media systems evaluate the shifting quality of news, *International Journal of Press Politics* 10, 47–68.

Poguntke, T ,Webb, P (eds), 2007, *The presidentialization of politics: A comparative study of modern democracies*, Oxford: Oxford University Press.

Powers, M, Benson, R, 2014, Is the internet homogenizing or diversifying the news?, *International Journal of Press Politics* 19, 246–65.

Rose, J, Mellon, H, 2011,When the message is the meaning: Government advertising and the branding of the state, in L Trimble, S Sambert (eds) *Mediating Canadian politics*, pp 75–92, Scarborough: Pearson.

Rumsfeld, D, 2011, *Known and unknown: A memoir*, New York: Penguin.

Savoie, DJ, 2008, *Court government and the collapse of accountability in Canada and the United Kingdom*, Toronto: University of Toronto Press.

Scheufele, DA, Tewksbury, D, 2007, Framing, agenda-setting and priming: The evolution of three media effects models, *Journal of Communications* 57, 11–20.

Schillemans, T, 2012, *Mediatization of public services: How organizations adapt to news media*, Frankfurt: Peter Lang.

Slater, D, Simmons, E, 2013, Coping by colluding: Political uncertainty and promiscuous power-sharing in Indonesia and Bolivia, *Comparative Political Studies* 46, 1366–93.

Speed, E, and Mannion, R, 2017, The rise of post-truth populism in pluralist liberal democracies: Challenge for health policy, *International Journal of Health Policy and Management* 6, 249-61.

Suiter, J, 2016, Post-truth politics, *Political Insight* 7, 25-27.

Thaler, RW, Sunstein, CR, 2008, *Nudge: Improving decisions about health, wealth and happiness*, New Haven, CT: Yale University Press.

Thomas, PC, 2011, Communications and prime ministerial power, in J Bickerton, BG Peters (eds) *Governing: Essays in honour of Donald J Savoie*, pp 53–84, Montreal: McGill/Queens University Press.

Vedung, E, 2013, Six models of evaluation, in E Araral, S Fritzen, M Howlett, M Ramesh, X Wu (eds) *Routledge handbook of public policy*, pp 387–400, London: Routledge.

Voltmer, K, 2013, *The media in transitional democracies*, Cambridge: Polity Press.Waisbord, S, 2013, Vox *populista: Medios, periodismo, democracia*, Buenos Aires; Gedisa.

Zahariadis, N, 2007, The multiple streams framework: Structure, limitations, prospects, in PA Sabatier (ed) *Theories of the policy process*, pp 65–92, Boulder, CO: Westview Press.

# CHAPTER TWO

# Media and public accountability: typology and research agenda

Sandra Jacobs and Thomas Schillemans

## Introduction

We live in a 'monitory democracy' (Keane, 2009). On the one hand, many executive functions have moved away from central governments in what Rhodes (1994) termed the 'hollowing out of the state'. On the other hand, monitoring functions have partially moved away from parliaments to a host of non-parliamentary institutions, ranging from independent regulators to societal organisations and the news media. The media play a key role in these networks, as they are the prime 'connecting mechanism' between the different entities monitoring governments. Critical mass media are increasingly important in the life of public sector organisations in democracies (Fredriksson and Pallas, 2016; Korthagen and Klijn, 2014; and see Chapter One).

Although considerable attention has been paid to the news media as a scrutiniser of governmental organisations (Jacobs and Wonneberger, 2017; Liu et al, 2012), the theoretical connection between news media on the one hand and public accountability on the other has not been investigated systematically. This chapter therefore theorises and explores the roles of media in public accountability (Jacobs, 2014; Maggetti, 2012). The core goal is to develop a theoretical model for understanding the roles of media in public accountability. The key assumption is that the media are an important trigger that 'activates' formal accountability institutions, that is, parliaments and regulators, and can also be instruments of accountability.

This chapter has two aims. First of all, the discussion on the role of the media in accountability is currently somewhat opaque. Many public administration scholars (including ourselves) have suggested that the media are highly important for accountability, yet they (and we) have failed to theorise this role in sufficiently clear terms (Flinders, 2012; Maggetti, 2012). In a different outpost of the academic landscape, political communication scholars have also looked at the role of media in accountability. These studies have generated interesting results (Arnold,

2005; Djerf-Pierre et al, 2013; Norris, 2014), yet the relevance of their studies for public accountability in systems of governance is underexplored.

Secondly, discussions on the role of the media in governance often land in the trenches, where some authors come to negative value judgements (Flinders, 2012) while others defend the media (Norris, 2014). Empirical claims and normative assessments go hand in hand. In this chapter, we try hard *not* to provide normative assessments of the role of the media. Rather, we aim to shift the focus to the more specific question: how can we theoretically distinguish between the functions of the news media in public accountability?

The chapter starts with a review of existing studies of public accountability and media. We then develop four roles of the media in public accountability: sparks, triggers, amplifiers and forums. We subsequently provide suggestions for research on this topic, in order to set out a an agenda for the empirical analysis of public accountability and the media. In addition, we operationalise the main roles of the media in relation to public accountability for use in empirical research.

## Public accountability

In the last decade, research on public accountability has grown almost exponentially (Bovens et al, 2014; Busuioc and Lodge, 2016; Schillemans and Busuioc, 2015). This chapter stands in a research tradition where authors employ a definition of accountability that focuses on the mechanisms by which actors in public administration are held accountable. In this tradition, many authors agree on a minimal definition: accountability is understood to refer to a communicative interaction between an actor (person or organisation) and an accountability forum, in which the former's behaviour (in the broadest sense of the word) is evaluated and judged by the latter, in light of possible consequences (see also Romzek and Dubnick, 1998, p 6; Mulgan, 2003, p 9). Accountability processes start with an *information phase* in which information on an actor's conduct in the broadest sense of the word is disclosed. The process ends with a *consequences* phase, in which the accountability forum passes consequential judgement on the actor and may support this judgement with formal sanctions (Bovens et al, 2014). Sanctions range from public disapproval on the one extreme to dismissal or termination on the other.

Accountability forums have several opportunities to establish their oversight. McCubbins and Schwartz distinguish between *police-patrol oversight*, which entails a forum that examines some organisations at its own initiative, 'with the aim of detecting and remedying any violations of legislative goals and, by its surveillance, discouraging such violations'

(McCubbins and Schwartz, 1984, p 166). *Fire-alarm oversight* in contrast involves 'less active and direct intervention', as a 'system of rules, procedures, and informal practices that enable individual citizens and organized interest groups to examine administrative decisions [and so on]' (McCubbins and Schwartz, 1984, p 166). The forum's role is 'limited' to ensuring the operation of this system.

Bovens (2010, pp 953-54) distinguishes various types of accountability by the nature of the relationship between actor and forum. Vertical, 'traditional', accountability refers to processes in which a superior demands accountability from a subordinate. Horizontal accountability in contrast refers to forms of accountability where the forum is not hierarchically superior to the actor. It may alternatively be understood as a form of accountability to third parties. For semi-autonomous agencies, independent evaluators, boards of stakeholders or commissioners, interest groups and clients – and the media – can all act as horizontal accountability forums (Mulgan, 2003; Schillemans, 2008).

The distinction between different *types* of accountability implies that public organisations are faced by a number of formal and (potential) informal forums. The news media can be seen as one of the informal forums demanding accountability from public organisations. The distinction also implies that different forums may influence each other and that distinctive accountability processes are linked sequentially: the media sometimes publish critical articles about organisations in response to critical questions in Parliament or after recommendations from inspectorates. The converse relationship, parliamentary scrutiny or inspections triggered by media reports, is also possible.

Figure 2.1 summarises the ideal-typical accountability regime of public organisations. The arrows pointing vertically (to government department, minister and Parliament), diagonally (to the inspectorate) and horizontally (to the news media) represent direct lines of accountability. The red arrow connecting the news media with Parliament and inspectorates represents how news media coverage as a form of informal accountability may alert vertical accountability to Parliament and diagonal accountability to inspectorates.

**Figure 2.1: Media, public accountability and public agencies**

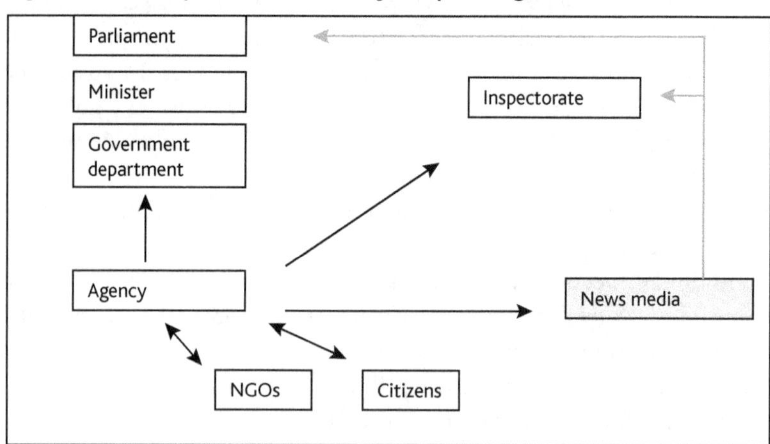


## Formal accountability vs accountability to the media: three core differences

Traditionally, news media have played a dual role in public accountability in democracies. On the one hand, the media *report* on public accountability processes, for instance by broadcasting question time in Parliament or by writing stories about formal accountability processes. In this way, public accountability functions as a media coverage topic. On the other hand, journalism has traditionally conceived of itself as a form of accountability in its own right (Entman, 2005, p 48):

> The ideal goal of traditional journalism has been to make power accountable: to keep ordinary citizens apprised of what government is doing, and how it affects them both individually and with respect to the groups and values that they care about.

Accountability to and in media contrasts with formal accountability in three respects: the motive that serves as a starting point for the accountability process, the accountability logic and the accountability procedure. The first one is the *motive* that moves the forum to start the accountability process. Whereas formal accountability processes are deliberately used by the forum to prevent corruption, induce organisational learning or improve democratic control (Bovens et al, 2014), journalists have two general reasons to ask organisations to account: keeping an eye on power (Entman, 2005) and providing news that fits the interests of their perceived publics (Eilders, 2006). When media ask public organisations to render account, they do not necessarily have the public good in mind (Chapter Seven).

This goal is also related to the *logic* by which accountability processes are guided. In formal accountability arrangements, public organisations work on their task fulfilment and are held accountable by official bodies, using formal norms and rules on a regular basis. The process is institutionalised and is designed as a means to reach stipulated goals. Formal accountability is predictable and is guided by an institutional logic that is dominated by bureaucratic and democratic values (Thorbjornsrud et al, 2014). When media are involved, the process between actor and forum is not oriented towards the same accountability goals. Journalists are driven by a media or, more specifically, news logic that teaches them to search for 'news' that is interesting to their perceived public (Thorbjornsrud et al, 2014). Their logic is guided by the rhythm and formats of their particular medium, and derives its power from the (self-fulfilling) notion that news media play an important role in organisational life (Thorbjornsrud et al, 2014). Accountability processes can arise as a consequence of journalistic news construction: journalists ask public organisations for information, evaluate the provided information and potentially criticise the organisation's behaviour (Cornelissen et al, 2009). Of course, journalists (ought to subscribe to) the democratic goal to hold those in power to account (Entman, 2005), but this democratic goal has a broader orientation than a specific organisation. Holding a specific organisation to account contributes to this general goal and can, as a byproduct, improve organisational operations or prevent corruption. Therefore the 'standard' democratic, constitutional and learning goals of accountability (Bovens et al, 2008) can be fulfilled as (unintended) byproducts of journalistic enquiries, yet they cannot be considered as the main goals of accountability to media.

A third difference between formal accountability and accountability to media is related to the *procedure* of accountability, thus the phases in the accountability process. In formal accountability processes, rules guide the procedures within the phases and the succession of these phases. When the media act as a forum, the process is different. During the information phase of the process, the forum – journalists – depend on freedom of information (FOI) legislation, the willingness of the organisation to provide information or their ability to lay their hands on classified information. The information phase thus largely depends on organisations that feel bound to render an account but are often not formally obliged to do so. Here, the organisation's spokespeople and communication professionals can act as gatekeepers (Meijer and Torenvlied, 2016). Organisations can also strategically disclose information to start an 'accountability process', thus trying to render social accountability (Klijn and Koppenjan, 2014, p 246). 'Stealing thunder' as a strategic communication act in times of crisis can also be characterised as an organisation-initiated way of starting an accountability process (Lee,

2016). From the perspective of the organisation, taking the initiative with information disclosure is considered to have strategic advantages as it – initially – gives the organisation control over the timing, content, amount and framing of information. In the accountability process between the organisation and the media, the information and discussion phases can be mixed up, as journalists gather their information and write it down or broadcast it at the same time. Contrary to formal forums, media do not have formal means to pass sanctions in the consequences phase. However, as organisations are heavily dependent on their reputation and legitimacy, negative coverage can have serious consequences for the ways they are viewed by stakeholders. Horizontal accountability to media can thus be effective through 'published voice' – i.e. critical coverage and published disapproval (Schillemans, 2008, p 179) – because it will reach important policy networks whose members are strongly media-oriented and media-influenced (McCombs, 2005).

## Media and accountability: towards a typology

The role of the media in public accountability has been analysed by a number of authors in recent years. The analyses are somewhat disparate and unconnected, and, also, tend to focus on the *direct* role of media as forums of accountability (Maggetti, 2012). However, when we accept that the news media can act as accountability forums on their own and may also play an important role in formal accountability processes, a wider number of possible roles emerge (Chapter Eight).

We have identified four different roles of the media in public accountability. We will describe them briefly below and then elucidate and illustrate them in the subsequent sections of this chapter. With this typology, we aim at disentangling the interplay between media and accountability in an analytical sense.

A first role follows directly from the natural task of news media: by simply covering organisations, the media already act as potential sparks for accountability, as organisations and their accountability forums may pre-emptively evaluate their policies and may – or may not – initiate an accountability process as a response to a media story. Accountability in response to mere media coverage is not guaranteed and will certainly not evolve in all cases. Nevertheless, it is well known that public sector decision-makers are highly media-sensitive (McCombs, 2005; Thorbjornsrud et al, 2014) and that media coverage triggers anticipatory reactions within organisations (Jacobs and Wonneberger, 2017; Schillemans, 2012). Media coverage of an organisation potentially leads to public accountability by formal accountability forums acting as accountability entrepreneurs. We therefore use the metaphor of the spark: a spark *may* lead to a fire but needs additional fuel from an external source. Many sparks will simply extinguish, yet when sparks fly through your living room, you are well advised to treat them all as potential causes of fire.

A second role is that the media operate as an accountability forum in their own right (Besley and Burgess, 2001; Maggetti, 2012). News media can ask critical questions on the basis of their own agenda, possibly supported by investigative journalism, and may aim to uncover untoward behaviour within public organisations through their publications. This role is in line with the classical role of watchdog journalism (Entman, 2005; Norris, 2014).

The third role of the media is that of an amplifier of accountability: the media report on formal accountability processes; they will for instance write about or broadcast Question Time in Parliament or the publication of reports by inspectorates. Media then magnify and potentially amplify the effects of formal accountability. It matters a great deal for accountability forums whether or not their critical comments and opinions 'hit' the media or not (Kepplinger, 2002) and lead to a prolonged news cycle with subsequent accountability demands.

The fourth and final role of the media extends from the above: the media may also trigger formal accountability processes. Media then function as a trigger for formal public accountability processes such as parliamentary questions (Van Santen et al, 2015). This function is comparable to fire-alarm oversight, as explained by McCubbins and Schwartz (1984). This role is analytically related to the previous role; one could say that the trigger role is similar to effectuated sparks (leading to real fires or, here, accountability). For research purposes, however, it is important to make this distinction, as will be discussed in the next sections.

The four roles are analytically distinctive but not mutually exhaustive (from the perspective of a single media report). Some roles might be a prerequisite for other roles (such as the spark or forum role for the trigger role) or media reports can fulfil two roles in one single report. From the perspective of an organisation, an issue might proceed from one role to another (for example, if media criticise the behaviour of an organisation in their forum role and the Parliament, subsequently, asks questions as a consequence of this media attention; the trigger role).

**Table 2.1: Typology of the roles of media in accountability**

| Role | Description | Phase | Accountability Forum |
|------|-------------|-------|----------------------|
| Spark | (Potential) media coverage may activate accountability forums | Information phase | Dependent on 'accountability entrepreneurs' |
| Forum | Media report critically on an organisation. Reports are based on either their own research or on information given by others (not being formal accountability forums) | Consequences phase | Media |
| Amplifier | Media depict formal accountability processes and potentially amplify their effects | Consequences phase | Formal accountability forums such as Parliament or Inspectorates |
| Trigger | Media coverage induces formal accountability processes | Information phase | Formal accountability forums such as Parliament or Inspectorates |

Table 2.1 summarises the four potential roles of media in public accountability. The different types will be described in more detail below, after presenting our research themes in the field of public accountability and the media.

## From typology to research approach

The aim of this research approach is to demonstrate how the typology can be used in research. For that reason, we indicate which research questions come up regarding our typology and present operationalisations of the four roles.

### Research themes

In general, this chapter treats the interplay between the concept of public accountability on the one hand and the media as an institution on the other. In an empirical sense, this process comes down to the relation between a public organisation (actor) that renders account to 'the media', which can play various roles in that accountability process. This relation did not receive much empirical scrutiny (Jacobs, 2014) and our typology yields several new research questions. Two aspects of this accountability relation serve as a source for research questions. The first one is related to empirical variation in the actor in the public accountability process: studying variations in actor type and their impact on accountability to media processes can generate new insights into actor characteristics that influence accountability to media. Second, opening up the concept of 'media' as an institution and focusing on different outlets and their interplay with different actor types yields new research questions that cover how accountability processes are started and develop over time. We will now elaborate a bit more on these two perspectives.

Public accountability processes are inherent to democratic societies. Defined as communicative interaction between an actor and a forum, they occur on micro-levels within public organisations, on meso-levels between organisations, and on the macro-level between democratic institutions (Strøm, 2000). If we focus on accountability processes within organisations, it is likely that accountability to media affects internal accountability processes (Jacobs, 2014). It is however not clear which characteristics of the accountability process play a crucial role and what the range of effects is. If we look at the content of the accountability process, we can conclude that there is a wide range of possible topics: finance, incidents, or administration for example (Bovens, 2010; Jacobs, 2014). As explained before, the accountability to media process can be expected to be guided by news logic. Thus, the topic of accountability is selected by a journalist who considers the topic relevant for their perceived public. This yields some interesting research questions. One could study the differences of the role of the media in relation to the nature of the actor. To what extent do the media function as an accountability forum for a specific type of organisations, for example, hospitals, compared to universities or ministries? How do the different roles of the media in accountability vary by type of organisation? And regarding the nature of the conduct, which topics are particularly relevant for the media as an accountability forum? It would be interesting to study the role of (crisis) history (Coombs, 2007): do organisations that have frequently figured in the news also attract more critical media attention in future reports? In addition, it would be relevant to look at spillover effects. If an organisation has to account for a specific type of behaviour (such as wrongdoing), to what extent does that topic also pop up in other accountability to media processes in the same sector or in other types of organisations (Zavyalova et al, 2012)? A comparative or longitudinal analysis could shed light on this issue.

If we take 'the media' as a starting point for analysis, several possibilities open up. One could focus on the difference between online and offline media in their roles as a forum, spark, amplifier or trigger. To what extent do outlets differ in their functions in accountability processes? The concept of intermedia agenda setting is relevant here. This concept describes how content 'transfers' between news media (Harder et al, 2017). Do online media for example function as a trigger for offline media to act as a forum? Do they vary in their topic selection? If we focus on the media in their role as a forum, the comparison between online and offline media could also focus on a related matter, namely the experience of the accountability process by the actor. To what extent do actors experience accountability to online media as an accountability process? How do accountability processes in which online media are a forum evolve? Thus, especially regarding the rise of new media, several new research questions emerge.

In sum, the following questions could be used to concretise a research problem regarding accountability and media:

1.  *Who is the actor?* Does the research focus on actors within an organisation, or on a specific type of organisation? What is the relation between actors, from the perspective of the research question? Do they operate in the same sector, have the same structure, or do they have the same tasks?
2.  *Who is the forum?* What types of media are taken into account? Which medium characteristics are relevant? Which aspects of the content are important?
3.  *What is the research goal?* Does the research aim at exploring or comparing accountability relations, in the present or compared to the past, or does it have an explanatory aim, focusing on identifying crucial factors in accountability?
4.  *Which method will be used?* Two methods are most likely for this kind of research: one could use a content analysis to analyse media content characteristics or employ a survey to analyse perceptions of organisation members, for example regarding the consequences of accountability to media for the organisation.

All of these research topics require further elaboration on their scope, method, sampling, and analysis when they are subjected to empirical analysis. The operationalisation of the roles of the media in accountability needs attention as well. In the following, we provide practical guidelines for the operationalisation of these media roles (as summarised in Table 2.1) that could serve as a starting point for the analysis of the role of the media in accountability. Some of them are operationalised with a content analysis in mind, but it is also argued that they could serve as a means to qualitatively discuss the media's meaning for the organisation in an in-depth interview or that they could be adapted to survey questions to explore the experiences of employees regarding the media.

### Sparks

Media can be sparks for accountability because the perceived risk of negative publicity invokes anticipatory reactions in public organisations and their accountability forums. Studies describe how media stories spark off a series of consequences in public organisations (Schillemans, 2012); even the anticipation of media stories can have profound effects within organisations. Some of the activities will be strategic, even Machiavellian, where officials seek to exploit the news. Other activities, however, will be introspective, aimed at the question: are we doing the right thing and are we doing it properly? People will gather data on the issue that has been reported on, just to be on the safe side and in order to review their policies. Experimental accountability research also suggests that accountability under uncertainty will trigger 'pre-emptive self-criticism' (Lerner and Tetlock, 1999). Furthermore, if one organisation is publicly rebuked in the press for a line of policy – for instance, excessive executive wages – most comparable organisations will critically look at their executive wages as well. In consequence, when media report on public organisations they spark off a string of pre-emptive and reflective activities in these and similar organisations and formal accountability forums. In that sense, the media are *sparks* for public accountability, although, of course, these sparks will not always be effective and many will simply fade.

A number of scholars from communication studies have adopted largely similar approaches. In his book on the role of the media in accountability, Arnold (2005) analyses the extent to which local American newspapers reported on the activities of 'their' local representatives in Congress in order to establish whether citizens were sufficiently informed about their representatives and thus were in a position to hold them accountable for their actions or lack thereof. Arnold focused on the *content* of media reports. While Arnold focused on the 'old' power centres in democracy, others have done similar research where they have chased the effects of media accountability in the sense of 'sparks' in other organisations. Davis (2003), for instance, zooms in on the consequences for accountability of the privatisation of police work – one of the core tasks of governments – in three countries. The study claims that privatisation of tasks creates an accountability deficit that may be dampened by the media. In a similar vein, Deacon and Monk (2001) investigated the role of the media in relation to quangos. In a more recent study, Maggetti (2012) looked at the role of the media in holding independent regulators accountable. He concluded that the media *can* be an accountability forum for these independent regulators when they report about them. And in a quite different study, Besley and Burgess (2001) analysed the macro-effects of media coverage in different Indian states. Their conclusion was that increased media coverage was positively correlated to government responsiveness to the needs of the people.

Besley and Burgess' work underlines that the media can only be effective as sparks when accountable agents anticipate potential media coverage and this, again, presupposes that the media are actually interested in their behaviours. It is common knowledge that political affairs are critically followed by the news media, but how about the relatively 'pastoral world' (Pollitt et al, 2004) of public organisations?

From a content analysis perspective, the media may act as sparks for accountability when they just mention organisations. Even non-critical media coverage in which an organisation is not the main actor can be perceived as a credible 'threat' from the perspective of the organisation when it points at (perceived) irregularities. Perception or 'implicit evaluation' is crucial here (Wonneberger and Jacobs, 2017). Thus, every report that mentions an organisation can potentially spark accountability. Keeping the previously discussed spillover effects in mind, we could also expect organisations to closely follow news in their sector or related topics that might affect them (Luoma-aho and Vos, 2010). Thus, media coverage on organisations or issues that are close to the organisation itself might also trigger introspection.

It is however questionable to what extent this role of the media can best be measured with a content analysis. Rather, one could use a survey or semi-structured interview to explore the media's role as a spark for accountability, as a spark only leads to a fire when all necessary circumstances are present. Attention and evaluation by employees are crucial here. In other words, if persons working for the organisation are either unaware of media reports or do not consider it important, the potential for the spark to lead to a fire (accountability process) is limited (Jacobs and Wonneberger, 2017). One could also combine content analysis and survey data here to measure differences in perceptions and content (De Vreese et al, 2017; Jacobs and Wonneberger, 2017). Questions could focus on the level of awareness of media coverage, monitoring practices and criteria that are used to label coverage as 'relevant' (Jacobs and Wonneberger, 2017).

### Forums

The second, and in theoretical terms most important, role of media in public accountability involves journalists in the role of accountability forum on their own (Maggetti, 2012). In this capacity, the journalist may question a public organisation, as the accountable actor, about its function, policies or performance. Investigative journalism leading to the discovery of malpractice or irregularities is the clearest example of direct accountability to media. This role can also be performed by a third party whom the media 'switches' to, such as an activist or whistleblower who can 'trigger a chain of unplanned events through media attention, political debate and action so that many audiences and criteria are mobilized in uncoordinated ways' (Olsen, 2013, p 452).

Some scholars have zoomed in specifically on this process of critical questioning by media. In a very interesting study, Clayman and Heritage (2002; see also Djerf-Pierre et al, 2013) focused their attention on the type of questions posed by journalists in the press conferences of Eisenhower and Reagan. They semantically analysed the questions that were posed, and one of these was the 'accountability question', in which the presidents were specifically requested to answer for malfeasance. Such studies implicitly assume that governments (and other powerful actors) are at least in part secretive organisations, and this allows journalists, in lieu of the public interest, to pursue issues and to uncover problems.

Other studies have adopted a similar perspective on media and accountability but they have zoomed in on the macro-level of the changing architecture of governance. In a series of case studies, political scientists have analysed how the media help to uncover and expose untoward behaviour. Smulovitz and Peruzzotti (2003) for instance analysed the role of the media in holding overtly centralised new democracies accountable in South America and Yankova (2006) explored how the media disclosed governmental misconduct in central and eastern Europe.

The media serve as accountability forums of their own when they act as critical commentators on their own capacity. Previous research that employs content analysis has clear operationalisations for the measurement of criticism in messages. In order to be considered 'critical', the story of an article or somebody in the story should explicitly evaluate the public organisation or mention dissatisfaction (Wonneberger and Jacobs, 2017). This could either be the journalist's or a third party's evaluation of the behaviour of a public organisation. The addition of a third party's negative evaluation is relevant since this includes the opportunity for whistle-blowers and others to use the media as a platform. Also, journalists often prefer to quote others' negative appraisals above making the negative judgement themselves. Criticism by MPs and inspectorates should not count as such, as they are formal accountability forums themselves; this is our third role (described in the next section).

The forum role could also be measured with a survey among members of the organisation to ask to what extent they feel criticised by the media

(Jacobs and Wonneberger, 2017) or among journalists to measure their role perceptions.

## Amplifiers

The third category is that of 'amplifier' or 'mirror' of accountability. The media then play no part in the accountability process as such but *display* the formal accountability process by mirroring and broadcasting the activities of formal accountability forums, such as Parliament or the inspectorate. Media coverage, then, is a reflection of accountability processes between two parties, a public organisation and a (formal) forum. The journalists have no active critical role; they are merely reporting, mirroring, accountability. However, by mirroring the exchange, the media may amplify and magnify the effects of accountability. The negative story can be seen as a form of additional punishment and as an informal sanction.

Furthermore, this mirroring-process is important, as it connects formal democratic accountability processes to the general public, which is ultimately the key principle in democracies. As almost all citizens know almost everything they know about public affairs via the media (McCombs, 2005), this role of the media is hugely important. Authorities aware that they are in the spotlight of the media can be expected to adapt their behaviour. Kepplinger (2002) has for instance shown how German MPs increasingly define their role as 'issuing statements' about current affairs. And Arnold (2005, p 12) aptly summarises:

> If legislators observe that journalists convey little information about legislative activity beyond what legislators reveal in their press releases, they may focus their creative talents on writing press releases rather than making laws.

With a content analysis, it can rather easily be measured whether accountability processes are topics of media reports.

## Triggers

A last role for the media in public accountability is that of *triggers* of formal accountability, extending from the spark role. Media are triggers of formal accountability, when their reporting is the cause of subsequent demands for accountability by formal accountability forums, such as Parliament or inspectorates. This is in line with existing studies analysing the extent to which questions in Parliament are based on media reporting (Wille, 2005; Van Aelst and Vliegenthart, 2014; Van Santen et al, 2015). The question of 'who follows whom' is a classic one in communication science, but these studies are usually not conducted from the theoretical perspective of public accountability. Van Aelst and Vliegenthart (2014, p 392), for example, conclude that 'the effect of media on written questions is stronger than the reverse' and indicate that 'most of the questions can be traced back to coverage in the days before'.

In order to investigate this empirical role of the media in public accountability with a content analysis, it is an option to focus on parliamentary questions. In those questions, one could look for 'traces' of follow-up accountability on media stories. However, social and political realities are complex and unidirectional forms of causation are difficult to come by. Despite these notions, it is interesting to investigate whether we can (more or less) for sure state that accountability processes that are found are 'triggered' by media coverage. By 'trigger' therefore is meant that in the parliamentary or inspectorate action a specific reference is made to media reports on the incident. For example, questions that are asked by MPs often start with a reference to a media report. A survey on members of parliament could also give insights into the role that media coverage plays in asking parliamentary questions.

## Conclusion and discussion

This chapter has developed, explained and operationalised a typology with which we can make sense of the role of the media in public accountability. We have made an effort to integrate existing views on the role of the media in society with existing models of public accountability. This has evolved into a typology in fours. The fact that media (potentially) cover acts of public organisations can stimulate self-reflection on behaviour and policies in public organisations. Next to that, media can function as an accountability forum and hold organisations to account. This is classical watchdog journalism (Entman, 2005; Norris, 2014), combined with the public accountability model (Bovens et al, 2008). A third role considers the amplification of formal accountability processes by simply reporting on them. This role is comparable to the role of the media as depicted by Keane (2009): media facilitate contacts between several monitoring institutions in 'monitory democracy'. Keane mentions a long list of highly disparate post-representative mechanisms of accountability. He writes about the rise of audit, independent regulators, participation mechanisms, social media, the blogosphere, integrity commissions and − the theme of this chapter − the news media. Ostensibly, these mechanisms do not have much to do with each other, but they are nevertheless comparable in the sense that they represent and inform the public, limit powers and control and establish public standards which they monitor. Lastly, media coverage can trigger formal accountability and thus serve as a fire alarm for formal accountability forums (McCubbins and Schwartz, 1984). Thus, media can act as a spark, forum, amplifier and trigger. It is an analytical typology: roles can overlap or interconnect in practice. Further research is needed to empirically analyse the presence, meaning and interaction of these roles. We provided directions for research that could gain more insight in the empirical value of this typology.

A remaining question to address is: how can we relate these roles to broader issues pertaining to the role of the media in contemporary governance? The role of the media in democratic processes is subject to permanent discussion (De Haan and Bardoel, 2012) or is even seen as being simply disruptive (Flinders, 2012). Sparrow (1999, p 25) has indicated that media are often compared with 'attack dogs' that are relentlessly critical of politics and 't Hart (2002) suggests that we now live in an 'inquisition democracy'. After a disaster or crisis, journalists and politicians both search for the institution which, or person who, is guilty and aim to hold them publicly accountable. This kind of 'inquisition democracy' prospers in a societal climate of 'guilty until proven innocent' ('t Hart, 2002). This observation ties in with Keane's (2009) claim that in modern democracies many other actors than Parliament – and especially mass media – fulfil monitoring functions. It may even be stated that mediatisation processes take place: politics and public sector organisations adapt themselves to their mediated environment (Mazzoleni and Schultz, 1999; Schillemans, 2012). The operational procedures and selection mechanisms of journalists – such as their focus on events and incidents, production logics and methods of framing – do make mass media in fact an informal forum for public sector organisations. Aggressive holding to account strategies may cause excessive caution. This is however not necessarily the case, as accountability to media can also spark functional adaptation of organisations (Jacobs, 2014). In conclusion, we can state that the media's main role lies in connecting critical external scrutiny with organisations on the one hand and formal institutions of accountability to citizens on the other. In this sense, the media are hubs in 'monitory democracies' in which 'power monitoring and power controlling devices have been shifting sideways and downwards through the whole political order' (Keane, 2009, p xxvi). News media are not only a monitoring tool in themselves, they are also a tool used by many of the other accountability forums and they thus provide information exchange and communication between all those other accountability forums. The media thus play an integrative role in fragmented processes of accountability in fragmented systems of public services.

# References

Arnold, RD, 2005, *Congress, the press, and political accountability*, Princeton, NJ: Princeton University Press.

Besley, T & Burgess, R, 2001, Political agency, government responsiveness and the role of the media, *European Economic Review* 45, 4-6, 629-40.

Bovens, M, 2010, Two concepts of accountability: Accountability as a virtue and as a mechanism, *West European Politics* 33, 946-67.

Bovens, M, Schillemans, T, Hart, PT, 2008, Does public accountability work? An assessment tool, *Public Administration* 86, 1, 225-42.

Bovens, M, Schillemans, T, Goodin, RE, 2014, Public accountability, in M Bovens, RE Goodin, T Schillemans (eds) *The Oxford handbook of public accountability*, pp 1-20, Oxford: Oxford University Press.

Busuioc, EM, Lodge, M, 2016, The reputational basis of public accountability. *Governance: An International Journal of Policy, Administration, and Institutions* 29, 2, 247-63, https://doi.org/10.1111/gove.12161

Clayman, SE, Heritage, J, 2002, Questioning presidents: Journalistic deference and adversarialness in the press conferences of US presidents Eisenhower and Reagan, *Journal of Communication* 52, 4, 749-75.

Coombs, WT, 2007, Protecting organization reputations during a crisis: The development and application of situational crisis communication theory, *Corporate Reputation Review* 10, 3, 163-76.

Cornelissen, JP, Carroll, C, Elving, WJL, 2009, Making sense of a crucial interface: Corporate communication and the news media, in C Chouliaraki, M Morsing (eds) *Media, organisation and identity*, pp 1-22, Basingstoke: Palgrave McMillan.

Davis, RC, 2003, The public accountability of private police: Lessons from New York, Johannesburg, and Mexico City, *Policing and Society* 13, 2, 197-210.

Deacon, D, Monk, W, 2001, 'New managerialism' in the news: Media coverage of quangos in Britain, *Journal of Public Affairs* 1, 2, 153-66.

De Haan, Y, Bardoel, J, 2012, Accountability in the newsroom: Reaching out to the public or a form of window dressing?, *Studies in Communication Sciences* 12, 1, 17-21.

De Vreese, CH, Boukes, M, Schuck, A, Vliegenthart, R, Bos, L, Lelkes, Y, 2017, Linking survey and media content data: Opportunities, considerations, and pitfalls, *Communication Methods and Measures* 11, 4, 221-44.

Djerf-Pierre, M, Ekström, M, Johansson, B, 2013, Policy failure or moral scandal? Political accountability, journalism and new public management, *Media, Culture & Society* 35, 8, 960-76.

Eilders, C, 2006, News factors and news decisions. Theoretical and methodological advances in Germany, *Communications* 31, 1, 5-24, https://doi.org/10.1515/COMMUN.2006.002

Entman, RM, 2005, The nature and sources of news, in G Overholser, KH Jamieson (eds) *The press*, pp 48-65, Oxford: Oxford University Press.

Flinders, M, 2012, *Defending politics: Why democracy matters in the 21st century*, Oxford: Oxford University Press.

't Hart, P, 2002, *De inquisitiedemocratie*, https://www.nrc.nl/nieuws/2002/02/09/de-inquisitiedemocratie-7576847-a37115 (last accessed 14 September 2018).

Fredriksson, M, Pallas, J, 2016, Characteristics of public sectors and their consequences for strategic communication, *International Journal of Strategic Communication* 10, 3, 149-52, https://dx.doi.org/10.1080/1553118X.2016.1176572

Harder, RA, Sevenans, J, Van Aelst, P, 2017, Intermedia agenda setting in the social media age: How traditional players dominate the news agenda in election times, *The International Journal of Press/Politics* 22, 3, 275-93, https://doi.org/10.1177/1940161217704969

Jacobs, SHJ, 2014, *Media & Verantwoording over incidenten: Gevolgen voor publieke organistaties*, Enschede: Gildeprint.

Jacobs, SHJ, Wonneberger, A, 2017, Did we make it to the news? Effects of actual and perceived media coverage on media orientations of communication professionals, *Public Relations Review* 43, 3, 547-59, http://dx.doi.org/10.1016/j.pubrev.2017.03.010

Keane, J, 2009, Monitory democracy and media-saturated societies, *Griffith Review* 27, 79-102.

Kepplinger, HM, 2002, Mediatization of politics: Theory and data, *Journal of Communication* 52, 4, 972-86.

Klijn, EH, Koppenjan, J, 2014, Accountable networks, in M Bovens, RE Goodin, T Schillemans (eds) *The Oxford handbook of public accountability*, pp 242-57, Oxford: Oxford University Press.

Korthagen, I, Klijn, EH, 2014, The mediatization of network governance: The impact of commercialized news and mediatized politics on trust and perceived network performance, *Public Administration* 92, 4, 1054-74, https://doi.org/10.1111/padm.12092

Lee, SY, 2016, Weathering the crisis: Effects of stealing thunder in crisis communication, *Public Relations Review* 42, 2, 336-44, https://doi.org/10.1016/j.pubrev.2016.02.005

Lerner, JS, Tetlock, PE, 1999, Accounting for the effects of accountability, *Psychological Bulletin* 125, 2, 255-75.

Liu, BF, Horsley, JS, Yang, K, 2012, Overcoming negative media coverage: Does government communication matter?, *Journal of Public Administration Research and Theory* 22, 3, 597-621, https://doi.org/10.1093/jopart/mur078

Luoma-aho, V, Vos, M, 2010, Towards a more dynamic stakeholder model: Acknowledging multiple issue arenas, *Corporate Communications: An International Journal* 15, 3, 315-31, https://doi.org/10.1108/13563281011068159

Maggetti, M, 2012, The media accountability of independent regulatory agencies, *European Political Science Review* 4, 3, 385-408.

Mazzoleni, G, Schultz, W, 1999, 'Mediatization' of politics: A challenge for democracy?, *Political Communication* 16, 3, 247-61.

McCombs, M, 2005, *Setting the agenda: The mass media and public opinion*, Cambridge: Polity Press

McCubbins, MD, Schwartz, T, 1984, Congressional oversight overlooked: Police patrol versus fire alarm, *American Journal of Political Science* 28, 1, 165-79.

McCombs, M, 2005, *Setting the agenda: The mass media and public opinion*, Cambridge: Polity

Meijer, AJ, Torenvlied, R, 2016, Social media and the new organization of government communications: An empirical analysis of Twitter usage by the Dutch police, *The American Review of Public Administration* 46, 2, 143-61.

Mulgan, R, 2003, *Holding power to account: Accountability in modern democracies*, Basingstoke: Palgrave MacMillan.

Norris, P, 2014, Watchdog journalism, in M Bovens, RE Goodin, T Schillemans (eds) *The Oxford handbook of public accountability*, pp 525-41, Oxford: Oxford University Press.Olsen, JP, 2013, The institutional basis of democratic accountability, *West European Politics* 36, 3, 447-73.

Pollitt, C, Talbot, C, Caulfield, J, Smullen, A, 2004, *Agencies: How governments do things through semi-autonomous organisations*, Basingstoke: Palgrave/Macmillan.

Rhodes, RAW, 1994, The hollowing out of the state: The changing nature of public service in Britain, *Political Quarterly* 65, 138-15.

Romzek, B, Dubnick, M, 1998, Accountability, in JM Shafritz (ed) *International encyclopedia of public policy and administration, vol. 1 A–C*, pp 6-11, Boulder, CO: Westview Press.

Schillemans, T, 2008, Accountability in the shadow of hierarchy: The horizontal accountability of agencies, *Public Organization Review* 8, 2, 175-94.

Schillemans, T, 2012, *Mediatization of public services: How public organizations adapt to news media*, Frankfurt: Peter Lang.

Schillemans, T, Busuioc, M, 2015, Predicting public sector accountability: From agency drift to forum drift, *Journal of Public Administration Research and Theory* 25, 1, 191–215, https://doi.org/10.1093/jopart/muu024

Smulovitz, C, Peruzzotti, E, 2003, Societal and horizontal controls: Two cases about a fruitful relationship, in S Mainwaring (ed) *Democratic accountability in Latin America*, Oxford: Oxford University Press.

Sparrow, BH, 1999, *Uncertain guardians: The news media as a political institution*, Baltimore: Johns Hopkins University Press.

Strøm, K, 2000, Delegation and accountability in parliamentary democracies, *European Journal of Political Research* 37, 3, 261–90.

Thorbjornsrud, K, Figenschou, TU, Ihlen, Ø, 2014, Mediatization in public bureaucracies: A typology, *Communications* 39, 1, 3–22, https://doi.org/10.1515/commun-2014-0002

Van Aelst, P, Vliegenthart, R, 2014, Studying the tango: An analysis of parliamentary questions and press coverage in the Netherlands, *Journalism Studies* 15, 4, 392–410.

Van Santen, R, Helfer, L, Van Aelst, P, 2015, When politics becomes news: An analysis of parliamentary questions and press coverage in three West European countries, *Acta Politica*, 50, 1, 45–63.

Wille, A, 2005, Kamervragen en de dagelijkse drang van politieke controle, *Bestuurswetenschappen* 5, 406–30.

Wonneberger, A, Jacobs, SHJ, 2017, Media positioning: Comparing organizations' standing in the news, *Corporate Communications* 22, 3, 354–68, https://doi.org/10.1108/CCIJ-11-2016-0075

Yankova, G, 2006, Political accountability and media scandals: A comparative exploration, *CEU Political Science Journal* 1, 3, 49–70.

Zavyalova, A, Pfarrer, MD, Reger, RK, Shapiro, DL, 2012, Managing the message: The effects of firm actions and industry spillovers on media coverage following wrongdoing, *Academy of Management Journal* 55, 5, 1079–101.

# CHAPTER THREE

# Political control or legitimacy deficit? Bureaucracies' symbolic responses to bottom-up public pressure

Saar Alon-Barkat and Sharon Gilad

## Introduction

A large body of public administration literature focuses on the response of bureaucracies – whether government ministries or separate agencies – to political signalling, pressure and control. Building on principal–agent theory, this literature demonstrates politicians' direct and indirect control over bureaucratic behaviour (for example, Moe, 1984; Wood and Waterman, 1991; Epstein and O'Halloran, 1999; Huber et al, 2001; West and Raso, 2013). Yet public bureaucracies are exposed not only to top-down political control, but also, increasingly, to direct bottom-up public pressure in the form of public opinion shifts and social protest. Moreover, the media play an important role in mirroring, actively shaping and amplifying such pressure (see Chapter Two). The direct responses of bureaucracies to such bottom-up public pressure and the mechanisms that underlie their responses have received limited theoretical and empirical attention to date. The small body of literature that analyses the direct responses of bureaucracies to public pressure focuses on their distinct reputation as the factor that guides and moderates their response (Rimkutė, 2018; Carpenter, 2002, 2004; Moffitt, 2010; Maor, 2011; Gilad et al, 2015; Maor and Sulitzeanu-Kenan, 2013, 2015; Maor et al, 2013). These studies, however, overlook the likely importance of subjection to (or independence from) political control for the response of bureaucracies to bottom-up public pressure. This study contributes to current research by analysing the extent to which political control moderates bureaucracies' direct response to salient signals from the public. In so doing, it complements other chapters in this book that analyse the implications of governance reforms involving the creation of semi-autonomous and independent agencies, for the public accountability and responsiveness of government (Schillemans, 2016; Jacobs and Schillemans, 2016).

The responses of bureaucracies to public pressure can be crudely divided into substantive responses (in terms of resource allocation, outputs and performance) and symbolic responses (most notably speeches, press releases and advertising campaigns). Symbolic responses, which are the focus of this study, may involve 'cheap talk'. Yet, even so, they may enhance bureaucracies' accountability and responsiveness to the public insofar as they shape citizens' expectations from government and expose bureaucracies to external scrutiny when their performance falls short of expectations (but see Alon-Barkat and Gilad, 2017).

We hypothesise two distinct micro-mechanisms through which political control moderates the direct response of bureaucracies to bottom-up public pressure. First, building, inter alia, on principal–agent theory, we expect more politically controlled bureaucracies to respond to public pressure in order to preempt intervention by politicians who are reliant on public support (hereafter, the principal–agent mechanism). Conversely, building on regulatory theory (Majone, 1997, 1998, 1999; Gilardi, 2008), we expect autonomous agencies to compensate for their legitimacy deficit by signalling their attentiveness to public concerns (hereafter, the legitimacy-deficit mechanism) (Black, 2008; Yeung, 2009; Maggetti, 2012; Neshkova, 2014; Puppis et al, 2014).

To investigate the above hypotheses, we explore the response of a diverse set of 36 bureaucracies, including central and local government ministries, semi-autonomous government companies and independent regulatory agencies, to the mass protests that erupted in Israel during the summer of 2011. These protests make a good case for our analysis insofar as no public bureaucracy could have ignored the profound criticism that the protests conveyed. Demonstrations involved hundreds of thousands of protesters, mainly of the young middle class, demanding that government engage in fundamental reforms of policy domains such as housing, food prices, education, welfare services, finance and transportation. Moreover, the influence of the protests on public opinion was boosted by intensive, supportive media coverage and active espousal by prominent journalists.

We analyse changes in the extent of bureaucracies' monthly expenditure on public campaigns as a proxy for their symbolic responses to the social protests. We argue that public campaigns are a strategic means for rendering bureaucracies and their contribution (to the public's wellbeing, health, security and so forth) more visible to the public over and above their educational and informative value. Our analysis shows that higher levels of political control, measured in terms of reliance on state budgets and politicians' authority to influence the nomination and decision-making of bureaucracies' executives, increased bureaucracies' inclination to advertise themselves and their contribution in response to the social protests. These findings are in line with the expectation that we derive from principal–agent theory. Conversely, our findings do not support the expectation that autonomous agencies are inclined to display their attentiveness to public discontent due to their legitimacy deficit.

## Political control as a moderator of bureaucracies' responses to bottom-up public pressure

Representative democracy theory assumes hierarchical lines of accountability in which politicians, who are accountable and responsive to voters, hold bureaucrats under their control. Empirically, media and the public blame for the execution of policies falls primarily on politicians compared with bureaucrats (Chapter Eight). Consequently, politicians have a strong incentive to monitor and control bureaucratic policy making and implementation (Besley and Burgess, 2001). It is therefore unsurprising that principal–agent theory has focused on the means of control via which politicians (the principals) shape bureaucracies' (the agents) actions and on bureaucratic responsiveness to political control (Moe, 1984; Wood and Waterman, 1991). However, inherent to principal–agent theory is the assumption that politically controlled organisations are responsive not only to top-down political control, but also directly to bottom-up public pressure. Given that bureaucracies are controlled by politicians who are themselves accountable to voters, bureaucrats should anticipate that public pressure would translate into political scrutiny (compare McCubbins and Schwartz, 1984; Chapter Two) and would therefore respond directly to this pressure to preempt political intervention. Consequently, we expect bureaucracies to respond directly to bottom-up public pressure, over and above their response to top-down political control. Thus, building on and extending principal–agent theory, we postulate that:

> H1: The more politically controlled is a bureaucracy, the more inclined it is to signal its attentiveness to bottom-up public pressure.

Whereas this hypothesis suggests that political control enhances bureaucracies' direct response to bottom-up public pressure, regulatory theory expects autonomous agencies that are formally insulated from political control to exhibit receptiveness to public pressure. This expectation is rooted in agencies' pursuit of public legitimacy as opposed to their attempt to preempt political control mechanisms. It builds on numerous studies theorising that independent agencies, which have gained increasing popularity over the past decades (Levi-Faur, 2005, 2006a, 2006b; Gilardi, 2008), nonetheless suffer from fragile and unstable public legitimacy (Majone, 1997, 1998, 1999; Lodge, 2004; Gilardi, 2008).

Consequently, these agencies may seek to buttress their legitimacy and cultivate their reputations by displaying direct accountability to the public through enhanced transparency, encouragement of public participation and public communications (Majone, 1999; Black, 2008; Yeung, 2009; Maggetti, 2012; Busuioc and Lodge, 2016; Puppis et al, 2014).

Recent studies support the expectation that independent agencies tend to deploy intensive public communications to enhance their legitimacy. Yeung (2009) documented the UK and Australian independent competition and consumer agencies' engagement in media campaigns in pursuit of enhancing their legitimacy. Puppis et al (2014) analysed the strategic communication activities of financial services, telecommunication and broadcasting regulatory agencies in the UK, Germany, Ireland and Switzerland. They showed that agencies engage in informing the public about regulatory decisions, actions and positions and in provision of explicit justifications for their actions. These findings indicate that independent agencies use communications as a means of direct accountability to the public. However, these studies were restricted to independent regulatory agencies (IRAs) and thus failed to analyse how IRAs' communications with the public compare to those of more politically controlled bureaucracies.

A third study, by Neshkova (2014), analysed the shaping of bureaucracies' engagement in 'participatory budgeting', namely involving the public in decisions over budget allocation. Her analysis indicated that agencies that enjoy greater budgetary autonomy from central administration are inclined to engage in 'participatory budgeting' so as to increase the legitimacy of their resource allocations, a finding which resonates with the legitimacy deficit hypothesis. However, Neshkova's study was restricted to one aspect of political control, namely budgetary autonomy, and to regulatory agencies. In conclusion, the regulatory literature regarding autonomous agencies' legitimacy deficit leads us to expect that:

> H2: The less politically controlled (that is, the more autonomous)
> is a bureaucracy, the more inclined it is to display its attentiveness
> to bottom-up public pressure.

The above hypotheses propose two distinct effects of political control and its absence. However, these effects are not necessarily contradictory, and may jointly influence the response of different bureaucracies to bottom-up public pressure. Congruently, politically controlled bureaucracies may seek to display their attentiveness because they anticipate political intervention, while autonomous bureaucracies may do the same in order to mitigate their democratic legitimacy deficit. Conversely, both hypotheses would be jointly rejected if politically controlled and autonomous bureaucracies both fail to display their attentiveness to public pressure.

## Case background: the Israeli 2011 social protests

The social protests that took place in Israel during the summer of 2011 exposed all Israeli public bureaucracies to a salient signal of public dissatisfaction, demanding at least deliberation of their response. The frame of the protesters' agenda initially focused on the cost of housing and dairy foods and thereafter shifted to encompass a wide array of policy issues such as the cost of early-years education, public health services, banks' extortionate fees and interest rates, public transportation, the employment conditions of contract workers and more.

The protests started in June 2011. The protesters set up tent encampments and organised weekly rallies in all the large cities. The largest of these demonstrations, in September 2011, attracted over 400,000 participants across the country, which amounts to 5% of the Israeli population. Alongside protesters' general criticism, certain businesses were condemned (and some boycotted), and a number of government agencies, mostly central ministries, were specifically blamed for failing in their duties.

The protest movement's leaders enjoyed favourable media coverage as well as the backing of economic and intellectual elites and political parties, and their message dominated the media agenda over a relatively long period (Ram and Filk, 2013; Rosenhek and Shalev, 2014). Their cause therefore gained the support of a vast majority of the public. Furthermore, unlike simultaneous anti-austerity protests in the US and southern Europe, Israel, at the time of the protests, enjoyed a low unemployment rate, relatively stable macroeconomic performance and no immediate security menace, thereby opening a space on otherwise crowded media and government agendas.

In August 2011, the prime minister, in response to the protests, established a public committee to solicit the public's views and to delineate recommendations for reducing the cost of living. The committee handed in its report at the end of September of the same year, and the government eventually adopted some of its recommendations. The last of the tent encampments was evacuated in October 2011, yet the impact of the social protests on the political and media agenda, while attenuated, continued through to mid-2012, when the protest movement leaders attempted, but failed, to replicate the previous summer's vast popular demonstrations (Cohen and Kobovic, 2012; Weissberg, 2012; Zarhia, 2012).

## Methodology

To analyse our hypotheses regarding the effect of political control on bureaucracies' symbolic responses to bottom-up public pressure, exemplified here in the form of the 2011 Israeli mass social protests, we have constructed a dataset of monthly investment in advertising campaigns of 40 bureaucracies. The researched period is January 2010 to June 2012, that is, from a year and a half before the social protests began until their decline. We focus on changes to expenditure on public campaigns as a proxy for the bureaucracies' strategic choice to demonstrate attentiveness to public concerns. A major advantage of this measure is that advertising expenditures are comparable across different organisations and over time, and can be estimated with great precision.

A potential challenge to our measurement concerns the extent to which bureaucracies can adjust their campaigns to external signals (such as the social protests) and their ownership over this process (vis-à-vis politicians and other government overseers). Insofar as flexibility and timing are concerned, producing entirely new advertising campaigns is likely to take a number of months. However, bureaucracies' adaptation to external signals may involve an immediate increase/decrease in the visibility of existing campaigns, through buying more/less media space or changing their location (for example, to prime time media and front pages). Moreover, rather than producing entirely new campaigns, bureaucracies can adjust their existing ads by changing the slogan or by adding new images and thereby change their message. Ultimately, however, adaptation to changing environments is intrinsic to professional advertising. Israeli bureaucracies, at the national level, have access to such professional services through the Government Advertising Agency (LAPAM), which is one of the largest advertising agencies in Israel, and is well known for producing and managing creative as well as effective advertising campaigns (for example, Epstein, 2012).[1] At the municipal level, bureaucracies are free to hire the services of any private advertising agency.

As to ownership, in Israel, bureaucracies' decisions to advertise are relatively free from administrative restrictions and from political direction. There is very limited regulation of public advertising, other than explicit prohibition on the exploitation of government campaigns for political/ partisan gains. Interviews with five spokespersons from different government ministries[2] suggest that a ministry's decision to advertise does not require consultation with and approval from other organisations. Campaigns are normally initiated by bureaucracies' professional departments, in collaboration with their spokespersons (who are career civil servants, and not political appointees), and managed by the spokesperson, with the professional assistance of LAPAM. In some ministries, political appointees and politicians approve the content of advertising. Nevertheless, given the spokespersons' professional involvement, the legal restrictions on political advertising, and the fact that there were no proximate, upcoming national or municipal elections during our research period (January 2010 to June 2012), the political influence on advertising is likely to have been rather low.

Public campaigns are a means for informing and educating the public (for example, eat at least five fruits and vegetables a day). Yet alongside their public educational value, public campaigns also convey a positive message about organisations and their operations (for example, we care for your health). Moreover, public campaigns often involve explicit promotion and branding of bureaucracies and their services (compare Eshuis and Klijn, 2012; Marvel, 2015; Alon-Barkat and Gilad, 2017) – displaying their effectiveness, efficiency, professional ethos and more. In addition, our preliminary qualitative analysis suggests that during the research period some bureaucracies overtly employed advertising to display their responsiveness to the protesters' agenda and demands.

An illustration of how bureaucracies' expenditures on public campaigns may reflect their symbolic response to the social protests is the Israeli Ministry of Housing and Construction's public campaign for housing-purchase grants. This campaign engaged with the high cost of housing, which was among the central themes of the social protests. The housing-purchase grants were preliminarily approved by the cabinet earlier in June 2011 (at the dawn of the social protests), and then extended and executed by the cabinet a few months later, alongside the expansion of the protests. Thereafter, the Ministry of Housing launched a public campaign in February 2012. This campaign shows newlywed couples and young families, who discover that they are entitled to a grant of up to 100,000 shekels to buy a house in the north or south of Israel. Figure 3.1 shows one of the campaign ads which was published in the newspapers. The slogan, in large green and blue Hebrew letters in the middle of the ad, is a pun. It means: 'What? Super!' (in Hebrew: ma? anak!), which sounds like the Hebrew word for 'grant' ('maanak'). The large colour picture above it shows a middle-class Israeli couple and their young child. The mother is looking surprised and exceedingly happy to discover that they are entitled to a grant to buy a house. At the lower left corner is the unique logo of the Ministry of Housing and Construction.[3] The campaign's ads were presented over a six-week period across television and radio channels, newspapers, billboards and internet websites, and were estimated to cost more than US$1.5 million. This was as much as three times the ministry's total annual advertising budget in 2009, 2010 and 2011.

**Figure 3.1: The Ministry of Housing and Construction's public campaign for housing grants (February–March 2012)**

The campaign provided the public with information about the availability of housing grants. Yet it also conveyed a positive message that the ministry is attentive to the protesters' agenda. Therefore, we consider it a symbolic response to the social protests. Moreover, even in the absence of direct conversation with the protesters' agenda, more communication of bureaucracies' activities via visibly located, colourful (and therefore more expensive) campaigns may have reflected strategic adaptation to social upheaval insofar as they enhanced bureaucracies' public visibility and sent an indirect message of the positive value of their operations, thereby signalling their attentiveness to the public.

## Sample selection

This study is a part of our larger multi-methods research project, which compares the responses of public and private sector organisations to the 2011 social protests in Israel (Gilad et al, 2016). Our sample of 40 bureaucracies (of which four were dropped due to insufficient information) is derived from the larger sample of 100 organisations that includes 60 business corporations and nongovernmental organisations (NGOs). The original sample of organisations was randomly selected from a comprehensive database purchased from Israel's leading market-research company – IFAT Business Information (hereafter IFAT). IFAT's database compiles information about the advertising expenditure of more than 16,000 organisations. To create the sample we restricted our population to organisations that use advertising as a regular means of communication, over six policy sectors (education, finance, housing, foods, transportation and tourism), of which some were central and some were peripheral to the social protesters' agenda. Further details regarding the construction of the sample are available from the Online Methodological Appendix (Alon-Barkat and Gilad, undated).

## Operationalisation of variables

Our dependent variable is individual bureaucracies' aggregated monthly expenditure on advertising (in US dollars) across different channels of communication, between January 2010 and June 2012. Consequently, the dataset consists of 30 data-points of expenditure on advertising for each of the 36 bureaucracies, giving an overall population of 1,080 monthly observations of organisations. The data, which we purchased from IFAT, covers bureaucracies' advertising expenditures across 120 media sources (including TV channels, national and local newspapers, radio channels, internet websites, cinema chains and billboards). IFAT's measure is an estimate based on the media channel (for example, the broadsheet *Yediot*), the exact location and size of the ad (for example, third page, medium size, colour ad) and the cost according to the media provider's price list.[4]

Our highly diversified sample includes bureaucracies of different sizes and functions, from state and local government levels, which therefore vary in their regular advertising trends. Some advertise all year long and at relatively consistent levels, whereas others fluctuate considerably in output. Therefore, in order to be able to compare across organisations and over time (to account for changes in advertising amidst the social protests), we transformed bureaucracies' advertising expenditures (in US dollars) into organisation-specific Z-scores. That is, the dependent variable scores represent bureaucracies' deviation from their own estimated mean divided by their own estimated standard deviation.[5] In other words, the observations represent the extent to which monthly advertising expenditure is typical or atypical of each bureaucracy's advertising trends.

Our two independent variables are the pre- and post-protest periods, and the degree of bureaucracies' subjection to political control. Our operationalisation of the research hypotheses is based on an interaction between these variables, as described below.

*Pre- and post-protest periods (PROTEST).* We operationalise the post-protest period as commencing in August 2011 (assuming a delayed response to the events initiated in June) and as ending by June 2012 (given the dramatic decrease in public and media support for the social protests in July 2012). Thus, we use a dummy variable to distinguish between the pre-protest period (January 2010 to July 2011) and the post-protest period (August 2011 to June 2012).

*Political control.* Based on current literature on bureaucratic autonomy/ independence (Gilardi, 2002; Verhoest et al, 2004; Yesilkagit and Van Thiel, 2008, 2012; Boin et al, 2010; Yesilkagit and Christensen, 2010; Gilardi and Maggetti, 2011; Van Thiel, 2012; Bach et al, 2015), our operationalisation of political control involves two dimensions. The first dimension is bureaucracies' relative reliance on public budgets (whether state or municipal), assuming that budget authorisation is an important device of political control. To account for bureaucracies' dependence on the state budget, we calculated their annual revenues from taxation and from the state or municipal budget as a fraction of their total annual revenues.[6] This measure varies from zero to one. A score of zero means that 0% of a bureaucracy's total revenue derives from the government budget, while a score of one means that 100% of its total revenue stems from the government's budget.

The second dimension of political control is the structural subjection of bureaucracies to political control. To account for this dimension we constructed an ordinal scale inspired by Van Thiel's (2012) typology, adjusted to the context of the Israeli public sector. The ordinal scale consists of three levels of structural control: (a) government ministry – a unit of national or local government, which is subject to direct control by elected politicians and thus has low formal autonomy; (b) a semi-autonomous agency – which is operationally detached from central or local government, yet lacks legal independence. Such organisations enjoy some operational autonomy, for example in relation to recruitment and pay; (c) a legally independent agency – which is formally independent from political intervention in its substantive decisions. To account for these three groups in the model, we used dummy variables for semi-autonomous agencies and government ministries, while setting independent agencies as a reference category.

The Israeli national-level public sector consists of three main groups of organisations: government ministries (including their functionally designated units), government-owned companies and statutory bodies (Galnoor, 2007, p 33). Local-level government consists of municipalities, regional councils and municipally owned companies. Government ministries, municipalities and regional councils are all headed and directed by elected politicians (whether ministers or mayors). Therefore, we categorised them as 'government ministry' to signify their similar subjection to a high degree of political control. Our sample contains 11 state government ministries (including two functionally designated units) and 15 municipalities and regional councils. Unlike ministries, government-owned companies are separate from the cabinet, and formally insulated from ministers through boards of directors. However, the Government-Owned Companies Act (1975) empowers ministers to appoint the companies' chief executive officers (CEOs) and board members and to direct their policy goals. The structural arrangement of municipally owned companies is similar to that of government-owned companies. We therefore categorised government-owned and municipally owned companies as semi-autonomous and not as independent agencies (compare Yesilkagit and Christensen, 2010). Our sample contains four government-owned and two municipally owned companies. Statutory bodies, like government companies, are also separate from the cabinet, yet their structural autonomy varies. Therefore, if they have a legislative mandate, their independence is formally stated and ministers are banned from intervening in their substantive decisions, they were coded as legally independent agencies (compare Gilardi, 2002). Otherwise, statutory bodies were categorised as semi-autonomous agencies. Our sample contains four statutory bodies, of which three were categorised as independent agencies, and one was categorised as semi-autonomous.

## Control variables

Specific targeting of an organisation during the protest period (TARGET): although the Israeli social protest movement tended to blame the economic system and the government as a whole (in accordance with its all-encompassing agenda), a few public bureaucracies (and businesses), mostly government ministries, attracted specific criticism (hereafter: targeted). Our hypotheses focus on the average response of all bureaucracies. However, we control for the additive effect of bureaucracies' response to criticism that specifically targeted their operations. This control is important to negate the possibility that politically controlled ministries reacted more, simply because they attracted more criticism than semi-autonomous and independent agencies. We therefore searched the electronic archive of 'TheMarker' – the daily economics section of *Haaretz* newspaper – over the entire social protest period for any mention of the individual bureaucracies in our sample combined with a set of keywords that are associated with the 2011 social protests and their linguistic variations ('protest', 'demonstration', 'boycott', 'cost of living' and 'social justice'). We chose TheMarker because it strongly supported the protests and both reflected and amplified the voice of the activists.[7] We use a dummy variable to account for bureaucracies that were specifically targeted at least once during the post-protest period versus those that were not. Of the 36 bureaucracies in our sample, 12 attracted specific criticism (33%), of which nine are government ministries, one is a semi-autonomous agency and two are independent agencies.

We further control for bureaucracies' (log) annual income (INCOME) to account for the variation in their size, and for an objective change in their financial capacity to advertise.[8] Additionally, to account for the panel structure of the data we include lagged dependent variables for the previous month (Advertising (Z scr) lag1), as well as for the same calendar month in the previous year (Advertising (Z scr) lag12) to account for seasonality in advertising. Furthermore, to deal with the correlation of errors within the 36 bureaucracies and panel heteroskedasticity we use a random effect Generalised Least-Squares (GLS) regression model with robust clustered standard errors (Petersen, 2009, pp 464–65).[9] Table 3.1 provides descriptive statistics regarding the distribution of the variables.

**Table 3.1: Descriptive statistics of the sample**

| Variable | Unit | Mean | SD | Min | Max |
|---|---|---|---|---|---|
| Advertising | $US (monthly) | 183,654 | 465,177 | 0 | 4,905,595 |
| Advertising (Z scr) | Organisation-specific Z-scores | -0.017 | 0.979 | -1.721 | 5.796 |
| Advertising (Z scr) lag1 | Organisation-specific Z-scores | -0.031 | 0.972 | -1.721 | 5.796 |
| Advertising (Z scr) lag12 | Organisation-specific Z-scores | -0.120 | 0.945 | -1.721 | 5.796 |
| PROTEST | 1=post-protest, 0=pre-protest | 0.37 | 0.482 | 0 | 1 |
| Structural political control (ref= Independent) | | | | | |
| Semiautonomous | 1,0 | 0.20 | 0.28 | 0 | 1 |
| government ministry | 1,0 | 0.08 | 0.45 | 0 | 1 |
| Economic dependence | Proportion | 0.726 | 0.271 | 0 | 1 |
| INCOME | Log transformed | 20.184 | 2.056 | 15.14 | 24.55 |
| TARGET | 1 = targeted organisation, | | | | |
| | 0 = non-targeted organisation | 0.33 | 0.472 | 0 | 1 |

## Results

As a preliminary, descriptive, observation, Table 3.2 compares bureaucracies' mean monthly expenditure on advertising before and after the social protests given their differential subjection to structural political control and their dependence on state budget. The average monthly expenditures are displayed in US dollars as well as in organisation-specific Z-scores with T-test estimates of the significance of the differences between each pair of Z-scores. This analysis indicates, in line with our first hypothesis, that higher levels of structural political control as well as of economic dependence on public budgets were associated with an inclination to increase expenditures on public campaigns after the social protests. Government ministries' average expenditure increased, significantly, by 27%, and similarly the expenditure of bureaucracies that derive more than 80% of their income from government budget, increased by 26% (though not significantly). The mean difference among semi-autonomous agencies is relatively small and far from significant. Finally, and counter to our second hypothesis, autonomous bureaucracies decreased their advertising expenditures: independent agencies' average expenditure decreased by 63%, and the expenditure of agencies that derive less than 60% of their income from the government budget decreased by 54% (though neither are significant).

Table 3.3 presents a set of random error regression models of advertising by bureaucracies over time (using organisation-specific Z-scores) between January 2010 and June 2012. Model 1a includes all the independent variables (structural political control; economic dependency; PROTEST) and controls (TARGET; INCOME; Advertising (Z scr) lag1 and lag12). Models 1b and 1c are designed to test the singular effects of each of the two dimensions of political control in interaction with PROTEST. Model 1b tests the effect of protest given bureaucracies' economic dependency on the government's budget, while model 1c tests the effect of protests given bureaucracies' subjection to structural political control. Finally, model 1d analyses the differential effect of protests in interaction with both dimensions of political control. We find that bureaucracies that are subjected to higher levels of political control, whether through structural control or economic reliance on the government budget, were more inclined to increase their expenditures on advertising. The interaction between economic dependence and the post-protest period is positive and significant in model 1b and marginally significant in model 1d ($p$ = 0.106). As for structural political control, in models 1c and 1d the coefficients for the interactions between protest and semi-autonomous agency are positive and insignificant and the interactions between protest and government ministry are positive and significant. Hence, in accordance with our first hypothesis, more politically controlled bureaucracies, and

**Table 3. 2: Comparing means of monthly expenditure on advertising before and after the social protest**

| | Mean monthly expenditure before protest | | Mean monthly expenditure after protest | | | | |
|---|---|---|---|---|---|---|---|
| | $US | Organisation- specific Z scores | $US | Organisation- specific Z scores | t | df | sig |
| All sample (n=36) | 168,748 (44,168) | -0.062 (0.032) | 209,401 (44,168) | 0.061 (0.321) | 1.557 | 35 | 0.128 |
| **Structural political control** | | | | | | | |
| Government ministry (n=26) | 216,104 (58,698) | -0.094 (0.036) | 273,369 (67,405) | 0.114 (0.064) | 2.218 | 25 | 0.036 |
| Semiautonomous agency (n=7) | 49,936 (11,888) | 0.021 (0.091) | 55,850 (16,531) | -0.027 (0.119) | - 0.265 | 6 | 0.800 |
| Independent agency (n=3) | 35,568 (19,278) | 0.023 (0.096) | 13,306 (8,951) | -0.186 (0.046) | - 1.544 | 2 | 0.262 |
| **Economic Dependence** | | | | | | | |
| 0-0.6 (n=6) | 60,095 (17,344) | 0.016 (0.099) | 27,800 (10,631) | -0.111 (0.097) | - 0.763 | 5 | 0.480 |
| 0.6-0.8 (n=14) | 85,026 (50,165) | -0.058 (0.050) | 120,108 (48,848) | 0.112 (0.086) | 1.321 | 13 | 0.209 |
| 0.8-1 (n=16) | 282,752 (82,007) | -0.095 (0.047) | 355,634 (97,096) | 0.082 (0.086) | 1.440 | 15 | 0.170 |

Notes: paired samples T-Test and significance levels refer to differences between organisation-specific Z scores with n-1 degrees of freedom; standard errors in parentheses; significance levels are two tailed.

most prominently traditional ministries, were inclined to increase their advertising in response to the social protests, which we interpret as a proxy for their display of attentiveness to public pressure. Conversely, in contrast

**Table 3.3: Effect of political control on organisations' expenditure on advertising**
(Non-standardised coefficients; robust standard errors in parentheses)

| DV= advertising (Z scr) | 1a | 1b | 1c | 1d |
|---|---|---|---|---|
| Structural political control (ref=Independent agency) | | | | |
| Semiautonomous | 0.065* (0.034) | - | 0.031 (0.078) | 0.016 (0.075) |
| Government ministry | 0.083 (0.020) | - | -0.037 (-0.052) | -0.032 (0.051) |
| Economic dependence | -0.001 (0.053) | -0.138 (0.094) | - | -0.116 (0.093) |
| PROTEST | 0.090 (0.067) | -0.191 (0.127) | -0.164* (0.096) | -0.391** (0.158) |
| Semiautonomous *PROTEST | - | - | 0.094 (0.170) | 0.132 (0.170) |
| Gov. ministry *PROTEST | - | - | 0.327*** (0.127) | 0.311** (0.122) |
| Economic dependence *PROTEST | - | 0.386** (0.182) | - | 0.318 (0.197) |
| TARGET | 0.054* (0.033) | 0.031 (0.031) | 0.055* (0.030) | 0.054* (0.033) |
| INCOME | -0.012*** (0.004) | -0.006 (0.005) | -0.012*** (0.005) | -0.012*** (0.005) |
| Advertising (Z scr) lag1 | 0.153*** (0.034) | 0.151*** (0.038) | 0.150*** (0.038) | 0.148*** (0.038) |
| Advertising (Z scr) lag12 | 0.086** (0.040) | 0.091** (0.040) | 0.084** (0.040) | 0.088** (0.040) |
| Constant | 0.123 | 0.173 | 0.216 | 0.300 |
| N organisations | 36 | 36 | 36 | 36 |
| N months | 30 | 30 | 30 | 30 |
| N observations (organisations *months) | 1080 | 1080 | 1080 | 1080 |
| R2 | 0.037 | 0.039 | 0.040 | 0.042 |

Notes: Table entries are non-standardised random-effects GLS-regression coefficients with robust standard errors, clustered at the level of organisations. * $p < 0.1$ ** $p < 0.05$ *** $p < 0.01$ (two tailed)

to the expectations of our second hypothesis, more autonomous agencies, and most prominently independent agencies, decreased their expenditure.

**Table 3.4: Simple effect of protest given organisations' levels of political control**

| Structural political control | Economic dependence (% of income derives from government's budget) | Expected change in expenditure on advertising after protest (Z scores) | Lower 95% confidence interval | Higher 95% confidence interval | Expected change in expenditure on advertising after protest ($US) |
|---|---|---|---|---|---|
| Government ministry | 100 | 0.238 | 0.046 | 0.430 | +65,806 |
| | 50% | 0.079 | -0.098 | 0.256 | +21,843 |
| | 0% | -0.080 | -0.396 | 0.236 | -22,119 |
| Semiautono-mous agency | 100 | 0.058 | -0.289 | 0.406 | +16,036 |
| | 50% | -0.100 | -0.369 | 0.168 | -27,649 |
| | 0% | -0.259 | -0.571 | 0.053 | -71,613 |
| Independent agency | 100 | -0.073 | -0.291 | 0.144 | -20,184 |
| | 50% | -0.232 | -0.419 | -0.046 | -64,147 |
| | 0% | -0.391 | -0.702 | -0.080 | -108,111 |

Notes: post-protest's simple effect coefficients and intervals are derived from model 1d; The expected change in expenditure after protest in $US was calculated by multiplying change in Z scores by the sample of organisations' mean expenditure standard deviation: 276,498$.

Table 3.4 depicts the expected change in the expenditure on public campaigns after the protests by bureaucracies under varying levels of political control according to model 1d. The left column shows the effects in Z-scores, while the right column displays the conversion of the Z-scores back into US dollars.[10] Accordingly, government ministries that derive 100% of their funding from taxes and state budgets are expected to significantly increase their expenditures on public campaigns by an average of 0.238 standard deviations (which amounts to $65,806). In comparison, government ministries that derive 50% of their income from taxes and state budgets are expected to increase their expenditures by only 0.079 standard deviations, which is not statistically significant. The change in expenditures of semi-autonomous agencies in response to the social protests is not significant and varies between an average increase of 0.06 and a decrease of 0.26 standard deviations. Finally, independent agencies that derive 0–50% of their funding from government's budget are expected to significantly decrease their expenditures on advertising by 0.232–0.391 standard deviations on average (which amounts to $64,147–$108,111).

As for our control variables, the coefficients for advertising in T-1 and T-12 are positive and significant in all four models, suggesting that advertising expenditure is both seasonal and correlated with previous expenditure. The coefficients for targeted organisations are positive and significant ($p < 0.1$) in models 1a, 1c and 1d, but not in model 1b. Similarly, the coefficients of an organisation's annual income (logged) are mildly negative and significant in models 1a, 1c and 1d, but not in model 1b. Given that our dependent variable measures organisations' monthly expenditure against their own 'normal' tendency, these effects may indicate variation in the skewedness of advertising by targeted/non-targeted organisations and between organisations with high/low income. These differences therefore appear irrelevant for our theoretical analysis. The R2 of our models is relatively low (0.04). This seems to be related to our use of organisation-specific Z-scores, which measure the deviation of each bureaucracy from its own mean, given its unique standard deviation. Moreover, the use of the random effect model accounts for the different effects on the dependent variable of the 36 organisations, and accordingly our model explains 0.53 of the variance between the organisations. We do not detect any problem of heteroscedasticity or high levels of multicollinearity (the mean VIF in model 1d is 1.78, and VIF of all variables is below 2.8). Model 1d is statistically significant (wald $X2(11) = 46.81$, $p < 0.001$).

## Discussion and conclusions

This study analysed the effect of political control on bureaucracies' symbolic responses to bottom–up public pressure as reflected by their expenditure on public campaigns in the aftermath of the 2011 social protests in Israel. Our analysis showed that traditional ministries and state-financed bureaucracies, which are subjected to higher levels of political control, were inclined to increase their expenditures on public campaigns in the post-protest period. These findings are in line with our first hypothesis that public bureaucracies are more attentive to public demands when they are at risk of political intervention by their political principals who are themselves reliant on public support. Their subjection to political control prompts them to display their attentiveness to public demands and/or their contribution to the public good so as to preempt political intervention. The generalisable prediction that we derive from these findings is that political control enhances the inclination of bureaucracies to respond to salient signals from the public and the media (at least) via symbolic interaction.

Conversely, we find that autonomous agencies were significantly inclined to decrease their expenditures on public campaigns in the post-protest period. These findings do not lend support for our second hypothesis that legitimacy deficit renders independent agencies inclined to seek public legitimacy and support in face of public discontent. Rather, they seem to imply that autonomous agencies strategically sought to keep a low public profile. By keeping a low public profile these agencies may have attempted to decrease their risk of being targeted by protesters and of attracting concrete demands for policy change. Such strategy was also documented in relation to Israeli private businesses during the same period (Dovrat-Mazritz, 2011; Gilad et al, 2016). Keeping a low public profile may be particularly effective as a means of avoiding attention amid a catchall type of social protest that cascades from one policy issue and organisation to another.

Overall, our study contributes to public administration theory by advancing the current understanding of bureaucracies' direct responses to public pressure. It shows that responses of bureaucracies to public pressure may be moderated not only by their distinct reputations (Carpenter, 2002, 2004; Moffitt, 2010; Maor, 2011; Gilad et al, 2015; Maor and Sulitzeanu-Kenan, 2013; Maor et al, 2013) and identities (Gilad, 2015), but also by their relative subjection to political control. These findings, if generalisable, have important implications for governance reforms. They suggest that the creation of autonomous agencies, in pursuit of a professional and non-politicised administration, may result in attenuated government attention and response to societal pressures that enjoy popular support and media amplification. Our findings further highlight a methodological weakness of existing studies of independent regulatory agencies' interaction with the public. Namely, the failure of these studies to compare the public interaction of the IRAs with that of politically dependent regulatory, and non-regulatory, bureaucracies.

Still, this study has limitations that we and others may seek to address in future. First, our study focuses on bureaucracies' response to one incident: the 2011 social protests in Israel with the possibility that our results were contingent upon the specific nature of this protest, its timing and favourable media and political conditions. Second, our chosen parameter for the symbolic response of the bureaucracies is their expenditures on public campaigns. We have explained and qualitatively demonstrated the validity of this measure. However, a systematic qualitative analysis of a deployment of advertising campaigns as a measure of response to external pressures is still to be done. Third, while symbolic responses are important, we lack an understanding of their association with material policy change. Thus, more qualitative analyses of public campaigns, studies of other cases of public pressure, as well as of other means of symbolic and material responses are needed to provide a well-rounded understanding of bureaucracies' responses to public pressure and demands.

## Notes

[1] Updated information about LAPAM and its campaigns is available from the agency's website: www.lapam.gov.il

[2] Interviews were carried out between June and December 2014. We asked the spokespersons about the initiation and production of advertising campaigns and about ministers' involvement in this process.

[3] A full-length television advertisement is available at www.youtube.com/watch?v=lZx92oJwfks

[4] The provided data does not account for price reductions to individual advertisers.

[5] For example, assume that the monthly advertising expenditure estimated mean of organisation 'a' is $100,000 and that its standard deviation is $50,000, if organisation 'a' spent $100,000 in August 2010 while in August 2011 it spent $150,000, its measure of the dependent variable (DV) will increase from 0 [(100,000–100,000)/50,000] to 1 [(150,000–100,000)/50,000] (an increase of 1 standard deviation).

[6] For state-level public agencies, data was collected from financial reports, which are available from the Ministry of Finance's website, and from agencies' reports, which are available from the Government Companies' Authority and from the agencies' websites. For local-level public agencies, we collected data from municipalities' financial reports, which are available from the Ministry of Interior's website.

[7] Research assistants read each individual article, and coded only those articles in which the relevant organisations were scrutinised in relation to the social protests. The first author thereafter conducted exactly the same media search and content analysis for five targeted organisations, over a period of three months, resulting in 87% intercoder agreement (Krippendorff's alpha = 0.71).

[8] For the collection of the data for organisations' incomes, see the above description of the data regarding the dependence on state budgets.

[9] We tested whether a random effect model fits our data using the Breusch–Pagan Lagrange Multiplier test and the Hausman test. The Breusch–Pagan test is significant ($X2$ (1) = 13.54, $p < 0.01$) and the Hausman test is insignificant (($X2$ (9) = 1.3, $p > 0.05$), thereby confirming our need to employ a random effects model.

[10] The conversion was calculated by setting the mean expenditure standard deviation − $276,498.

## Acknowledgements

We thank Noam Brenner, Nimrod Leher and Elyasaf Keller for their research assistance. An early version of this chapter was presented at the 2014 ECPR General Conference in Glasgow. We thank the participants of this session. We also thank David Levi-Faur, the editors, and two anonymous reviewers for their valuable comments and suggestions. This research was supported by the Israel Science Foundation (grant number 538/13).

## References

Alon-Barkat, S, Gilad, S, 2017, Compensating for poor performance with promotional symbols: Evidence from a survey experiment, *Journal of Public Administration Research and Theory*, 27, 4, 661-75.

Alon-Barkat, S, Gilad, S, undated, Online methodological appendix, http://public-policy.huji.ac.il/.upload/staff/21/ONLINE%20 METHODOLIGICAL%20APPENDIX%20-%20Alon-Barkat%20 and%20Gilad.pdf (last accessed 30 August 2018)

Bach, T, Ruffing, E, Yesilkagit, K, 2015, The differential empowering effects of Europeanization on the autonomy of national agencies, *Governance* 28, 3, 285–304.

Besley, T, Burgess, R, 2001, Political agency, government responsiveness and the role of the media, *European Economic Review*, 45, 4-6, 629–40.

Black, J, 2008, Constructing and contesting legitimacy and accountability in polycentric regulatory regimes, *Regulation & Governance* 2, 2, 37–64.

Boin, A, Kuipers, S, Steenbergen, M, 2010, The life and death of public organizations: A question of institutional design?, *Governance* 23, 3, 385–410.

Busuioc, EM, Lodge, M, 2016, The reputational basis of public accountability, *Governance* 29, 2, 247-63.

Carpenter, D P, 2002, Groups, the media, agency waiting costs, and FDA drug approval, *American Journal of Political Science*, 46, 3, 490.

Carpenter, D, 2004, Protection without capture: Product approval by a politically responsive, learning regulator, *American Political Science Review* 98, 4, 613–31.

Cohen, G, Kobovic, Y, 2012, Clashes in Tel Aviv: 85 are arrested at the end of violent demonstrations by social activists, *Haaretz* Online, www.haaretz.co.il/news/education/1.1738420

Dovrat-Mazritz, A, 2011, We do not know what consumers want, TheMarker, www.themarker.com/advertising/1.1577390

Epstein, D, O'Halloran, S, 1999, *Delegating powers: A transaction cost politics approach to policy making under separate powers*, Cambridge: Cambridge University Press.

Epstein, M, 2012, Shaking the dust from the government advertising, TheMarker, www.themarker.com/technation/1.1886523

Eshuis, J, Klijn, E-H, 2012, *Branding in governance and public management*, London: Routledge.

Galnoor, I, 2007, *Public administration in Israel: Development, structure, functions and reforms*, Jerusalem: Hebrew University Publishing.

Gilad, S, 2015, Political pressures, organizational identity and attention to tasks: Illustrations from pre-crisis financial regulation, *Public Administration* 93, 3, 593–608.

Gilad, S, Alon-Barkat, S, Braverman, A, 2016, Large-scale social protest: A business risk and a bureaucratic opportunity, *Governance* 29, 3, 371-92.

Gilad, S, Maor, M, Ben-Nun Bloom, P, 2015, Organizational reputation, the content of public allegations, and regulatory communication, *Journal of Public Administration Research and Theory* 25, 2, 451–78.

Gilardi, F, 2002, Policy credibility and delegation to independent regulatory agencies: A comparative empirical analysis, *Journal of European Public Policy* 9, 6, 873–93.

Gilardi, F, 2008, *Delegation in the regulatory state: Independent regulatory agencies in Western Europe*, Cheltenham, UK, and Northampton, USA: Edward Elgar.

Gilardi, F, Maggetti, M, 2011, The independence of regulatory authorities, in D Levi-Fair (ed) *Handbook on the politics of regulation*, pp 201–14, Cheltenham: Edward Elgar.

Huber, JD, Shipan, CR, Pfahler, M, 2001, Legislatures and statutory control of bureaucracy, *American Journal of Political Science* 45, 2, 330–45.

Jacobs, S, Schillemans, T, 2016, Media and public accountability: Typology and exploration, *Policy and Politics*, 44, 1, 23-40.

Levi-Faur, D, 2005, The global diffusion of regulatory capitalism, *The Annals of the American Academy of Political and Social Science* 598, 1, 12–32.

Levi-Faur, D, 2006a, Regulatory capitalism: The dynamics of change beyond telecoms and electricity, *Governance* 19, 3, 497–525.

Levi-Faur, D, 2006b, Varieties of regulatory capitalism: Sectors and nations in the making of a new global order, *Governance* 19, 3, 363–66.

Lodge, M, 2004, *Accountability and transparency in regulation: Critiques, doctrines and instruments*, Cheltenham: Edward Elgar.Maggetti, M, 2012, The media accountability of independent regulatory agencies, *European Political Science Review* 4, 3, 385–408.

Majone, G, 1997, From the positive to the regulatory state: Causes and consequences of changes in the mode of governance, *Journal of Public Policy* 17, 2, 139–67.

Majone, G, 1998, Europe's 'democratic deficit': The question of standards, *European Law Journal* 4, 1, 5–28.

Majone, G, 1999, The regulatory state and its legitimacy problems, *West European Politics* 22, 1, 1–24.

Maor, M, 2011, Organizational reputations and the observability of public warnings in 10 pharmaceutical markets, *Governance* 24, 3, 557–82.

Maor, M, Sulitzeanu-Kenan, R, 2013, The effect of salient reputational threats on the pace of FDA enforcement, *Governance* 26, 1, 31–61,

Maor, M, Gilad, S, Ben-Nun Bloom, P, 2013, Organizational reputation, regulatory talk, and strategic silence, *Journal of Public Administration Research and Theory* 23, 3, 581–608,

Maor, M, Sulitzeanu-Kenan, R, 2015, Responsive change: Agency output response to reputational threats, *Journal of Public Administration Research and Theory*, http://jpart.oxfordjournals.org/content/early/2015/03/05/jopart.muv001.short

Marvel, JD, 2015, Unconscious bias in citizens' evaluations of public sector performance, *Journal of Public Administration Research and Theory* 26, 1, 143-58.

McCubbins, MD, Schwartz, T, 1984, Congressional oversight overlooked: Police patrols versus fire alarms, *American Journal of Political Science* 28, 1, 165–79.

Moe, TM, 1984, The new economics of organization, *American Journal of Political Science* 28, 4, 739–77.

Moffitt, SL, 2010, Promoting agency reputation through public advice: Advisory committee use in the FDA, *The Journal of Politics* 72, 3, 880–93.

Neshkova, MI, 2014, Does agency autonomy foster public participation?, *Public Administration Review* 74, 1, 64–74.

Petersen, MA, 2009, Estimating standard errors in finance panel data sets: Comparing approaches, *Review of Financial Studies* 22, 1, 435–80.

Puppis, M, Maggetti, M, Gilardi, F, Biela, J, Papadopoulos, Y, 2014, The political communication of independent regulatory agencies, *Swiss Political Science Review* 20, 3, 388–412.

Ram, U, Filk, D, 2013, The 14th of July of Daphni Leef: The rise and the fall of the social protest, *Theory and Criticism* 41, 17–43 [in Hebrew].

Rimkutė, D, 2018, Organizational reputation and risk regulation: The effect of reputational threats on agency scientific outputs, *Public Administration* 96, 1, 70-83.

Rosenhek, Z, Shalev, M, 2014, The political economy of Israel's 'social justice' protests: A class and generational analysis, *Contemporary Social Science* 9, 1, 1–18.

Schillemans, T, 2016, Fighting or fumbling with the beast? The mediatisation of public sector agencies in Australia and the Netherlands, *Policy and Politics*, 44, 1.

Van Thiel, S, 2012, Comparing agencies across countries, in K Verhoest, S Van Thiel, G Bouckaert, P Lægreid (eds) *Government agencies: Practices and lessons from 30 countries*, pp 18–26, Basingstoke: Palgrave Macmillan.

Verhoest, K, Peters, BG, Bouckaert, G, Verschuere, B, 2004, The study of organisational autonomy: A conceptual review, *Public Administration and Development* 24, 2, 101–18. Weissberg, H, 2012, Supporting, yet less: Decrease in popular support of the social protest, TheMarker, www.themarker.com/news/protest/1.1747654

West, WF, Raso, C, 2013, Who shapes the rulemaking agenda? Implications for bureaucratic responsiveness and bureaucratic control, *Journal of Public Administration Research and Theory* 23, 3, 495–519.

Wood, BD, Waterman, RW, 1991, The dynamics of political control of the bureaucracy, *The American Political Science Review* 85, 3, 801–28.

Yesilkagit, K, Christensen, JG, 2010, Institutional design and formal autonomy: Political versus historical and cultural explanations, *Journal of Public Administration Research and Theory* 20, 1, 53–74.

Yesilkagit, K, Van Thiel, S, 2008, Political influence and bureaucratic autonomy, *Public Organization Review* 8, 2, 137–53.

Yesilkagit, K, Van Thiel, S, 2012, Autonomous agencies and perceptions of stakeholder influence in parliamentary democracies, *Journal of Public Administration Research and Theory* 22, 1, 101–19.

Yeung, K, 2009, Presentational management and the pursuit of regulatory legitimacy: A comparative study of competition and consumer agencies in the United Kingdom and Australia, *Public Administration* 87, 2, 274–94.

Zarhia, Z, 2012, This is how the 2012 social protest looks like: The violence, the rallies and the banks burglary, TheMarker, www.themarker.com/news/protest/1.1738485

# Mediatised local government: social media activity and media strategies among local government officials 1989–2010

Monika Djerf-Pierre and Jon Pierre

## Social media and local government

The advent of social media such as Facebook, Twitter and blogs provide government institutions with both challenges and opportunities (Klang and Nolin, 2011; Magro, 2012). On the one hand there is potential to increasing legitimacy through involvement, collaboration and dialogue (Knox, 2013). Social media allows citizens to communicate directly with government institutions and government actors may respond directly to the public. However, there are also difficulties with accommodating large flows of direct public feedback into public organisations (Knox, 2013).

What is more important is that social media may alter the power relations between conventional media institutions (press, radio and television) and government actors, that is, transforming the very trajectory of mediatisation itself (for example, Schulz, 2004; Miller, 2014). Social media provide the political elite with opportunities to circumvent the filtering and gatekeeping practices of professional news organisations and communicate directly with citizens. This poses a challenge to the power of conventional media and the dominant news media logic; that of professional journalism in press, radio and television.

To date, most studies on how government actors relate to social media have focused on national elections and politics (for example, Schweitzer, 2011; Southern, 2014) while local government has received less attention (Larsson, 2013). The key issues to explore in this context are thus if social media have similar implications for local governance as studies suggest they have at the national level, and to what extent the advent of social media has changed the ways in which local politicians and bureaucrats relate to the news media, particularly the local press. Our main research questions are thus how local political and administrative elites relate to the media, and to what extent social media complement or replace conventional news media in local governments' public communication.

This chapter first examines the development of local government-media relations across time, on the basis of a unique survey-based data set comparing the local political and administrative leadership's media strategies in 1989 and 2010. We surveyed the local senior political and administrative leadership in all municipalities in Sweden, including the Chairman of the Executive Board (CEB) who is the top elected politician and de facto mayor of the city; the city manager (the top, non-elected, public servant and the Head of the city administration); and the financial manager (the senior economic manager in the city administration).

The 2010 survey also included questions on social media use. Drawing on the survey, the chapter proceeds to explore how these local officials in Sweden use social media in their work, that is, Facebook, Twitter and blogs. We examine the level of social media usage within different institutional settings and identify the micro- and meso-level factors that influence local officials' social media activity.

Finally we study the relationship between the officials' social media activity and the contacts with conventional news media. By bringing together the analyses of media strategies across time and the study of the social media use among officials we can assess if and how social media affect the relationship with conventional news media at the local level.

The extensive time period between the two points of measurement has witnessed profound changes both in the media landscape and in the local authorities. Indeed, social media did not exist in 1989 and local authorities had limited professional staff charged with managing media relations. In 2010, social media had become the defining feature of the web 2.0 and most local authorities had specialised, professional staff to manage the institution's media relationships. Our dataset thus allows us to explore how these transformations have affected the media strategies of the local leadership and their ramifications on local governance. The analysis demonstrates that the advent of social media seems to reinforce existing patterns. Social media do not replace conventional media but, on the contrary, actually *increase* interactions with traditional news media.

## Local governance and the media

The basic rationale of this theme issue is our limited knowledge about the role of the media in governance. Klijn et al (2014) suggest that the research on the relationship between the media and public managers can be categorised into three broad traditions: the public relations tradition, the agenda-setting tradition and the mediatisation tradition. Political scientists, judging by the literature, tend to be aware of the first two traditions whereas mediatisation is much less noted or understood.

The role of the media in governance is particularly neglected in studies of local government. On the precious few occasions when the media is at all mentioned it is for the most part lumped together with other societal actors such as citizens, private businesses and organised interests (see for instance Clark, 2000; DiGaetano and Strom, 2003; Pierre, 2011). The media is typically perceived as an arena or a channel of communication. There is essentially no understanding of the media as an actor or active participant in governance, let alone of the mediatisation of local politics.

Interestingly, the perhaps most important exception to this pattern is found in the urban political economy literature of the 1970s and 1980s. Here, city politics is seen as closely tied to economic development and some scholars describe cities as 'growth machines' (Molotch, 1976; Logan and Molotch, 1987). This metaphor signifies that essentially all actors in urban politics – not just businesses and the local authority but NGOs, neighbourhood organisations and the media – have a 'unitary interest' (Peterson, 1981) in economic growth. Local media have huge stakes in urbanisation and growth in the local economy as this increases circulation and ad revenues. This point was made rather bluntly when the publisher of the San Jose Mercury News was asked why the newspaper had supported the devastation of orchard gardens where now the city is sprawling: 'Trees do not read newspapers' (Downey, 1974, 112, cited in Logan and Molotch, 1987, 96).

A mutual lack of integrity between the sphere of politics and that of the media is evident in this account of urban politics, raising issues about transparency and accountability. In addition to reviewing and reporting city politics or the local business community, local media also have an interest in marketing or 'branding' the city. This takes place in news reporting in conventional media but increasingly so also through social media (Nielsen and Houlberg Salomonsen, 2012). Such confluence of social constituencies is not merely explained by economic factors. Just as nations that come under attack rally behind unifying symbols and leaders, so do societal actors in cities that come under external scrutiny. Social media provide an alternative forum where citizens can display criticism and discontent with local politics, and municipalities must respond if they become the target of extensive social media criticism.

Local media also differ from national media in terms of resources and conditions, particularly in smaller municipalities. There is rarely an abundance of news stories to choose from and reporting often relies on the continuous flow of information from local officials; the same officials that journalists are supposed to scrutinise. There is also a lack of resources in terms of staff; a problem that has been exacerbated by the decline in readership and the loss of advertising due to the spread of the internet

(Franklin and Murphy, 2005). Journalistic scrutiny thus encounters several problems at the local level and investigative journalism is indeed a peripheral phenomenon in Swedish local journalism (Ekström et al, 2006). Also, some local governments operate in media shadow (Nord and Nygren, 2002); there simply is no media of any consequence covering their jurisdiction. The lack of media coverage may work as a driver for local politicians and bureaucrats to develop social media platforms as an alternative route to communicate with the local citizenry.

Thus, understanding the role of social media and the mediatisation of local governance is a somewhat different academic challenge compared to analyses of mediatisation at the national level. Analyses of local governance must depart from the economic and structural features of that governance which shape the behaviour of both the officials of the local state and the media. The specific political and economic context within which local media relates to local elites constitute institutional and structural factors which set the preconditions for the relationship. Our focus is precisely on political agency within those confining parameters where changes in the media system, not the least through the advent of social media, create new interactions between the media, the local elites and the citizens.

## Mediatisation and social media use in local government

Research on mediatisation is currently flourishing. Alongside the increasing amount of research there is an ongoing debate over the definition of the concept, its scope and qualities and its historical trajectories (for example, Hjarvard, 2008; Strömbäck, 2008; Krotz and Hepp, 2011; Esser, 2013; Hepp, 2013; Marcinkowski, 2014). The specific study of the mediatisation of politics has so far given most attention to parliamentary politics, political parties and (particularly) national elections. We know much less about the extent to which the media shapes the non-elected, administrative element of the political system such as the public bureaucracy (Schillemans, 2012; Thorbjornsrud et al, 2014) and local government.

The process through which political institutions integrate and accommodate to new forms of media, and how the diffusion of social media impacts on the relationship to conventional news media (press, radio, and television), is a key issue for mediatisation research (for example, Schulz, 2004; Hjarvard, 2014; Miller, 2014). Although there has been a surge in research on both e-government and the mediatisation of politics in recent years, studies of how *local* politicians and bureaucrats relate to social media are less common. Existing studies usually examine the municipalities' webpages (for example, Haug, 2007; Wohlers, 2009; Larsson, 2013) while there is a lack of studies that survey how individual officials use and relate to social media (Winsvold, 2007).

In this study we depart from an institutionalist perspective on mediatisation; it refers to the process where the media have become integrated into the operations of other social institutions (such as political institutions), while they have also acquired the status of social institutions in their own right (Hjarvard, 2008, 113). The notion that political actors and government institutions adapt to and accommodate the institutional logic ('modus operandi') of the news media is fundamental to the institutionalist perspective on mediatised politics (Marcinkowski, 2014). That argument notwithstanding, we also regard mediatisation as an interactive process where government institutions do not just passively submit to the (fixed) media logic but also actively develop strategies to handle and engage with the media.

This perspective highlights the media activities of individual officials as 'a *constituent* of the processes in which mediatisation is reconstructed and enacted', that is, the 'micro-dynamics of mediatisation' (Pallas and Fredriksson, 2013, 421). It also puts a focus on how individual and structural factors (organisational settings) influence how individual officials in different organisations relate to both conventional and social media.

In the study we perceive of the interactions with conventional news media and social media activity *as two different, but integral, parts of the officials' media relations*. Although mediatisation entails adapting to, accommodating, and integrating media into government institutions (for example, Schultz, 2004; Hjarvard, 2008; 2014), there are differences between individual officials within the same organisation with regard to how they relate to the conventional news media and how they accommodate social media in their professional work. There is also variation in the extent and quality of integration and adaptation among different organisations.

## Exploring local government mediatisation

In order to explore the mediatisation of local government in Sweden, this study addresses three, related, issues.

## Characterisation

The first issue is how the media strategies of individual officials can be characterised. We analyse their contacts with news media journalists on two salient dimensions: the frequency of contacts with journalists and the initiative for contacts. Results can be combined into four different media strategies:

- A *proactive* strategy entails frequent (daily/weekly) contacts with journalists in which the official generally initiates contact or contacts are initiated by both parties to the same degree.
- The *defensive* strategy involves frequent contacts with journalists but contacts often occur on the journalist's initiative.
- The *selective* strategy means that officials have few contacts with journalists (less frequently than on a weekly basis). Nevertheless, the official generally initiates contact or contacts are initiated by both parties to the same degree.
- The *passive* strategy, finally, entails few contacts with journalists and signifies that those contacts often occur on the journalist's initiative.

## Explanation

The second issue is how to *explain* officials' media relations. To this end we focus on micro- and meso-level factors such as personal motivations and the structural and organisational environment within which the actors operate that can explain individual officials' news media strategies and social media use.

- *Publicness of position* Obviously, the chairmen of the executive board (CEB), the city manager and financial manager have very different requirements vis-à-vis the public sphere. Answerability and public accountability require elected officials to communicate with the citizenry and stakeholders through the media (Bovens et al, 2008). City managers, too, have a public position although they are senior civil servants. Public management reform has accorded city managers a more prominent and autonomous role as the chief operational and executive officer of the city, thus to some extent removing them from the sheltered privacy of their offices (Moore, 1997; Pollitt and Bouckaert, 2011). The financial manager, on the other hand, is not expected to deal directly with the media and thus experiences less of a push to develop media practices as part of her professional work.
- *News media experience and social media competence* Dealing with the news media and fostering personal networks with journalists is a skill cultivated over time and it is reasonable to expect that the officials' contacts with the news media increase significantly with age (that is, experience). Since social media use, particularly being an active blogger or tweeter, follows from an inclination or need to be visible in the public sphere, we assume that individuals who are opinion makers in the public sphere and regularly work proactively vis-à-vis conventional journalists, also are social media users. Officials who

have developed routines for dealing with conventional news media would also find it easier to engage social media. The expectation is consequently that officials' contacts with conventional news media and their social media activity are positively related.

- *Media scrutiny*  The notion that effective external communication will yield positive media coverage is widely embraced in political and administration research (Liu et al, 2012). Equally widespread is the idea that effective communication, including the management of media relations, contributes to favourable media coverage which in turn will help maintain or increase political legitimacy and citizens' trust. This hypothesis largely explains the professionalisation and expansion of governments' strategic communications. Empirical research has however not unequivocally supported this hypothesis (compare Liu et al, 2012; Fredriksson et al, 2015). Since studies of the association between communication activities and media publicity often rely on cross-sectional data it is difficult to determine the causal direction between the two, that is, if organisations become more media-active as a response to increasing levels of attention or scrutiny or the other way around. In any case, there is probably a positive correlation between the level of media scrutiny and the officials' media contacts so that they increase when the municipality is the target of media criticism.
- *Organisational capacity* The amount of media attention that a municipality attracts is most likely related to its size. Large municipalities have bigger resources and capacity to influence decisions at the national level (Rhodes, 1986; Gustafsson, 1987) and are thus more likely to attract media attention to their undertakings. Larger entities also have more resources to put into their communications activities (compare Fredriksson et al, 2015).
- *Media focus or shadow* Not all municipalities are of interest to the media; particularly the national media tend to pay only scant attention to what some see as the political hinterland. Also, the amount of attention that local or regional newspapers pay to different municipalities varies greatly and, indeed, some areas do not even have a local newspaper. Municipalities located next to metropolitan regions, particularly the nation's capital, often find it hard to attract any media attention at all. Nord and Nygren (2002) refer to this phenomenon as 'media shadow'. Social media can also be used to attract media attention and thus alleviate the media shadow. We thus expect that officials will be more active social media users in municipalities that lack a local newspaper.
- *Media competition* The local media situation presumably influences both the officials' relations to conventional news media and the incentive to engage in social media. Local media concentration has been seen

as a democratic problem for a very long time and it was the main reason for the introduction of press subsidies that have been in place in Sweden since the 1960s (Djerf-Pierre and Weibull, 2009). The existence of more than one local newspaper in a municipality is seen as a safeguard for opinion diversity and pluralism and as a prerequisite for effective opinion formation. Officials in municipalities marked by local monopolies, that is, where a municipality is dominated by a single newspaper, are possibly more inclined to widen the space for public communication and opinion formation by engaging in social media. If, on the other hand, there is diversity of media outlets, officials would feel less induced to develop alternative communication channels through social media.

### Assessment

The third issue brings together the advent of social media and the changes in media strategies in an assessment of how social media affect the relationship with conventional news media. There are three theoretically conceivable patterns of interaction:

- *Substitution* For individual officials, social media activities can *substitute* or replace interacting with conventional news media. If this is the case, social media activity would decrease the overall level of news media interaction, at least among the heavy users of social media.
- *Complement* On the other hand, social media can also be regarded as *complementary* to conventional media, providing yet another communication platform for officials' public communication. In the latter case, social media would not have an impact on the level of conventional media activity.
- *Reinforcement* A third potential outcome is that social media and conventional media activities actually *reinforce* each other so that heavy social media users also have intense relations with conventional media, contributing to an intensification of the officials' media related activities overall.

## Method and data

The study draws on two surveys conducted in 1989 and 2010, both led by the present authors (Djerf and Pierre, 1991). The surveys targeted senior local government officials and included all senior politicians (the chairmen of the executive boards (CEB)), city managers and financial managers in *all* Swedish municipalities (284 municipalities in 1989 and

290 in 2010). The surveys thus include the entire population of officials and not a sample.

The 1989 survey used a mail questionnaire while the 2010 study was a web-based questionnaire. The response rate was much higher in 1989 (85 per cent) than in 2010 (40 per cent). The declining response rate over time is consistent with a general trend in survey studies. The distribution of respondents in both surveys, however, equals the 'population of municipalities' in 1989 and 2010, respectively. The distribution of the responses from officials in municipalities with different political situation (political majority), tax base (measure of the economic situation of the municipality), media situation (the level of competition and the political stance of newspapers) and population were almost identical to the municipality population, except for the population indicator in the 2010 sample, where smaller municipalities were slightly overrepresented. There was no significant difference in the response propensity of different categories of officials. Both surveys are thus representative for the larger group of municipalities in Sweden, and the lower response rate in 2010 should thus not bias the results.

Since the surveys include the entire population of officials, the procedure of statistical inference (that is, drawing conclusions regarding a population from a random sample) and the calculation of significance levels are not fully applicable. The correlations that are found exist 'as is' in the population. Significance levels nonetheless will be presented in all tables to indicate the robustness of the results.

The main *dependent variables* in the study are the level of social media activity and the frequency of contacts with journalists in conventional news media.

*Social media activity* was measured by the following question: 'Do you use social media in your work?'. The specified categories of social media use were: 'Writing blogs/twittering', 'Reading/following blogs or twitter', and 'Using Facebook'. The response alternatives were 'Daily', 'Weekly', 'Monthly', 'Yearly', 'More seldom', and 'Don't know'. The correlations between the different types of activity is fairly high; it varies between 0.461★★★ and 0.569★★★ and a reliability test shows a Cronbach's alpha of 0.800. We thus constructed an index of social media activity by adding the responses for 'Writing blogs/twittering', 'Reading/following blogs or twitter', and 'Using Facebook' and assigning them the following values: (5) 'Daily', (4) 'Weekly', (3) 'Monthly', (2) 'Yearly', (1) 'More seldom' and (1) 'Don't know'. This created an index ranging from 3 to 15. The final social media activity index (SMAI) was calculated by rescaling the index to range from 0 to 1 where 0 = no social media activity, 1 = active in all three social media categories every day.

The frequency of *media contacts* with news media journalists was measured by asking the respondents, 'How often do you have contact with journalists from the following media?' The specified media categories were: 'Local press', 'Local/regional radio/ TV', and 'National media (national press, radio, TV)'. The response alternatives were 'Daily', 'Weekly', 'Monthly', 'Yearly', 'More seldom', and 'Don't know'. Although the responses were completely dominated by the local press, the correlations between the different types of media contacts are quite high. A reliability test returns a Cronbach's alpha of 0.802, indicating the plausibility of constructing an additive index by assigning the following values to the responses: (5) 'Daily', (4) 'Weekly', (3) 'Monthly', (2) 'Yearly', (1) 'More seldom', and (1) 'Don't know'. The addition of the values for all three conventional media categories results in an index that ranges from 3 to 15. The final Media Contacts Index was calculated by rescaling the index to range from 0 to 1 where 0 = do not have contact with any of the three conventional media categories, 1 = have daily contact with all three media categories (local, regional, national press, radio and television).

Throughout the survey very few respondents used the 'Don't know' alternatives or chose not to answer individual questions. We know from previous studies of media use that non-users sometimes use the 'Don't know' categories or abstain from responding because of the lack of familiarity with the object. The 'Don't know' responses were thus recoded into the 'More seldom' category. We also tested the models with the 'Don't know' coded as 'missing' and concluded that the recoding did not significantly change the results.

The *independent variables* used in the study consist of a combination of individual level and municipal level factors. The individual level factors include the officials' personal characteristics and experiences (gender, age, position) whereas the municipal level factors refer to contextual and structural circumstances surrounding the individual official, that is, media situation, municipality population, level of media scrutiny of the municipality. The individual characteristics are all derived from the survey; the municipality level factors are collected both from the survey (respondent were asked how they perceive certain characteristics of the municipality) and from official statistics sources.

To measure the effect of *gender* and *age (social media competence and media experience)*, the respondents in the survey were asked to indicate their gender (1 = male, 2 = female) and age (33–69).

To measure the differences in media relations between senior politicians, city managers and financial managers, the variable *position* was dummy coded and the financial manager category is used as the reference category.

*Media initiative*, which measures whether the individual official is proactive vis-à-vis the news media and initiates contacts with journalists, was gauged by the question, 'Who does normally initiate these contacts?' with regard to the specified media categories: 'Local press', 'Local/regional radio/ TV', and 'National media' (national press, radio, TV). The response alternatives were 'You yourself', 'The journalists', and 'Both equally often'. Media initiative was calculated by identifying the respondents who chose the alternatives 'You yourself' or 'Both equally often' with regard to any of the media categories. This resulted in a dichotomous variable: 0 = does not initiate contacts with conventional news media, 1 = initiates contacts with conventional news media.

The perceived intensity of *media scrutiny/criticism* towards the local government was measured by asking the officials, 'How often has the local government been the object of critical scrutiny or debate in various categories of media in the last year?' The specified media categories were: 'In the local press', 'In national media' and 'In social media'. The response alternatives were: 'Daily', 'Weekly', 'Monthly', 'Yearly' and 'Seldom/ never' and 'Don't know'. There is a correlation between the perceived level of scrutiny of the municipality in different categories of media, but the correlations are only moderately strong (Kendall's Tau, 0.300★★★ to 0.447★★★, and Cronbach's alpha is 0.631). This indicates that the extent to which the local government has been the subject of media scrutiny/ criticism in the local press, national media and social media should be regarded as different factors/variables and the effect of each is investigated independently. In the analysis we constructed three separate media scrutiny variables that range from 1 to 5 by assigning the response alternatives the following values: (5) 'Daily', (4) 'Weekly', (3) 'Monthly', (2) 'Yearly', (1) 'Seldom/never' (1) and (1) 'Don't know'.

To measure *organisational capacity* we use the population size of the municipality as an indicator. We constructed a dichotomous variable where 1 = a large municipality that has a population of 26,000 or more and 0 = a smaller municipality with less than 26,000 inhabitants.

The extent to which a community is in a *media focus* or resides in 'media shadow' is indicated by the presence or absence of a local newspaper in the municipality. This is measured by a dichotomous variable, 1 = a local newspaper is published (has its main office) in the municipality, 0 = no local newspaper.

Finally, *media competition* was measured as a dichotomous variable, 1 = newspaper competition (a second newspaper has 10 per cent or more of the readership in the municipality; this pertains to about 50 per cent of the Swedish municipalities) and 0 = local monopoly, (one newspaper is totally dominant; this pertains to about 50 per cent of the municipalities).

## Results

We start with an examination and *characterisation* of the local officials' news media strategies across time. The next step is to examine the officials' use of social media and how individual and structural factors *explain* differences in social media activity by employing a multivariate analysis. Finally we *assess* how social media use relates to the local elite's strategies vis-à-vis conventional news media.

### The officials' news media relations: surprisingly small changes across time

The first step in exploring how social media influence the relations with conventional news media is to *characterise* and *compare* the officials' media strategies in 1989 and 2010.

In the 1989 study (Djerf and Pierre, 1991) we established the predominance of the local press in the public communication system at the local level. Indeed, media contacts of all Swedish officials were completely dominated by the local press; 85 per cent of the senior politicians and about 66 per cent of the city managers had contact with local press on a weekly or daily basis. The few media contacts reported by the financial managers were with the local press as well. Local/regional radio and television, all of which were part of the public service broadcasting services at the time, yielded much lower levels of contact. National press, radio and television were considered so irrelevant for local politics that the contacts with national media were not even measured. Indeed, in 1989 the local press was at its all-time high with regard to profits and readership (Djerf-Pierre and Weibull, 2009) while genuinely local radio and television were virtually absent. However, newspaper concentration was fairly high and about a quarter of the communities had local newspaper monopolies.

In 2010 the media landscape looked completely different. Newspaper readership and profits were plummeting and numerous local papers had been bought up by their local competitor, further increasing concentration. Internet was widely accessible, exacerbating local competition for advertising and audiences, and commercial television and radio were established since the 1990s.

Despite the expansion of commercial broadcasting, however, in the 2010 study the news media contacts were still dominated by the local press; 84 per cent of the senior politicians, 43 per cent of the city managers, and 4 per cent of the financial managers had regular contacts (weekly/daily) with the local press. Local/regional broadcast media still only yielded low contacts; only 8 per cent of the officials had regular (weekly/daily) contacts. This time, contacts with national media were surveyed, but very few of the officials had any contacts with national press, radio and television; only 1 per cent of the officials had regular contacts (weekly/daily).

Overall, the results point to remarkably small changes in how frequently local officials interact with conventional media since the 1980s, despite the significant changes in the media environment. Local newspapers have been an integrated part of local political life for a very long time. However, with increasing mediatisation we assumed that the media pressure on local officials would increase across time. On the other hand, an increasing institutional pressure does not necessarily entail that individual officials will have more intense media contacts. The professionalisation of the local government's media relations (where specialised departments are formed and agents are employed to handle the news media) increased significantly in the 1990s (Larsson, 2005), and may instead have alleviated some officials from interacting personally with journalists.

In Table 4.1 we distinguish between the officials' contact intensity (frequency of contacts) and contact initiative (if it is the journalist or the official who initiates the contact) in relation to the media in 1989 and 2010. This distinction enables us to identify four general media strategies which we applied to the local officials' relations to the local press. The *proactive* strategy entails frequent (daily/weekly) contacts with the local press

**Table 4.1: Local press strategies among local officials 1989 and 2010 (percent)**

|  | CEB (senior politicians) | | City managers** | | Financial managers* | |
|---|---|---|---|---|---|---|
|  | 1989 | 2010 | 1989 | 2010 | 1989 | 2010 |
| Proactive | 36 | 42 | 15 | 13 | 4 | 2 |
| Defensive | 49 | 42 | 51 | 30 | 8 | 2 |
| Selective | 5 | 5 | 9 | 14 | 13 | 7 |
| Passive | 10 | 11 | 25 | 43 | 75 | 89 |
| Sum | 100 | 100 | 100 | 100 | 100 | 100 |
| N = | 237 | 118 | 240 | 114 | 202 | 112 |

Note: ** $p <0.01$, * $p <0.05$ (Cramer's V). The table is constructed on the basis of the responses to the question about the official's contact frequency and contact initiative with the local press. Proactive: the official has daily or weekly contact with the local press and the official initiates contact or contacts are initiated by both parties to the same degree. Defensive: the official has daily or weekly contacts with the local press but contacts often occur on the journalist's initiative. Selective: the official has contacts with the local press less frequently than on a weekly basis but the official initiates contact or contacts are initiated by both parties to the same degree. Passive: the official has contact with the local press less frequently than on a weekly basis and the contacts often occur on the journalist's initiative.

and the official initiates contact or contacts are initiated by both parties to the same degree. The *defensive* strategy involves frequent contacts with the local press but contacts often occur on the journalist's initiative. The *selective* strategy means few contacts with the local press (less frequently than on a weekly basis) but the official initiates contact or contacts are initiated by both parties to the same degree. The *passive* strategy, finally, entails few contacts with the local press and that the contacts often occur on the journalist's initiative.

Table 4.1 shows that there is a small but noticeable shift in the officials' local press strategies between 1989 and 2010. In 1989, senior politicians were generally proactive or defensive in relation to the local press, and in 2010 the two active approaches were still as evident. A shift from a defensive stance to a proactive stance can be observed but the shift is not statistically significant. The city managers have moved from a defensive stance to a passive one. The financial managers were mostly passive vis-à-vis the local press already in 1989 and the passive stance was even more pronounced in 2010. Senior politicians are thus slightly more active vis-à-vis the media while city-managers and financial managers are less active.

The findings indicate that the elected officials still see fostering personal contacts with journalists as essential and give a first indication that the advent of social media has not changed this relationship to any large extent. Instead, the small but significant shifts in strategies are mainly indicative of the professionalisation of media relations in Swedish local authorities. Since we are asking the officials about their individual contacts with conventional media, some of these interactions are now handled by professional press secretaries or communications officers. Senior politicians still maintain personal contacts with journalists while city managers to a greater extent have delegated this task to professionals.

## Social media use: only moderate appropriation

One of the main changes since 1989 is obviously the advent of social media. As a second step of our exploration, we examine the degree to which actors in local government have appropriated social media in their professional lives. From the outset it could be expected that social media use would be quite widespread and common in our population. Sweden ranks among the countries with the highest overall penetration of social and digital media in society (Westlund, 2012) and the advent of social media is often seen as a path-breaking change in the media landscape. However, when our 2010 survey was conducted, social media was not yet widely spread among Swedish local officials.

Table 4.2 shows that for all three categories of social media use – 'Writing blogs/twittering', 'Reading/following blogs or twitter' and 'Using Facebook' – the response category with most replies was the minimum level of usage, that is, 'more seldom'. Overall, Facebook topped the list of social media activities, followed by reading blogs and tweets. Officials were thus more inclined to be consumers rather than producers of social media content such as blogging and tweeting. In total, 44 per cent of the senior politicians, 38 per cent of the city managers and 5 per cent of the financial managers used Facebook as part of their work at least once a week. No financial managers were blogging or tweeting on a weekly basis, compared with 11 per cent of the city managers and 20 per cent of the senior politicians.

In order to create a baseline for assessing the extent of the social media activity, we must compare the officials' social media use with that of other social groups. The officials' activity level is on par with that of the general population; in 2010, 6 per cent of Swedes write blogs, 22 per cent read blogs at least once a week while 34 per cent use social media such as Facebook at least weekly (Bergström, 2011). However, when we compare local officials' social media activity with that of Swedish journalists (a study conducted about the same time as the present survey), we note that journalists – the counterpart in the politics-media interaction – are much more active users of social media (Hedman and Djerf-Pierre, 2013). Among journalists, 77 per cent use social network sites such as Facebook and 65 per cent read blogs at least once a week.

Table 4.2 clearly indicates that social media activity varies significantly between different groups of officials. Our 2010 analysis included independent variables with which the variations in social media use of local government actors can be tentatively *explained*. Those relate to *personal* factors (gender and age), *professional* factors (position, media contacts, and media initiative), *organisational* factors (capacity/size) as well as *media-related* factors (media scrutiny, media focus, and media competition). Together, these factors turned out to be helpful in explaining variance in social media use.

We examine the local officials' social media activity, by means of OLS regression. Table 4.3 shows the multivariate analysis, with the Social Media Activity Index (SMAI) as the dependent variable. The multivariate analysis indicates that age (being young), position (being a senior politician or city manager), media contacts (having frequent contacts with journalists in conventional media), social media scrutiny/criticism (local government being the target of criticism/debate in social media, but not in national or local conventional media), and the size of the municipality (large population) are factors that contribute to increase the level of social media activity among local officials. Altogether, the included factors explain about 30 per cent (Adjusted $R^2$ 0.298★★★) of the variation in social media activity.

**Table 4.2: Social media activity among local officials (per cent)**

| | | Daily | Weekly | Monthly | Yearly | More seldom | Sum | N = |
|---|---|---|---|---|---|---|---|---|
| Blogging or writing tweets*** | CEB (senior politicians) | 6 | 14 | 7 | 5 | 68 | 100 | 119 |
| | City managers | 5 | 6 | 3 | 2 | 84 | 100 | 114 |
| | Financial managers | 0 | 0 | 1 | 2 | 97 | 100 | 114 |
| Reading blogs or tweets*** | CEB (senior politicians) | 9 | 17 | 14 | 3 | 57 | 100 | 119 |
| | City managers | 11 | 10 | 10 | 8 | 61 | 100 | 114 |
| | Financial managers | 3 | 3 | 4 | 6 | 84 | 100 | 114 |
| Using Facebook*** | CEB (senior politicians) | 25 | 19 | 13 | 5 | 38 | 100 | 119 |
| | City managers | 14 | 24 | 7 | 5 | 50 | 100 | 114 |
| | Financial managers | 1 | 4 | 4 | 34 | 88 | 100 | 114 |

Note: *** p <0.001 (tau-c). Social media activity was measured by the following question: 'Do you use social media in your work?' The specified categories of social media use are: 'Writing blogs/twittering', 'Reading/following blogs or twitter', and 'Using Facebook'. The response alternatives are 'Daily', 'Weekly', 'Monthly', 'Yearly', and 'More seldom'.

The findings generally correspond with our expectations. Social media use is indeed related to personal factors (age, that is, social media competence), media contacts, organisational capacity and publicness of position.

With regard to media-related factors social media scrutiny display a significant effect on the level of social media activity. Social media activity is thus mostly a reactive response, triggered by social media criticism. Contrary to our expectations, however, variables relating to media situation (that is, if the municipality is a media centre or the presence of local media competition) do not have unique effects on social media use. This means that local government officials in municipalities with local media monopolies and/or that are in media shadow do not counter the lack of opportunities for news media visibility by becoming more active in social media.

The results also indicate that social media activity and contacts with conventional media are positively related (that is, the effect of media contacts on social media activity is 0.335★★★) and the next section looks more closely at how social media and conventional media interact in the professional lives of local officials.

**Table 4.3: Effects of individual and municipal level factors on local officials' social media activity (OLS regression)**

| OLS regression, unstandardised b coefficients (std. errors in parenthesis) | Dependent: Social media activity index (SMAI) (0–1) |
| --- | --- |
| **Gender** = female | 0.046 (0.029) |
| **Age** (30–69) | -0.008 (0.002) *** |
| **Position** (reference category = Financial manager) | |
| Senior politician | 0.157 (0.046) ** |
| City manager | 0.137 (0.037) *** |
| **Media initiative** | 0.011 (0.031) |
| **Media contacts** (index, 0–1) | 0.335 (0.091) *** |
| **Media scrutiny/criticism** | |
| Local press (1–5) | -0.026 (0.015) |
| National press (1–5) | -0.004 (0.021) |
| Social media (1–5) | 0.044 (0.010) *** |
| **Organizational capacity**: Population = Large | 0.084 (0.032) ** |
| **Media focus** = Has local newspaper | 0.024 (0.032) |
| **Local newspaper competition** = Yes | 0.003 (0.026) |
| Intercept | 0.164 (0.072) * |
| N = | 347 |
| Adjusted $R^2$ | 0.298*** |

Note: *** $p < 0.001$, ** $p < 0.01$, * $p < 0.05$. The dependent variable is the Social media activity index, ranging from 0–1.

## *Assessment: social media reinforce existing patterns*

If mediatisation entails that news media become integrated into the professional lives of public officials and that these public officials negotiate with and adapt to the requirements of the news media, it is possible that the advent of social media alters the process of mediatisation itself.

For individual officials, social media activities can *substitute* or replace interacting with conventional news media. If this is the case, social media activity would decrease the overall level of news media interaction, at least among the heavy users of social media. On the other hand, social media can also be regarded as *complementary* to conventional media, providing yet another communication platform for officials' public communication. In the latter case, social media would not have an impact on the level of conventional media activity. A third potential outcome is that social media and conventional media activities actually *reinforce* each other so that heavy social media users also have intense relations with conventional media, contributing to an intensification of the officials' media related activities overall.

The analysis of how conventional and social media activities are related at the individual level requires a shift of analytic focus. The next step is thus a multivariate analysis where we use media contacts as the dependent variable and include social media activity as the main independent variable. We also control for all the other factors that previously were identified as important predictors of the officials' inclination to engage in mediated communication (Table 4.4).

The results show most importantly that – other factors held constant – social media activity indeed increases the level of conventional media contacts; officials who are actively using social media have more contacts with conventional news media. There is thus little evidence for the substitution and complementarity hypotheses. It appears that social media actually increases the interactions with conventional news media at the local level. By being active in social media the local official probably signals accessibility and a desire to be visible in the public sphere and this attracts additional news media attention – thus creating a spiral of activity in social *and* news media. Our findings consequently support the reinforcement thesis.

**Table 4.4: Effects of individual and municipal level factors on local officials' news media contacts (OLS regression)**

| OLS regression, unstandardized coefficients (std. errors in parenthesis) | Dependent: Media contacts index (0–1) |
| --- | --- |
| **Gender** = female | -0.041 (0.017)* |
| **Age** 30–69 | 0.002 (0.001) |
| **Position** (ref = financial manager) | |
| Politician | 0.319 (0.021)*** |
| City manager | 0.145 (0.021)*** |
| **Social media activity** (index, 0–1) | 0.119 (0.032)*** |
| **Media scrutiny/criticism** (1–5) | |
| Local press | 0.026 (0.009)** |
| National press | 0.039 (0.012)** |
| Social media | 0.002 (0.006) |
| **Organizational capacity**: Population = Large | -0.021 (0.019) |
| **Media focus** = has local newspaper | 0.051 (0.019)** |
| **Local newspaper competition** = yes | 0.022 (0.016) |
| **Intercept** | 0.027 (0.039) |
| N = | 347 |
| Adjusted $R^2$ | 0.555*** |

Note: *** $p < 0.001$, ** $p < 0.01$, * $p < 0.05$. The dependent variable is the Media contacts index, ranging from 0–1.

## Conclusions and discussion

This chapter examines how local government officials in Sweden use social media and to what extent the emergence of social media has altered the relationship to conventional news media.

Local officials have appropriated social media in their work, but only to a moderate extent. Senior politicians are the most frequent users; a pattern we attribute to the publicness of their position that creates a need for public visibility also in social media. The senior politicians display the highest level of usage, but they are still less active than their counterpart in the local politics–media interaction – journalists (Hedman and Djerf-Pierre, 2013). We attribute these differences to the professional roles of politicians and journalists; politicians see public communication as a means to reach voters and, not least important, their own staff (Page and Jenkins, 2005), whereas communication to a journalist could be seen as an end in itself. On the other hand, journalists that use social media the least are those working in the local press (Hedman and Djerf-Pierre, 2013). Government–media relations at the local level clearly differ from those at the national level and social media, possibly, play a more limited role in local politics (Winsvold, 2007).

Local government officials may engage in social media out of choice or out of perceived necessity. The drivers of social media use can be perceived in terms of 'push' and 'pull' factors. Pull factors indicate that social media use is motivated by choice in order to attain professional or organisational goals. Push factors, on the other hand, are reactive; social media use is motivated by a 'necessity' in order to cope with organisational and professional challenges. Our findings indicate that local government officials are engaged in social media both out of choice and out of perceived necessity.

What is important is that the most revealing result is that local officials engage in social media if and when the local government becomes the target of social media scrutiny. Social media activity is thus provoked when criticism are put forward in social media. Criticism in the local or national press, on the other hand, primarily increases contacts with conventional media and does not induce officials to try to bypass the journalistic filtering by communicating directly in social media.

The (relatively) limited use of social media must be understood within the context of the specific conditions for local political communication in Sweden. Local newspapers have a very long tradition, readership is reasonably high and the local press is consequently still the nexus of the local public sphere. We find only minor changes in the strategies local officials employ vis-à-vis the news media, despite the transformative changes in the political and media environment between the 1980s and the 2010s. The identified shifts, most notably the city managers' move from a defensive to a passive strategy, should be attributed to the professionalisation of local governments' public communication rather than the advent of social media. The local press remains the hub of the public communication system at the local level.

Contrary to what we expected, we found that the local media context is not a push-factor for social media use. If a municipality is in 'media shadow' or has a local press monopoly, it does not significantly influence how much officials' use social media.

Officials in larger municipalities are more active social media users. The causal mechanism that induces these officials to turn to social media is, most likely, that large municipalities are more visible in national politics. Social media are mostly activated when the local government appears on the national political radar or when social media become a tool to safeguard the 'local interest' against external criticism. Social media activity, at least in 2010, seems to have less to do with influencing the local polity.

This observation speaks to the role of social media in local governance. Despite the high level of internet penetration of Swedish society, local political and administrative elites use social media sparingly. A study by Larsson (2013) suggests that the Swedish municipal governments' social media activity declined between 2010 and 2012, which further corroborates the slow appropriation of social media in local government. Although social media allow the local elite to communicate directly with the polity, they have not replaced conventional media as a means of communication with constituencies.

Indeed, officials who *are* active social media users have more contacts with conventional media compared to less active officials. Social media thus contributes to an *intensification* of the mediatisation of local governance rather than *replacing* conventional media in local political communication. Many media scholars have theorised that the evolution of 'new media' will contribute to an intensification or reinforcement of mediatisation (for example, Schulz, 2004; Miller, 2014). The present study provides empirical evidence for why this is actually the case.

## References

Bergström, A, 2011, Valår på nätet [Election year online], in S Holmberg, L Weibull, H Oscarsson (eds) *Lycksalighetens ö*, pp 477–88, Gothenburg: SOM-institutet, University of Gothenburg

Bovens, M, Schillemans, T, 't Hart, P, 2008, Does public accountability work? An assessment tool, *Public Administration* 86, 1, 225–42

Clark, TN, 2000, Old and new paradigms for urban research: Globalization and the fiscal austerity and urban innovation project, *Urban Affairs Review* 36, 1, 3–45

DiGaetano, A, Strom, E, 2003, Comparative urban governance: An integrated approach, *Urban Affairs Review* 38, 3, 356–95

Djerf, M, Pierre, J, 1991, Massmedierna som omvärld: De kommunala beslutsfattarnas relationer till massmedierna [The media as environment: Local officials' relationship to the mass media], in J Pierre (ed) *Självstyrelse och omvärldsberoende: Studier i lokal politik*, pp 244–81, Lund: Studentlitteratur

Djerf-Pierre, M, Weibull, L, 2009, *Ledarskap i framgångsrika tidningsföretag* [Leadership in successful newspaper organizations], Gothenburg: JMG, University of Gothenburg

Ekström, M, Johansson, B, Larsson, L, 2006, Journalism and local politics: A study of scrutiny and accountability in Swedish journalism, *Journalism Studies* 7, 2, 292–311

Esser, F, 2013, Mediatization as a challenge: Media logic versus political logic, in H Kriesi, S Lavenex, F Esser, J Matthes, M Bühlmann, D Bochsler (eds) *Democracy in the Age of Globalization and Mediatization*, pp 155–76, Basingstoke: Palgrave Macmillan

Franklin, B, Murphy, D (eds), 2005, *Local Journalism and local media: Making the local news*, London: Routledge

Fredriksson, M, Pallas, J, Schillemans, T, 2015, Determinants of mediatization: An analysis of the adaptation of Swedish government agencies to news media, *Public Administration*, DOI: 10.1111/padm.12184

Gustafsson, G, 1987, *Decentralisering av politisk makt* [Decentralization of political power], Stockholm: Carlssons

Haug, AV, 2007, Local democracy online, *Journal of Information Technology and Politics* 4, 2, 79–99

Hedman, U, Djerf-Pierre, M, 2013, The social journalist: Embracing the social media life or creating a new digital divide?, *Digital Journalism* 1, 3, 1–18

Hepp, A 2013, The communicative figurations of mediatized worlds: Mediatization research in times of the 'mediation of everything', *European Journal of Communication* 28, 6, 615–29

Hjarvard, S, 2008, The mediatization of society: A theory of the media as agents of social and cultural change, *Nordicom Review* 29, 2, 105–34

Hjarvard, S, 2014, From mediation to mediatization: The institutionalization of new media, in A Hepp, F Krotz (eds) *Mediatized worlds: Culture and society in a media age*, pp 123–42, Basingstoke: Palgrave Macmillan

Klang, M, Nolin, J, 2011, Disciplining social media: An analysis of social media policies in 26 Swedish municipalities, *First Monday* 16, 8, http://firstmonday.org/ojs/index.php/fm/article/view/3490/3027

Klijn, E-H, Van Twist, M, Van der Steen, M, Jeffares, S, 2014, Public managers, media influence, and governance: Three research traditions empirically explored, *Administration and Society*, doi: 10.1177/0095399714527752

Knox, CC, 2013, Public administrators' use of social media platforms: Overcoming the legitimacy dilemma?, *Administration and Society*, doi: 10.1177/0095399713503463

Krotz, F, Hepp, A, 2011, A concretization of mediatization: How 'mediatization works' and why mediatized worlds are a helpful concept for empirical mediatization research, *Empedocles: European Journal for the Philosophy of Communication* 3, 2, 137–52

Larsson, AO, 2013, Bringing it all back home? Social media practices by Swedish municipalities, *European Journal of Communication* 28, 6, 681–95

Larsson, L, 2005, *Upplysning och propaganda: Utveckling av svensk PR och information*, Lund: Studentlitteratur

Liu, BF, Horsley, JS, Yang, K, 2012, Overcoming negative media coverage: Does government communication matter?, *Journal of Public Administration Research and Theory*, doi: 10.1093/jopart/mur078

Logan, JR, Molotch, HL, 1987, *Urban fortunes: The political economy of place*, Berkeley, CA: University of California Press

Magro, MJ, 2012, A review of social media use in e-government, *Administrative Sciences* 2, 4, 148–61

Marcinkowski, F, 2014, Mediatisation of politics: The reflections on the state of the concept, *Javnost – The Public* 21, 2, 5–22

Miller, J, 2014, Intensifying mediatization: Everywhere media, in A Hepp, F Krotz (eds) *Mediatized worlds: Culture and society in a Media Age*, pp 107–22, Basingstoke: Palgrave Macmillan

Molotch, HL, 1976, The city as a growth machine, *American Journal of Sociology* 82, 2, 309–55

Moore, MH, 1997, *Creating public value: Strategic management in government*, Cambridge, MA: Harvard University Press

Nielsen, JA, Houlberg Salomonsen, H, 2012, Why all this communication? Explaining strategic communication in Danish local governments from an institutional perspective, *Scandinavian Journal of Public Administration* 16, 1, 69–89

Nord, L, Nygren, G, 2002, *Medieskugga* [Media shadow], Stockholm: Atlas bokförlag

Page, EC, Jenkins, B, 2005, *Policy bureaucracy: Government with a cast of thousands*, Oxford: Oxford University Press

Pallas, J, Fredriksson, M, 2013, Corporate media work and micro-dynamics of mediatization, *European Journal of Communication* 28, 4, 420–35

Peterson, PE, 1981, *City Limits*, Chicago, IL: The University of Chicago Press

Pierre, J, 2011, *The politics of urban governance*, Basingstoke: Palgrave

Pollitt, C, Bouckaert, G, 2011, *Comparative public management reform*, Oxford: Oxford University Press

Rhodes, RAW, 1986, *The National World of Local Government*, London: Allen, Unwin

Schillemans, T, 2012, *Mediatization of public service: How organizations adapt to news media*, Frankfurt: Peter Lang

Schulz, W, 2004, Reconstructing mediatization as an analytical concept, *European Journal of Communication* 19, 1, 87–101

Schweitzer, EJ, 2011, Normalization 2.0: A longitudinal analysis of German online campaigns in the national elections 2002–9, *European Journal of Communication* 26, 4, 310–27

Southern, R, 2014, Is web 2.0 providing a voice for outsiders? A comparison of personal web site and social media use by candidates at the 2010 UK general election, *Journal of Information Technology and Politics* 12, 1, 1–17

Strömbäck, J, 2008, Four phases of mediatization: An analysis of the mediatization of politics, *The International Journal of Press/Politics* 13, 3, 228–46

Thorbjornsrud, K, Ustad Figenschou, T, Ihlen, Ø, 2014, Mediatization in public bureaucracies: A typology, *Communications: The European Journal of Communication Research* 39, 1, 3–22

Westlund, O, 2012, *Cross-media news work: Sensemaking of the mobile media (r)evolution*, Gothenburg: Department of Journalism, Media and Communication, University of Gothenburg

Winsvold, M, 2007, Municipal websites in the local public debate: Supplying facts or setting agenda?, *Nordicom Review* 28, 2, 7–23

Wohlers, TE, 2009, The digital world of local government: A comparative analysis of the United States and Germany, *Journal of Information Technology and Politics* 6, 2, 111–26

# CHAPTER FIVE

# Fighting or fumbling with the beast?
# The mediatisation of public sector agencies in Australia and the Netherlands

Thomas Schillemans

## Introduction

In recent years, the 'mediatisation' of many parts of the political process have been analysed, as a way of studying the media's influence on politics (see Strömbäck, 2008; Hjarvard, 2013; Landerer, 2013). 'Mediatisation' generally refers to processes of organisational or institutional adaptation to the (news) media. It is a very subtle form of influence, where the media affect the structure or operations of other actors, simply because these have to some degree become dependent on the media and have accordingly adapted themselves to the 'rules' and 'logics' of the media. As in most political communications research, the gist of these studies focus – quite naturally – on the central actors and defining moments in democracies, such as political parties, presidents, elections and campaigns (Brants and Van Praag, 2006). In addition, however, a new stream of research has evolved that focuses on the mediatisation of public agencies and state bureaucracies (Deacon and Monk, 2001; Maggetti, 2012; Thorbjørnsrud et al, 2014). Researching the mediatisation of agencies is relevant, because agencies invest large sums of money in media management (see Cook, 2005), have obtained important *political* powers in contemporary systems of governance (James and Van Thiel, 2011) and as they are the subjects of around a third of the daily news (Schillemans, 2012).

The initial research focus of mediatisation studies was explicitly *normative* and the path-breaking studies in the field developed critical analyses of how politics was crucially transformed – if not colonised or mutilated – by mediatisation (Mazzoleni and Schulz, 1999; Meyer, 2002). In more recent years, successful attempts have been made to 'reconstitute' mediatisation as an analytical concept with which processes of institutional or organisational transformation can be described (Schulz, 2004; Hjarvard, 2008; Strömbäck, 2008). However, *country comparisons* are largely absent from the literature.

Against this background, this chapter will explore the mediatisation of public sector agencies in Australia and the Netherlands with a multi-methods research design. The central question is: to what extent have public agencies in Australia and the Netherlands become mediatised? As will be explained below, we will work from the general hypothesis that mediatisation is likely to be more advanced in Australia than in the Netherlands, due to the more competitive and combative political and media systems in Australia.

## Comparing Australian and Dutch agencies

Australian and Dutch public sector agencies operate in distinctive political systems and media systems. As we will explain below, the Australian agencies operate in a more combative political system and in a more competitive media system which makes it likely that Australian agency experience more (media) pressure which will lead to more advanced levels of mediatisation.

### *Public sector agencies*

The last decades witnessed many major administrative reforms in the Netherlands and Australia with fairly large and fairly similar impacts on the landscape of public sector agencies. Both countries have in some ways been at the forefront of the waves of new public management reforms that swept through the developed world since around 1990 (Pollitt and Bouckaert, 2004; Christensen and Lægreid, 2011). In the Netherlands, there have been some large government reforms that were more or less explicitly inspired by new public management thinking, although it is sometimes difficult to tell rhetorical strategies from real administrative reforms (Van Thiel, 2000). A substantial field of reform has been the delivery of public services. Following closely on examples set in the UK, Scandinavia and New Zealand, many public agencies were hived off from the administrative centre of government departments and were reformed into quangos (quasi autonomous non-governmental organisations) (Van Thiel, 2000; Smullen, 2010). At present, there are hundreds of quasi-autonomous agencies delivering public services in the Netherlands. In addition, many public services in education, healthcare and social housing are delivered by third sector organisations.

Australian public services are delivered by a broad variety of public agencies and third sector organisations, just as in the Netherlands, although there are some differences in forms. Many of the social services that in the Netherlands are delivered by third sector organisations are in Australia delivered through the public agencies of the different states although there are also non-profits involved. On the national level, there is a variety of public agencies that are generally directly answerable to the minister. A number of often complex tasks or regulatory services are delivered by a host of statutory authorities (see Wettenhall, 2003; Aulich et al, 2010). There has been a notable centralisation in the agency domain in recent years and the political centre has 'reasserted its control' (Halligan, 2006). In addition, many of the services to the public are in Australia delivered at the state level, for instance in housing, healthcare and education. In addition, large national agencies such as Centrelink operate with local offices. The state level is considered to be strong and also more innovative. State-reforms have served as a 'laboratory' for changes at the federal level (Pollitt and Bouckaert, 2004, 210).

Overall, the 'agency-landscape' in Australia is different from but not dissimilar to the Dutch landscape. In both countries, public services are provided by a plethora of agencies with various legal and financial relations to the government.

## Different political systems

The Dutch political system was famously described by Lijphart as a form of consociational democracy. Consociationalism refers to the fragmented but surprisingly stable form of democracy that was traditionally found in countries such as the Netherlands, Belgium and Austria (Lijphart, 1969, 211). It is fragmented, as numerous societal subgroups are represented in Parliament by a large number of political parties. The political institutions of consociationalism traditionally compel party elites to cooperate across party boundaries, and they have to be more sensitive and respectful towards their political opponents than is common in dualistic political systems. This basically lowers the levels of political antagonism in parliament, as most parties and politicians know that they are likely to be forced to cooperate with their opponents in the near future. The cooperation between elites ensures the stability of the democratic system but also leads to a spread of responsibilities and institutions, as the different parties to a coalition government carve up the 'benefits' of the office and divide the spoils among a large number of beneficiaries. In the past decades, this 'pillarised' system is in transformation and the old more or less corporatist style of politics is giving way (Andeweg and Thomassen, 2011). However, the corporatist style of governance remains a constant factor in the Dutch governance (Kickert, 2003) even though political rhetorics have become stronger. Many of the institutions of consociational rule do still exist, including systems of service provision where central state control is limited (Andeweg and Thomassen, 2011).

The Australian political system in contrast, is much more centralised as is common in the Westminster tradition. The 'first past the post' electoral system normally – although not in the 2010 elections – provides either Labour or the Coalition with an absolute majority and majoritarian rule is thus customary. The political concentration of power spills over into the public service, where the level of centralisation is also much higher as the prime minister's relative powers are much stronger than those of his counterpart in the Netherlands, who is generally considered as nothing but the primus inter pares of a group of equally weighted ministers. The virtual two-party system of Australia lowers the necessity for cooperation between the political antagonists and – perhaps together with some cultural features – explains the strongly antagonistic features of Australian political life, particularly when compared to the political tradition in the Netherlands. John Uhr and John Wanna for instance described parliament as: 'An unruly bear pit in which politics is a ruthless adversarial contest between disciplined parties' (quoted from Smullen, 2010).

### Different media systems

Media systems can be expected to be important for mediatisation, as they define the rules of conduct for media and their interactions with political entities, such as public sector agencies. Media systems refer to 'all mass media organised or operating within a given social and political system (usually a state)' (Hardy, 2008, 5). The most common characterisation of media systems is Hallin and Mancini's (2004) typology of three, western media systems. They considered the Netherlands as a clear example of their north/central European model. Australia was not formally implicated in their study, but it is a fair bet to include the country in the list of liberal models alongside the UK and the US.

The liberal model of Anglo-Saxon countries such as Australia is characterised by a relatively strong focus on media *markets* and a relatively limited level of government regulation. The model of journalism in liberal media systems is most clearly facts-based, 'neutral' and focused on balanced reporting. Media in Anglo-Saxon systems have no enduring formal ties with political parties (although newspapers may take 'sides' in election campaigns). In addition and somewhat to the contrary, however, liberal media have also developed a tabloid tradition.

In the Dutch north/central European model, the links between civil society, political parties and media have traditionally been much stronger than in Anglo Saxon countries. Early newspapers were sometimes literally the member's magazines of political parties, trade unions or other social organisations. The Dutch public broadcasting system is not, unlike the Australian Broadcasting Corporation (ABC) 'neutral' but is a platform where different associations representing social groups (Catholics, social democrats, different brands of Christians, and so on) enjoy regulated air-time. The Australian media landscape is also much more commercialised: even public broadcasting depends for 70 per cent of the revenue on advertising (Tiffen and Gritten, 2004).

## From political and media systems to mediatisation

The political and media systems in both countries are likely to have a similar effect on public agencies. It can generally be expected that mediatisation is more advanced in Australia than in the Netherlands. The characteristics of the political systems and media systems have in common the fact that they are likely to heap up more pressure on policy actors, such as agencies. The *pressure* of the media is likely to be higher in the liberal, competitive and partially tabloid-driven system of Australia than in the Netherlands. The Australian media landscape is more 'risky'. Agencies may also be more vulnerable in 'blame games' in the media in Australia and it only seems rational to set off more resources to media monitoring and media management (Ward, 2007). In the same vein, the *willingness* to exploit the news as an 'instrument of power' would be naturally higher in the competitive political system Down Under than in the consensual system in the Low Countries. Australia is renowned for its more combative political style, where the winner takes all in elections and political agents are more readily prepared to do what it takes to arrive at their goal. This also leads to politicisation of the civil service and agencies (Hamilton and Maddison, 2007; Young, 2007).

## Mediatisation of public sector agencies

Mediatisation is a meta-concept that refers to a large set of institutional changes (Krotz, 2007, 257; Couldry and Hepp, 2013). It refers to specific forms of mediation, where the mass media as mediators have a specific impact on – here – public sector agencies. At base, mediatisation is a relatively simple concept. It refers to all those situations where communication via mass media replaces other activities and to the ensuing adaptation of processes, rules, routines and structures in order to do so effectively. When organisations (or other entities) 'mediatise', they 'integrate' the media logic in their own operations (Hjarvard, 2008, 113).

Even though the base definition is straightforward, the process of adaptation to the media is highly complex in its consequences. One could say, with a slight reference to Tolstoy's Anna Karenina, that every entity mediatises in its own way. On the micro level, mediatisation has been used to analyse dyadic relationships between individuals and it has been used to study specific social interactions or practices (Livingstone, 2009, 7–9). On a meta level, mediatisation has been used to analyse the development of society at large or of distinct social institutions, such as politics (Mazzoleni and Schulz, 1999), religious life (Hoover, 2009) and culture (Hjarvard, 2013). For our purposes, however, the analysis of mediatisation focuses on the meso-level of public sector agencies (Pallas et al, 2014).

Strömbäck's (2008, 236–40) typology of mediatisation is helpful in detecting the mediatisation of public agencies. He argued that the process consists of a sequential trajectory of four phases. In the first phase, media become important or even the most important source of information to entities. In the second phase, media operate increasingly independent from governments and start operating on their own terms, through their own choices and according to their own internal rules, procedures and routines. In the third phase, the media as an independent institution start affecting other social organisations and institutions. As public sector agencies to some extent are dependent on the media (phase 1) and the media operate on the basis of their own, institutional logic (phase 2), the agencies need to adapt in order to be able to operate successfully in their media-saturated contexts. This implies that agencies invest in their skills to operate the media. In this third phase, agencies for instance create a media-team that reports directly to the CEO, invest in media training or may even adapt their own routines to fit the schedules of journalists.

In the fourth phase of mediatisation, public sector agencies internalise the external media rules and thus change in a fundamental way. For instance, journalists find colourful stories about specific clients who are treated badly more interesting than abstract stories about complex, structural obligations that might have more detrimental effects on the clients in general. Media need the human face. When agencies internalise this media rule, they shift their focus from structural problems to individual problems. Whether this is a good or a bad thing is still a matter to be disputed, it nevertheless serves as an illustration of the logic of mediatisation, where an organisations' mission and problem definition is adapted to the media's perception of problems. It also shows that mediatisation refers to very subtle forms of media influence, where the media–context may have deep effects within agencies.

In order to gauge how public sector agencies may 'mediatise', it is useful to apply the concept to three standard processes in organisations. We may understand public sector agencies as systems receiving *inputs* (all sorts of information, potentially including media-information), processing these inputs in *throughputs* (where the media may be important) and finally producing *outputs* (again potentially involving communications with, via or devised for the media). Agencies are found to be mediatising when they are putting more resources into media monitoring (as a form of inputs), when they attach more value on media-information in their throughputs and when they put more resources into media communication (outputs).

## A multi-method approach

In order to gauge the mediatisation of agencies in Australia and the Netherlands, a combination of two types of qualitative and quantitative research methods has been used. The general idea has been to operationalise the concept of mediatisation and to use it in an exploratory comparison of agencies in two countries. The research questions and items in the survey were theoretically derived from mediatisation theory as applied to the idea of an organisation as processing inputs, throughputs and outputs. The very same questions and items were used in 1) a questionnaire, 2) focus groups and 3) interviews.

### Survey

Respondents in the focus groups started by filling out a survey covering a number of statements relating to different forms of mediatisation (see Table 5.1). The survey was filled out *after* a short introduction (not mentioning the concept 'mediatisation') but *prior* to the discussion. This allowed respondents to qualify and explain some of their answers in the questionnaire and additionally helped the researcher to contravene the potentially distorting effect of group processes on the discussion in the focus group. The small-N survey reached 50 respondents (with a slight over-representation of Australian respondents); the 42 participants in focus groups and an additional eight respondents who for some reason or another were unable to participate in one of the focus groups. Table 5.1 displays the items used in the questionnaire. Respondents answered on a 4-part scale from 'strong agreement' to 'strong disagreement'.

### Focus groups

The focus groups were the starting point of the qualitative research process. There were seven focus groups with senior staff from agencies; largely not communications staff. In total there were 42 respondents. The idea was to speak with senior strategic officers from agencies, both national and on the state level, not being the highest executives or communications staff. In addition there was one focus group specifically with communications officials. Respondents primarily represented organisations providing services to the public. The seniority of respondents was evidenced by their average age (42.3 yrs) and average length of tenure (13.1 yrs).

**Table 5.1: Measuring organisational mediatisation**

| | |
|---|---|
| Subjective perception of media pressure | • "My policy field receives a lot of media-attention"<br>• "In my perception, the media is de facto a positive watchdog for governments and the public sector"<br>• "The media give a lot of attention to the organisations in our field"<br>• "At work, we often speak negatively about the media" |
| Mediatisation of inputs | • "It is important for my line of work to follow closely on what appears in the media"<br>• "Media-stories often contain information that is relevant for my work" |
| Mediatisation of throughputs | • "Our organisational executives are highly sensitive to media stories"<br>• "Media stories often influence the things I do during a day"<br>• "In meetings with internal and/or external people, there will often be references to recent media stories"<br>• "Incidents in the media often influence the way I prioritise"<br>• "In my daily work, the question 'How will this be seen by the media' is always in the back of my head"<br>• "Public communication now plays a central role in internal processes"<br>• "It is important in our work to be able to see reputational and communication risks in advance" |
| Mediatisation of outputs | • "It is important for organisations such as ours to avoid damage to their reputations"<br>• "Our organisation handles the media competently" |

The focus groups served as a great way of initiating a dialogue between respondents from similar types of organisations. The focus groups generally produced animated discussions, where participants would follow up on each other and also sometimes expressed dissent. The focus groups trigger group processes which help to map out the terrain and in which respondents follow up on each other, provide examples and expand the topic. There are also drawbacks in terms of suppressed variance and limited anonymity. The survey and the interviews served to compensate for this.

*Interviews*

There were 40 elite interviews, in which respondents were asked the same sets of questions that was used in the focus group. Elite interviews focused on organisational CEOs with a few additional communications officers. Now the interviewees were given much more time to describe and explain and to go into detail. The interviewer now also started from a more informed position, given the earlier input from the focus groups.

The focus groups and interviews were recorded (with the exception of three interviews where we had technical problems). In the analysis, all excerpts from the interviews and focus groups relating to media pressure, inputs, throughputs and outputs were ordered as the basis for the analysis. For example, all quotes from the interviews and focus groups where people would speak about why and how they followed the news were collected and ordered under the head 'inputs'.

All in all, with the combination of interviews, focus groups, the questionnaire and content analyses, the mediatisation of agencies in the two countries have been explored. This has led to a broad snapshot of organisational adaptations to the media.

## Results

We will now discuss the results, focusing on perceived media pressure, and the mediatisation of organisational inputs, throughputs and outputs. By and large the exploratory results will follow our guiding hypotheses about the stronger mediatisation of Australian agencies. Somewhat surprisingly, however, some of the perception data from the Netherlands suggest that Dutch agencies experience more media pressure than was expected.

*Media pressure*

The many different organisations delivering public services in Australia and the Netherlands occupy a substantial niche in the most important news media (Deacon and Monk, 2001; Jacobs, 2014). Of course, political actors are at the heart of the majority of news stories and the leaders of the most important political parties are the subjects of the majority of the stories. There is nevertheless a substantial niche of news stories that involve the different agencies.

Anglo-Saxon media systems are generally seen as 'tougher' and more critical than northern western media systems, particularly with their traditions of talkback radio and tabloids. Our interviews and focus groups clearly underscored this point. Australian respondents were generally more outspoken and more critical about the media, and also provided many more stories about people in the public sector who were afraid of the media.

Australian respondents, for example, spoke about how some colleagues would "much rather have their arm eaten off than appear on radio. Some of our media people have basically been begging, preparing talking points, really holding their hands, but some of them just won't." The effect may be that people who were involved "won't speak to the media, even if it's on the local sports edition. They're terrified, they run miles to avoid the press." Others followed in line with strong claims, such as: "It can leave a community traumatised for years", or "it's a body blow if you have been at the centre of attention", "I sometimes need to lie down." None of the Dutch focus groups and interviews led to similarly strong-worded claims, suggesting that the media pressure on Australian agencies is, indeed, higher (which would suggest more advanced levels of mediatisation in response).

The perception data on media pressure from the survey provide an apparently contrasting picture, however. The respondents were asked whether they (strongly) agreed or (strongly) disagreed with the propositions that their policy fields and the organisations in their policy fields received a lot of media attention. In addition, respondents were asked whether the media served as a watchdog (classical role of investigative journalism, see Norris, 2014), and whether they often talked negatively about the media at their work. The subjective experience of media pressure was thus tapped.

Figure 5.1 provides an overview of the answers. The maximum score of 4 corresponds with strong agreement on the proposition, a 3 is 'agreement', 2 is 'disagree', and 1 is 'strongly disagree'. The neutral value in this – and the following figures – is 2.5.

**Figure 5.1: Subjective perceptions of media pressure**

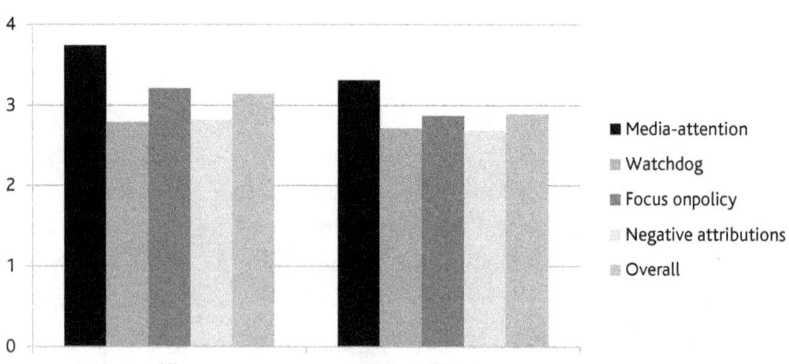

The figure clarifies that the respondents generally perceive a high media attention for their policy fields but the figure also shows how the Dutch responses were somewhat stronger than those of their counterparts on the other side of the globe. Dutch respondents also speak more often negatively about the media while at work. These results seem to contain a paradox: where the levels of media coverage in Australia are generally higher and the tone of coverage is more negative and critical on public authorities, the subjective perception of media pressure, as suggested by our exploratory research, seems to be lower in Australia. This is the central paradox that will resurface throughout this chapter.

### Mediatisation of inputs

Public agencies devote resources to media monitoring. Here again the same paradox resurfaced as above: whereas the Dutch survey-respondents gave somewhat more firmly confirmatory responses to the statements about whether it was important to 'know' and 'follow up' on the news, the Australian organisations clearly devoted more resources to this end.

To begin with the perception data. Figure 5.2 provides an overview of two important dimensions, in isolation and combined, of the mediatisation of organisational inputs. The survey aimed to find out whether senior strategic staff in public agencies claimed that it was important to 'know' what is in the news and also the extent to which news coverage was somehow informative to them in their professional capacities. The figure suggests that responses in both countries were strongly confirmatory on both propositions; people generally thought that they needed to know the news (question 1) and the news generally provided them with valuable information (question 2). Nevertheless, the Dutch responses were, again, more outspoken than the Australian responses.

**Figure 5.2: Mediatisation of organisational inputs**

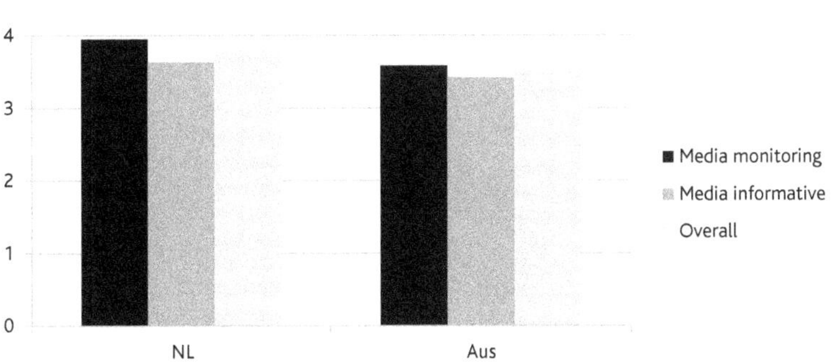

During the interviews and focus groups, however, the Australian respondents demonstrated and described far more advanced forms of media monitoring than their Dutch counterparts. The Dutch attached more value to monitoring whereas the Australians simply devote more resources to the task. The interviews and focus groups suggested, as has also been described in the literature, that at least almost all large Australian agencies have invested in external media monitoring services (see also Ester, 2007). These monitoring services report steadily on developments in the news, sending round clippings and reports at reliable intervals of sometimes one per hour. The monitoring service will scan all media for references to specific search words, the name of the organisation or service that is provided or will measure the media-impact of campaigns or decisions. If we conceive of media reporting as an emergent yet fractured story-line, then external media monitors allow organisations to gauge and analyse the stories as they evolve. The monitoring services produce large stacks of analyses that provide 'snapshots' of what the 'touchstone issues' are.

Some of the large organisations add that they make thematic or periodical analyses of the media-monitors that they receive. Organisations then look for trends in reporting, sources of dissatisfaction or success or associations with related issues. The organisations will also monitor all media requests, will sometimes analyse trends in media requests, and will monitor the effects of specific target actions by the organisations. "We produce a sort of 'travel journey' of the media team", a respondent notes. Furthermore, once the CEO or another spokesperson appears in the media, analyses are often made of his or her performance.

The three types of monitoring activities described above all lead to documentation in the form of clippings, email alerts, reports and conclusions that are actively sent through the organisation. It is a process of warning, signalling and dissemination. This process primarily aims at the executive level of the agency, but many more people are included in the stream of information as "we want our people to know what the news is". A respondent notes: "As a civil servant, I started every day with the media monitor by Rehame, who operated on a million dollars contract. The report would set the agenda of the day." Many others have the same experience. The basic difference between the organisations is the time at which the report on the media is produced. People in the media team often have contact with the media until late at night and very early in the morning. For many other people, especially close to the executive level, the first reports are sent in at 6 or 7 in the morning for media-sensitive agencies. In early meetings, the organisation decides whether or not to respond or act on the impending news.

For persons in executive positions, the stream of information from the different monitoring mechanisms can be quite absorbing. A regional director from a very media sensitive organisation recalls:

> We have two different monitors on the phone. One on the state level that warns on news stories, the other gives more contextual information to the news. I read them both every morning; we have three to five media emergencies every week. Anything happening near one of our centres, whether or not it has anything to do with us or whether or not the person even is a client, is news. So I start the day at 6.30 in the morning with the monitor and also finish my day that way. If you'd respond to everything that is passing, it would be a full-time job.

Our findings all in all suggest that the level of mediatisation in Australian agencies may have been advanced much further than in the Netherlands. The descriptions of the media strategies, the instrumentation of media monitoring, was all far more extensive and explicit in Australia. This does not imply that the Australian actors thought the media were more important than their Dutch counterparts, there was nothing to suggest this point, but some of the harshness of the media and particularly the level of professional investment in media monitoring was just much further advanced.

## Mediatisation of throughputs

Mediatisation of organisational throughputs is essentially about the question whether people in public agencies 'are aware' of the media 'out there' while at work on the policy process in ways that potentially affect those policies. One of the very specific forms is how people record and document issues in a context where journalists use freedom of information clauses to extract information from formerly sealed organisations. There is a general trend, for instance noted by Barker (2007, 130), that civil servants will quickly learn not to put things in emails as they may be 'FOI-ed'. The respondents in interviews and focus groups all conferred to this view; there were very little differences here between the Dutch and the Australian respondents. However, Australian respondents were clearly more outspoken in their descriptions and explained how they were always alert to potential FOI concerns.

Australian respondents for instance stated that those requests for information came in "increasingly and often by journalists". One respondent noted how (s)he always reminded people "what they put in emails, in letters or reports. Always be aware it might be FOI-ed." New staff is "briefed on how to document things as they may well arrive in the public arena". The general line is, according to one respondent, thus: "You just don't put anything, anywhere, you know, that could end up in the wrong place." People may be asked: "How is it going to look on the front page of the *Herald*, you know?" As a result, personal comments are filed less and less often. People are very cautious, they feel they have to, and "start ringing each other a bit more often to let off steam". The cautiousness not only refers to what is documented in and on memos and reports, but may also refer to more virtual types of information. In one case, for instance, names, pictures and addresses of the responsible workers were published on the internet. One respondent refers to communications via mobile phone equipment that can be tapped by citizens. The respondent noted: "They have to be careful how they tell their colleagues about responses that can be heard, because it could end up [in public] and be defamatory."

These are all personal responses to the potential threat of public disclosure of intentionally classified information. Earlier research also pointed to institutional mechanisms with which public organisations check the potentially negative effects of publication, such as restrictive interpretations of the law, acts of omissions and other administrative routines that allow public services some information control (Roberts, 2005, 6). The respondents in our research additionally indicated a few more options. One option would be to change periodical reporting in order to decrease the number of media storms. One agency, for example, recalls that they used to provide two reviews a year that always attracted a lot of media attention and a lot of critical discussion. In response they decided to limit themselves to only one review a year. In a Dutch case a similar solution is mentioned: a service provider with a large, varied and controversial portfolio decided to stop publishing individual reports on its diverse activities but chose to integrate everything in one big report, as this substantially lowered the level of discussion, reporting and criticism. The point is not that the organisations behave more secretively, but rather that they use deliberate timing and crowding to lower the level of criticism and media activity. The same recipe should be followed in crisis management, one of the communications officers noted: organisations should establish all damaging facts as soon as possible, and then "shovel it out at once". This assures negative publicity but also abbreviates the media-episode as the chances of follow-up stories diminish. Another respondent adds that, following the increased critical attention by the news media, they now "publish more, so they [the journalists] don't have to seek and think: 'There must be a reason why it is buried.'"

A telling indicator for the difference between Australia and the Netherlands is how the social media are treated differently in the public sectors in both countries. In the Netherlands, the ministry of the interior started *encouraging* government employees to use social media in 2010. In Australia, on the contrary, many public and third sector organisations actually forbade their people to do so. An executive manager from a small service provider explains: "People see Facebook as a personal photo album and don't realise it is a publication. Our people need permissions and I generally check."

When we turn to our questionnaire, however – and the narrative may become predictable now – a contrasting picture evolved. As visualised in Figure 5.3, a number of statements referring to the mediatisation of throughputs – or on how media affect non-media activities in organisations – were given to the respondents. Again the Dutch responses were a little stronger in their confirmatory responses on almost all dimensions.

Figure 5.3 again shows how all responses are strongly supportive of mediatisation, and even more so in the Netherlands than in Australia. The Dutch respondents thought that their executives were more sensitive for media stories (column 1), they were more influenced by media stories in their daily activities (column 2), they were more often and more severely affected by incidents (column 4), they spoke about it more often with their colleagues (column 3), and they felt it was more important to gauge potential media risks of new policies (column 7). This all suggests that organisational throughputs in Dutch agencies are more strongly mediatised.

There was only one, interesting, exception. On the statement whether communication with the media was now 'in the heart of the policy process', a highly instrumental statement, the Australians respondents suddenly gave somewhat stronger answers. This finding is in line with the qualitative findings that gave so many suggestions that the Australian

**Figure 5.3: Mediatisation of organisational throughputs**

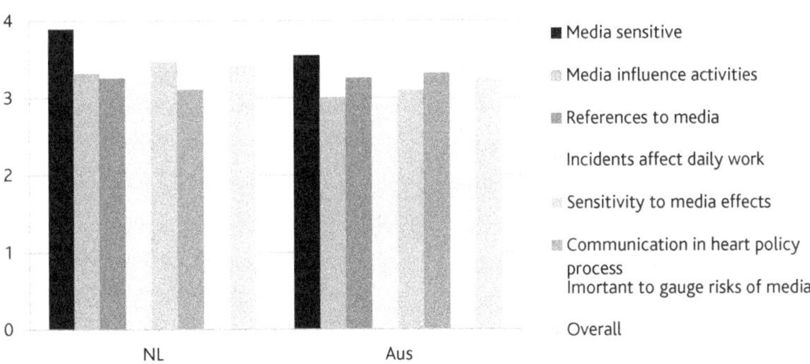

agencies have been able to 'instrumentalise' their relations with the media more pragmatically and thoroughly than Dutch agencies. This distinction between the mental awareness of the importance of the media 'out there' and the strategic and operational instrumentalisation of media-related measures 'inside', resurfaces in the next section on outputs.

## Mediatisation of outputs

The mediatisation of outputs, which refers to the ways in which organisations use the media and communicate with the media as part of their strategy, is the last of our four empirical sub-paragraphs. It is the only one of the four where the findings from the different methods were consistent and where perception data, focus groups and interviews suggested further advanced states of mediatisation in Australia than in the Netherlands.

Figure 5.4 visualises how the Australian respondents thought that 'reputation' is even more important than their Dutch counterparts already do and it also sketches their assessment of their overall capacity to 'handle the media'. The findings suggest that they do so more thoroughly, more competently and more deliberately.

One of the clearest examples of the difference between Australia and the Netherlands was in the way how public agencies sometimes struggle to enter the news as they wish. They do so, with some room for manoeuvre in both countries, yet the explicit Australian strategies provide testimony to the statement (Patrick Weller, quoted in Young, 2007) that 'Australian politics is played like Australian sport, up front, down to earth and with a blatant desire to win at any cost.'

**Figure 5.4: Mediatisation of organisational outputs**

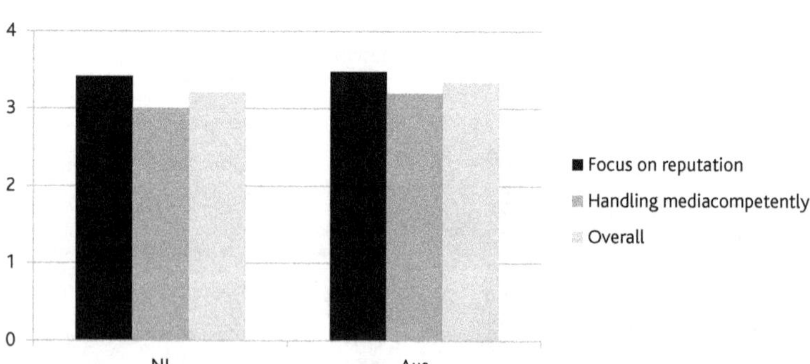

The struggle over content seems to be far more explicit and outspoken in Australia than in the Netherlands. A number of Australian respondents described a level of planning of positive stories that seems to be unheard of in the Netherlands, particularly for agencies operating close to the political centre. One respondent for instance notes: "We have a target for the number of positive stories we want every week, with certain numbers of radio, TV, etcetera." Another respondent adds: "We have a strategy for the day; like on Tuesday we want this and on Wednesday that. We battle constantly to get into the media. There is always a plan, and we all agree it is a real battle."

This struggle over content is fuelled by the fact that most news media operate on the basis of predetermined *news holes* that need to be filled. The news hole refers to all the space that is left after the removal of the advertorial space and it can actually be measured (McCombs, 2004, 27). Newspapers may, for example, have two education reporters that will run a more or less fixed number of stories on education. In addition, the different news outlets appear with an almost metrical regularity. Almost irrespective of the events of the day, there are empty time slots to be filled each day for designated types of news, and there are specialised journalists looking for stories with a predictable (and high) regularity, and there are, as one of the respondents states: "Just so many columns to fill." The strategic response to this fact is highly similar for all agencies operating in more or less newsworthy policy areas: "We", describes an Australian respondent "try to press news from anything." Many respondents spoke in similar and slightly cynical terms: "We are there to produce grist for the mill", or: "We have a method to ascertain that we appear in the news on a regular basis", and: "There is a space that needs to be filled, so you provide the content to fill it yourself." It echoes the famous words from the Blair team: you have to feed the (media) beast.

The obvious advantage of filling the news hole yourself is that it ascertains that there are less negative stories. Some of the respondents understand this as a real competition between potential stories. "If we don't do it, someone else will, so there's a real competition." And another adds: "It's also explicit. They [the journalists] would say, 'We are going to run this on Sunday, unless you got something better...'" And a third respondent states: "In our policy field, we deal in hope and fear. That's the choice. If you provide them [journalists] with something good, about real lives, with specifics, real people, and you tell it well, that is attractive to them and better than a story of fear."

## Conclusions and discussion

This chapter set out to explore the relative mediatisation of public sector agencies in Australia and the Netherlands. Our exploration generally suggests that almost all respondents – mostly representing larger public sector agencies – report fairly advanced forms of mediatisation. The contents of media stories are important *inputs* in public agencies, where people are expected to 'know the news', where they find news stories important and informative and where all organisations invest in some form of media monitoring. The media environment is also important to organisational *throughputs*. Daily activities are often altered by sudden news stories, people will weigh the perceived communicative consequences of substantive policy choices and will be careful how to make notes on paper because of freedom of information requests. In general, almost all respondents agreed that communicative concerns had become integrated in the heart of policy processes. Agencies finally do also cater specifically to the news media with their *outputs*. They will devise specific outputs for the media but will also try to maximise the media exposure of some of their strategic key activities. All in all, thus, the answer to our central question is that public agencies in Australia and the Netherlands have clearly and in consequential ways become mediatised. Furthermore, the findings overall suggest that Australian agencies have equipped themselves to a larger degree to their media environment than their Dutch counterparts who, in turn, seemed to be more 'bothered', 'distracted' and critical of the media's external presence.

In the 1990s, Tony Blair's team made some furore by claiming that governments need to feed the media beast. This chapter now suggests that public sector agencies also go to some length to feed the media and report, in not dissimilar phrases, how this is a critical contingency for their organisations. The differences between Australian and Dutch agencies in this respect can, in an allusion to the original expression, and with some hyperbole, be summarised as 'fighting' versus 'fumbling' with the beast. Australian agencies have gone to greater lengths in adjusting their organisations to the media, are more explicit in the ways they seek favourable media coverage and couch their strategies in more belligerent terms. Many Australian agencies seem to be engaged in an explicit *fight* with the media beast. Dutch agencies, in contrast, are *fumbling* with the beast. They seem to be even more aware of the media environment than their Australian counterparts yet they are more restricted and hesitant in their instrumental handling of the media.

These findings above should be read carefully. The found differences could be a simple – and deflating – product of our research approach. This chapter has deliberately cast a wide net, aiming to 'catch' a large number of indications of mediatisation, with a variety of research methods. This exploratory approach was adopted because organisational mediatisation is a relatively new concept relating to a large number of 'things'. Our comprehensive research approach has entailed a trade-off in terms of precision which might explain our findings. Furthermore, the different findings in Australia and the Netherlands could also be a by-product of the implicit benchmark used by our respondents. For instance, when respondents were reporting on the extent to which their executives were media sensitive, it could well be that relatively high answers were caused by implicitly low benchmarks. More specified research with larger numbers – for instance on media monitoring, media rules of conduct and media training in agencies – would be necessary to refute or substantiate our findings.

There are, however, some reasons to at least take the exploratively established differences between Australian and Dutch agencies seriously as *informed hypotheses* for future research.

For future research on the mediatisation of public sector agencies, three avenues of progress seem imminent. The first logical road would be a full-fledged comparative and quantitative analysis of public agencies in different jurisdictions. The relevance of the questionnaire has been corroborated in this chapter, and our analyses suggest that there may be important variations between agencies in different countries. In a new research project, the comparison could be improved with a full survey among a much larger number of agencies.

Such a quantitative approach would still suffer from a major drawback: it sketches a static snapshot of what is essentially a dynamic historical process. In studies of the mediatisation of politics, some important historical analyses have been made (Kepplinger, 2002; Brants and Van Praag, 2006; Elmelund-Praestekaer et al, 2011; Djerf-Pierre et al, 2013). A historical analysis of the mediatisation of agencies would ideally focus on historical data of organisational investments in media monitoring, media events and media staff.

A third way forward would be to look in more detail at what is the puzzling outcome of our own exploration: the difference between the relatively stronger instrumental mediatisation of Australian agencies and the more outspoken mental 'suffering' experienced by respondents from Dutch agencies. This finding could be related to differences in appreciation of the media. Public trust in the media in Australia is among the lowest in the world (Mumbrella, 2014), which might explain why the Australian respondents were simultaneously *more eager* to 'fight' the media while they were simultaneously less concerned about the media 'out there'. A different explanation could be that the two findings are really twins; perhaps it is exactly the relative *lack* of instrumentalisation of media-management in Dutch agencies which explains why the respondents seemed a little more bothered by and concerned about the media.

Our analysis has been a necessary first step in the empirical assessment of the mediatisation of public sector agencies. Important questions about causation, variance and consequences constitute the agenda for future research.

## References


Andeweg, R, Thomassen, J, 2011, *Democratie doorgelicht: Het functioneren van de Nederlandse democratie*, Leiden: Leiden University Press

Aulich, C, Batainah, H, Wettenhall, R, 2010, Autonomy and control in Australian agencies: Data and preliminary findings from a cross-national empirical study, *Australian Journal of Public Administration* 69, 2, 214–28

Barker, G, 2007, The public service, in C Hamilton, S Maddison (eds) *Silencing dissent: How the Australian government is controlling public opinion and stifling debate*, pp 124–47, Crows Nest, Australia: Allen and Unwin

Brants, K, Van Praag, P, 2006, Signs of media logic: Half a century of political communication in the Netherlands, *Javmost – The Public* 13, 1, 25–40

Christensen, T, Lægreid, P, 2011, *The Ashgate Research Companion to new public management. Autonomy and regulation: Coping with agencies in the modern state*, Cheltenham, UK: Edward Elgar

Cook, T, 2005, *Governing with the news: The news media as a political institution*, Chicago, IL and London, UK: University of Chicago Press

Couldry, N, Hepp, A, 2013, Conceptualizing mediatization: Contexts, traditions, arguments', *Communication Theory* 23, 3, 191–202

Deacon, D, Monk, W, 2001, New managerialism in the news: Media coverage of quangos in Britain, *Journal of Public Affairs* 1, 2, 153–66

Djerf-Pierre, M, Ekström, M, Johansson, B, 2013, Policy failure or moral scandal? Political accountability, journalism and new public management, *Media, Culture and Society* 35, 8, 960–76

Elmelund-Praestekaer C, Hopmann, D, Norgaard, A, 2011, Does mediatization change MP–media interaction and MP attitudes toward the media? Evidence from a longitudinal study of Danish MPs, *International Journal of Press/Politics* 16, 3, 382–403

Ester, H, 2007, The media, in C Hamilton, S Maddison (eds) *Silencing dissent: How the Australian government is controlling public opinion and stifling debate*, pp 101–23, Crows Nest, Australia: Allen and Unwin

Halligan, J, 2006, The reassertion of the centre in a first generation NPM system, in T Christensen, P Lægreid (eds) *Autonomy and regulation, coping with agencies in the modern state*, pp 162–80, Cheltenham, UK: Edward Elgar

Hallin, C, Mancini, P, 2004, *Comparing media systems: Three models of media and politics*, Cambridge, UK: Cambridge University Press

Hamilton, C, Maddison, S (eds), 2007, *Silencing dissent: How the Australian government is controlling public opinion and stifling debate*, Crows Nest, Australia: Allen and Unwin

Hardy, J, 2008, *Western media systems*, Abingdon: Routledge

Hjarvard, S, 2008, The mediatization of society: A theory of the media as agents of social and cultural change, *Nordicom Review* 29, 2, 105–34

Hjarvard, S, 2013, *The mediatization of culture and society*, London: Routledge

Hoover, SM, 2009, Complexities: The case of religious cultures, in K Lundby (ed) *Mediatization, concept, changes, consequences*, pp 123–38, New York, NY: Peter Lang

Jacobs, S, 2014, *Media & verantwoording over incidenten: Gevolgen voor publieke organisaties*, Utrecht University (dissertation)

James, O, Van Thiel, S, 2011, Structural devolution and agencification, in T Christensen, P Laegreid (eds) *Ashgate Research Companion to new public management*, pp 209–22, Aldershot, UK: Ashgate

Kepplinger, H, 2002, Mediatization of politics: Theory and data, *Journal of Communication* 52, 4, 972–86

Kickert, WJM, 2003, Beneath consensual corporatism: Traditions of governance in the Netherlands, *Public Administration* 81, 1, 119–40

Krotz, F, 2007, The meta-process of 'mediatization' as a conceptual frame, *Global Media and Communication* 3, 3, 256–60

Landerer, N, 2013, Rethinking the logics: A conceptual framework for the mediatization of politics, *Communication Theory* 23, 3, 239–50

Livingstone, S, 2009, On the mediatization of everything: ICA presidential address 2008, *Journal of Communication* 59, 1, 1–18

Lijphart, A, 1969, Consociational democracy, *World Politics* 21, 2, 207–25

Maggetti, M, 2012, The media accountability of independent regulatory agencies, *European Political Science Review* 4, 3, 385–408

Mazzoleni, G, Schulz, W, 1999, 'Mediatization' of politics: A challenge for democracy? *Political Communication* 16, 3, 247–61

McCombs, M, 2004, *Setting the agenda: The mass media and public opinion*, Cambridge, UK: Polity Press

Meyer, T, 2002, *Media democracy: How the media colonize politics*, Cambridge, UK: Polity Press

Mumbrella, 2014, *Public trust in Australian media among worst in the world*, http://mumbrella.com.au/public-trust-in-australian-media-among-worst-in-the-world-39477

Norris, P, 2014, Watchdog journalism, in M Bovens, RE Goodin, T Schillemans (eds) *The Oxford handbook of public accountability*, pp 525–44, Oxford, UK: Oxford University Press

Pallas, J, Strannegard, L, Jonsson, S, 2014, *Organizations and the media: Organizing in a mediatized world*, London: Routledge

Pollitt, C, Bouckaert, G, 2004, *Public management reform: A comparative analysis* (revised 2nd edn), Oxford, UK: Oxford University Press

Roberts, A, 2005, Spin control and freedom of information: Lessons for the United Kingdom from Canada, *Public Administration* 83, 1, 1–23

Schillemans, T, 2012, *Mediatization of public services: How organizations adapt to news media*, Frankfurt: Peter Lang

Schulz, W, 2004, Reconstructing mediatization as an analytical concept, *European Journal of Communication* 19, 1, 87–101

Smullen, A, 2010, *Translating agency reform: Rhetoric and culture in comparative perspective*, Basingstoke: Palgrave MacMillan

Strömbäck, J, 2008, Four phases of mediatization: An analysis of the mediatization of politics, *International Journal of Press/Politics* 13, 3, 228–46

Thorbjørnsrud, K, Ihlen, Ø, Ustad Figenschou, T, 2014, Mediatization in new areas: The changed role of public bureaucracies, in J Pallas, L Strannegård, S Jonsson (eds) *Organizations and the media: Organizing in a mediatized world*, pp 162–75, New York: Routledge

Tiffen, R, Gritten, R, 2004, *How Australia compares*, Melbourne, Australia: Cambridge University Press

Van Thiel, S, 2000, *Quangocratization: Trends, causes, consequences*, Utrecht: ICS

Ward, D, 2007, Mapping the Australian PR state, in S Young (ed) *Government communication in Australia*, pp 3–18, Melbourne, Australia: Cambridge University Press

Wettenhall, R, 2003, Exploring types of public sector organizations: Past exercises and current issues, *Public Organization Review* 3, 3, 219–45

Young, S, 2007, *Government communication in Australia*, Melbourne, Australia: Cambridge University Press

# The mediatisation of university governance: a theoretical and empirical exploration of some side-effects

Andres Friedrichsmeier and Frank Marcinkowski

## Theoretical considerations

### Mediatisation of stakeholder relations in a knowledge society

The 'mediatisation of science' is a widely acknowledged concept in studies on science communication (for example, Rödder et al, 2012), but it is far less recognised in studies on the governance of higher education institutions (HEI). The mediatisation thesis states that academic institutions and individual scholars are increasingly oriented towards the media and therefore adopt a strategy of becoming visible in the mediated public sphere. The general public, which is represented by mass media, is said to be increasingly significant for legitimising the public funding of academic institutions, a scenario which has repercussions on science itself. The mediatisation of HEI governance has been substantiated in a number of studies (for example, Carvalho, 2007; Peters et al, 2008). For example, universities have increased resources in their communication offices, and obliged their academic staff to contribute to the corporate image in their public appearances (Marcinkowski et al, 2014a, 115–16). Exhaustive survey results have revealed that German HEI attach great importance to being visible in news media. Empirics also point to a particular relevance of higher education policy. The more HEI decision-makers attempt to become visible in mass media, the stronger they perceive politicians to be susceptible to mass media coverage (Marcinkowski et al, 2013, 270–4).

The vision of a 'knowledge society' has become increasingly influential in HEI-politics (Vällima and Hoffman, 2008) and bolsters 'governments' attempts to make higher education more responsive to a nation's socio-economic needs' (Capano, 2011, 1636), since HEI are thought to be 'destined to play a fundamental role in knowledge societies' (UNESCO, 2005, 96). The visibility of a HEI in the media can be used as a proxy for its efforts in connecting with a widening spectrum of social actors. In expert-interviews, officers in pending German state authorities report that they would actually make extensive use of this proxy, but unsystematically (Friedrichsmeier and Gohr, 2013, 8–11). However, media coverage lacks the kind of precision that most HEI administrators aspire to obtain from performance measurements. The main goal of recent HEI reforms in various countries can be said to be a 'rationalising' of governance (Seeber et al, 2014, 8). In an 'industrial' notion of the knowledge society, knowledge production is treated as if it consisted of accumulating objective, isolated facts 'behind the walls of academic institutions' (Rifkin, 2014, 114). However, knowledge dissemination by universities is lateral in nature and consists of sharing with stakeholders. Universities deal with vague objects that have no actual, if any, 'value, which only has to be discovered' or measured; instead, the 'recognition and auditability' of an HEI's knowledge-sharing have to be generated (Mouritsen, 2000, 211). A mediated public arena is capable of generating auditability and recognition, but so far HEI-reformers primarily have sought to assign that task to market mechanisms. Governments in all western countries therefore took efforts 'to enhance competition among institutions' (OECD, 2008, 86) and constituted various quasi-markets, for example, systems of performance financing. But representing public needs by means of these politically constituted markets is limited. Governors are usually aware of this (Friedrichsmeier and Gohr, 2013, 12–4, 30–2). In a classic market, a service is valued by consumers' effective demand. In politically constituted quasi-markets, things proceed differently (Marginson, 2007). Given a lack of customer willingness or inability to cover full costs, service effectiveness requires an additional evaluation. For example, if a quasi-market indicates a deficient public demand, little 'information about desired direction of change' can be obtained from that outcome (Meijer and Schillemans, 2009, 256). So the participants of quasi-market competition are compelled to resort to additional sources of information, such as in media coverage, given that they are actually interested in meeting that consumer demand in the first place.

In quasi-markets, *politics* constitute supply, demand, or both, and consumer demand mostly takes the form of a symbolic representation. What actually constitutes quasi-markets are audited representations of performance and not performance itself. This contributes to the emergence of 'expressive organisations' (Mouritsen, 2000) geared towards visualising their value in an 'attention economy' (Davenport and Beck, 2001). Striving for corporate reputation enables HEI to face the complex 'needs for orientation' (compare McCombs and Weaver, 1973), a knowledge society confronts them with. 'Reputation' is a form of global evaluation that lacks formal organisation but serves as an effective means of social coordination (Luhmann, 1992, 251), as it is capable of transmitting beliefs.

Reputation is a meta-belief, that is, a belief about the belief of others. Believing in the reputation of Harvard, for example, equals believing that almost everybody else does as well. Corporate reputation is capable of serving various stakeholders at the same time, without presupposing that all of them actually have to be reached (compare Meijer and Schillemans, 2009, 271). Mere indication of a credible chance to reach them, such as media coverage, can suffice to uphold the meta-belief. Meta-beliefs need to be represented in a discourse. If you would never hear someone's name mentioned, you would not believe others share high beliefs concerning this person's value. On an individual level, an academic's reputation is represented by a disciplinary discourse. But academic disciplines can only attribute disciplinary reputation, so a considerable share of performance auditing at the level of whole universities needs to be represented in the general public, that is, in mass media. Accordingly, current research sees reputation at the university level to be ascribed by 'civil society at large' (Paradeise and Thoenig, 2013, 195).

Expectations that universities should become recognised at the organisational level also relate to the aforementioned efforts to rationalise HEI governance. Scholars are employed to progress a knowledge base, as opposed to subjugating given evaluation criteria and protocols, so considerable discretion is typical of their work. Consequently, hierarchies in university governance (state, local, disciplines) tend to contradict one another in a rather obvious manner (Brunsson and Sahlin-Andersson, 2000, 735). Further, knowledge specialists generally identify less with their home institution than with their profession, whose participants are located all over the world (Clark, 1983, 30). To characterise this lack of organisational unison, current research refers to classic universities as 'arenas' (Seeber et al, 2014) with 'weaknesses as regards identity' (Brunsson and Sahlin-Andersson, 2000, 735). In order to build up a corporate identity, an HEI has to frame itself as an outcome of collective goals. A visualisation of the output from different disciplines, side-by-side, only takes place in one locus in modern society. This locus is the mediated public sphere. Leaving to add that the mass media usually contribute to the public expectation that an HEI should behave as if it were a unitary institution and not just 'loosely coupled systems' (Weick, 1976).

An effective means to raise local identification is experiencing competition. Monitoring competitors in news media (Friedrichsmeier et al, 2013, 14) and competing with them for visibility may fuel internal identification and corporate reputation at the same time. A focal point of corporate public visibility, reputation and competition are constituted by public rankings broadcasted by the news media. We therefore apply the example of public rankings when examining potential side effects in the second part of the chapter. HEI research further ascertains that '[o]ne crucial element to bind all those theories and risks together can be found in the concept of reputational risk that emerges as a genuine type of academic risk' (Huber, 2011, 15). At this point, an important hint at potential side effects of the rationale of HEI to worry about their corporate reputation is given: as reputation is more easily damaged than built up, we expect HEI to be interested in avoiding public blame in the media and we will present some empirical support for this claim in this chapter.

The function of reputation as a generalised means of academic coordination, depends on a certain degree of non-recognition of its significance, which may lead to unintentional effects. As Huber (2011) points out, if HEI-reputation could 'be traced back to the interests of certain persons, groups or organisations, the reputation will be considered manipulated, corrupted and in turn, worthless as far as scientific communication is concerned'. If regarded as significantly influenced by non-academic actors such as politicians or the media, HEI-reputation would appear invalid in the eyes of academics, who depend on the use of reputation as a means of orientation in academia. In the case of Germany, this has been illustrated by empirical research. When interviewed,[1] HEI-executives as well as full professors tend to give rather low estimates on the impact of media coverage on the corporate reputation of their home institution. On the other hand, in a standardised survey the same group of academics report attaching great value to favourable media coverage of their university (Friedrichsmeier et al, 2013, 16).

A closer observation of the peculiarities of governing knowledge specialists may identify further potential drivers of mediatisation, for example, the relevance of public appearances (publications, conferences, and so on) to the career of academic staff. Without denying such arguments, this chapter focuses on the organisational level of analysis (also compare Marcinkowski et al, 2014b).

Summing up our previous argument, an industrial notion of a knowledge society gave grounds to the rise of the expectation that HEI should react uniformly to multitudes of stakeholder expectations. This argument centres on media's role in a corporate evaluation of HEI contributions to society. In the case of public universities, there is also a political side to the issue.

### Steering at arm's length

In the last two or three decades, most governments retracted from detailed decision-making for the 'public good'. Instead, HEI were expected to become more responsive to multitudes of stakeholder demands. This change is most evident in countries with a pronounced tradition of state responsibility for HEI expenditure and regulative framework, such as in Central Europe.[2] But more or less in all other western countries, HEI governance at the state level has scaled up the significance of decentralised controls. Irrespective of some national peculiarities, observers concur with one another in noting 'overall a shift…in particular towards…the steering-at-a-distance mode of governance' (Capano, 2011, 1636).

Similar to other branches of the public sector (compare Jacobs and Schillemans, in this book), a former 'system of hierarchical organisational and political accountability relations has given way to a much more diversified and pluralistic set' (Bovens, 2007). HEI and other public sector organisations are now expected to respond to an opaque setting of stakeholders. Previously, government decisions were claimed to represent the whole spectrum of public interests at stake and to map their relative weighting. Evaluating differing societal demands was regarded to culminate in the domain of public authorities elected democratically. In decentralised governance, it does not. Hence, mediated public discourse comes into play, which is deemed to indicate public demands and expectations (compare Fuchs and Pfetsch, 1996). Classic vertical accountability takes place via elected bodies and bureaucratically mandated service organisations aligned to a hierarchical chain of delegation, with the drawback that democratic agency is remitted at every step of this chain (Strøm, 2000). In contrast, steering at arm's length nudges public organisations to a direct orientation towards a plurality of stakeholder demands, which constitutes a shift to a more 'horizontal' type of public accountability (Bovens, 2007). Accounting directly to stakeholders dispenses of a formal chain of democratic representation but introduces a new need for stakeholder intermediation. Accordingly, a study on horizontal accountability in the Dutch public sector revealed that stakeholder influence is mostly indirect and is particularly strong when 'external pressure, from political actors and the media, combined with organisational concerns for reputation-management' (Meijer and Schillemans, 2009, 285). These findings correspond with the need for reputation as discussed above. So reputation management may enhance horizontal accountability while also being an instrument of make-believe at its core. A reputational orientation of HEI therefore gives not only a rationale of public transparency but also of blame avoidance strategies in order to avoid reputational losses.

As highlighted in the findings of Meijer and Schillemans, political authorities have not been rendered irrelevant. On the contrary, pressure by politicians and a 'shadow of hierarchy' may enhance horizontal accountability. From the perspective of public authorities, media coverage can serve as a means of exerting influence. With the waiver of direct controls, exerting indirect influence via news media is even a pre-condition of successful implementation of formal instruments and controls.[3] As observed by Meyer in as early as the 1970s, 'national discussion had rather powerful effects' on educational organisation in the USA, via its potential to 'set agendas and define problems' (Meyer, 1992, 257, today still supported by 'overall empirical evidence'; Seeber et al, 2014, 26). The same applies all the more to policy-making by international bodies without legislative powers of their own (for multi-level constellations also compare Klijn, 2015 and Hasler et al, 2015, in this book). For the EU, public discourse is a major venue for 'intruding into higher education by disseminating common legitimating policy discourses' (Magalhães et al, 2013, 109).

Most higher education policies would 'require decades to produce measurable impacts, especially regarding complex issues' (Seeber et al, 2014, 10). Evaluating outcomes in real-time by positive publicity allows monitoring of public legitimation at the same time. Considering that office holders tend to seek media recognition (for example, Mazzoleni and Schulz, 1999), there is also a rationale for HEI to present themselves favourably in the media arena. Similarly, this lays foundations that HEI use the media to lobby for funding. Without exception in all OECD countries, public authorities are the predominant sources of university funding, with an average of only 12.1 per cent of expenditures originating from private sources (OECD, 2013, 205). This even applies to the USA or Chile when accounting for public research funding, public study grants, and the tax deductibility of tuition fees and study loans. The superior role of public financing implies a certain need to publicly justify a given resource allocation in relation to other public purposes.

In German HEI, the role of tuition fees is insignificant, which makes it obvious that there is no 'natural' market situation at play, but only a politically constituted one, for example, a public performance financing that utilises student numbers as an indicator. In our view, this peculiarity of Germany and other Central European HEI facilitates a comparison with other branches of the public sector without a presence of paying customers.

## A model of mediatised university governance

Summing up, the media plays a multifaceted role in higher education governance, which is depicted in Figure 6.1.

Public authorities *steering at arm's length* exert influence indirectly via public discourse and monitor outcomes and public resonance of their policies in news media.[4] HEI have a rationale to be visible in the media in order to *lobby for public funding*.[5] In order to meet political expectations associated with the notion of a knowledge society, HEI are compelled to *raise profile* in relation to their stakeholders. A favourable portrayal in the

**Figure 6.1: Mediation of actor interactions in higher education governance**

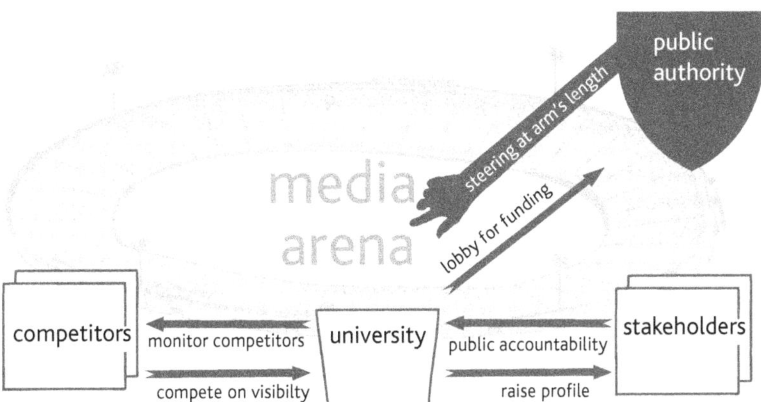


media emerges as an indispensable ticket to mobilising public support and financing. It also functions as a means of *competition*. The auditing of competitive outcomes of entire universities is transdisciplinary by nature and therefore is best *monitored* by resonance within news media,[6] in contrast to the recognition of individual academic performance given by a professional audience of peers.

As a result of reforms decentralising governance, news media now play a role in what recent discussions in this journal referred to as 'a wider reconfiguration of state–citizen relations, which…are now characterized by extreme reflexivity' (Leggett, 2014, 12). In our model (Figure 6.1), this reflexivity is represented by the public arena, which mediates all of the depicted actor relations at the same time. For analytical understanding, the media's conflating mediation of different actor relations complicates matters, but in practical terms, it is an invaluable simplification for the parties involved. The arena of news media coverage bears a multifocal capacity and allows for addressing a wide range of actors at once. For anyone lacking the time and knowledge to communicate directly with each potential external stakeholder or office holder, monitoring the media instead is a practical choice. The same applies to monitoring potentially relevant public expectations and their trends. At the same time, the risk of unintentional effects prevails. In a simple two-actor relationship, a mediation of the interaction via news media might have a skewing effect, but probably little more. If a university feels that its efforts towards a specific target group are evaluated via the media by that target group, and by other target groups at the same time, objectives that are congruous only with regard to a single target group can crosscut and intermingle. But it is more or less the same news media that is utilised for a number of aims. First, HEI attempt outside lobbying of the government. Second, public affairs management addresses external stakeholders. Third, the media are an arena in which a university competes for visibility with a view to competitors, not in the least to motivate its own staff. The objective of being observable as a complete university exacerbates the risks of intermingling incompatible goals.

## Two empirical illustrations

Based on our theoretical considerations about the interrelation of mediatisation and notions of a knowledge society, we expect unintentional policy outcomes in the context of policy efforts derived from this notion. Our empirical expectation is that HEI will react to these policy efforts by means of strategies that ought to enhance corporate reputation. Side effects can be expected to result from a rationale to avoid any reputational risks. For HEI activity associated with reputational risks, we expect to detect an affinity of *blame avoidance* behaviour. This includes 'back cover checking behaviour', 'cocooning', and laying out bureaucratic 'paper audit trails' (Hood, 2011).

Our second expectation is that media-related strategies for enhancing university responsiveness to a specific group of stakeholders can also cause accidental effects on other stakeholders. In consequence, goal attainment in relation to a particular stakeholder group has side effects on goal attainment in relation to other HEI stakeholder groups.

### Accidentally reinforcing the mismatch between research and teaching

The most prominent example of an HEI policy with a potential for side effects can be found in the political intention to rebalance the significance of teaching and research in HEI. Policy recommendations by international institutions concerning an upcoming knowledge society, for example, the EU Lisbon Strategy, emphasise the teaching function of universities. The 'Wissenschaftsrat', Germany's primary consultancy agency and brain trust in higher education policy, with 50 per cent staffing by politicians in its central boards, concludes that a knowledge society advances 'teaching quality' to an 'important societal goal' (Wissenschaftsrat, 2013, 40). Consonant to this, supranational organisations emphasise the need for academic training of the national workforce (compare calculations on the public return of investment in tertiary education, OECD, 2013, 131–35).

Apart from the conciliatory style typical of policy declarations, the main obstacle to increasing teaching efforts is perceived to be a 'research fixation' of the universities. The German 'Wissenschaftsrat' assumes a still-prevailing 'reputation asymmetry' between research and teaching to be responsible for a fairly poor implementation of policy efforts to strengthen teaching quality (Wissenschaftsrat, 2008, 84). This asymmetry is confirmed by studies in a number of European countries (for example, Young, 2006; Turner, 2012), and is thought to be rooted in the disciplinary academic communities. Academic reputation in a discipline primarily relies on research achievements, not on teaching performance in a specific university. In contrast, corporate reputation is attributed at the level of a whole university and has been upvalued by recent reforms (Blümel et al, 2011, 110f). Before these reforms, national academic systems with a comparatively high level of branding at the organisational level, as in the USA, revealed comparatively high attention to teaching achievements (Clark, 1983, 95). Correspondingly, recent high-stake policy initiatives to advance teaching quality in Germany, namely a €2 billion programme, require HEI to officially commit to teaching quality as an essential part of their corporate profiles (BMBF, 2012). Nevertheless, recent studies indicate that the intended advancement of teaching did not take place (Wilkesmann and Schmid, 2011; Bogumil et al, 2012) without providing a sufficient explanation for the policy failure. Studies from different countries report many promising programmes for strengthening teaching quality management, but also on poor implementation and 'lack of consistency', which have thwarted these programmes (HEA and GENIE, 2009, 22). Empirical indications are a low corporate reputation of teaching quality managers (for example, Whitchurch, 2009), 'management vacuums' (Schneijderberg and Teichler, 2013, 397) and unclear task profiles (Kloke, 2014, 318f) in teaching management. In addition, recent findings indicate that HEI do not attribute reputational risks to teaching and research in a uniform manner. Huber reports that HEI in the UK perceive considerable risks linked to 'students' perception of teaching', as these 'may lead to a loss of reputation' (Huber, 2011, 11). At the same time, they 'largely ignore risks inherent to the research process or research strategies at university level. They are not assessed or evaluated in terms of risk, although they are decisive for the competitive success' (Huber, 2011, 13).

In our view, blame avoidance behaviour in teaching management might be the key to an adequate understanding of these findings. Blame avoidance implies that vested interests perceive some risk of being blamed. Most likely, though not necessarily, this indicates public scrutiny in the news media. The converse of 'blame avoidance' is 'credit-claiming' (Weaver, 1986), a strategy of taking credit for popular activities and receiving positive recognition. Blame avoidance prevails when the chances of positive recognition are low and the risk of blame is high, since decision-makers tend to react more strongly to blame risks than to chances of claiming credit (for example, Hood and Heald, 2006). Building on the growing importance of positive publicity for organisational reputation, we assume that teaching is associated with a lower ability to raise the public profile and a higher risk of attracting public blame than research. More precisely, we expect the news media to cover teaching at the university level more rarely and mainly negatively, while research efforts are covered more often and mainly positive in tone.

### Empirics

To check these expectations, a detailed content analysis of media coverage in the top ten national news media outlets in Germany was conducted. Media titles[7] were selected according to the assessment of the HEI's collegial executives in the form of a standardised questionnaire (Friedrichsmeier et al, 2013, 21). We accounted for coverage on a sample of ten universities that were selected via building subgroups among the 100 largest universities in Germany according to their visibility in the national media in relation to their number of personnel.[8] The period covered was January 2010 to April 2013. Of a total of 14,902 national media reports, a random sample of 2,192 national media reports was selected for detailed content analysis. Inter-coder-reliability (five coders) was tested: 0.897 (Holsti) on issues of media coverage (Table 6.1) and 0.952 on the reporting of problematic organisation (Table 6.2).

The findings displayed in Table 6.1 overwhelmingly support the first part of our expectation. Apart from organisational matters, research and expertise is 25 times as likely to attract national media coverage compared to teaching.

A simple explanation of these results is provided by news value theory (compare Kepplinger, 2008). The low news value attached to teaching probably renders it of little use in attaining media visibility. If the media constitute an important channel through which a university can reach its

**Table 6.1: Main issues of media coverage for 10 German HEI, content analysis, 2010–13 (%)**

| | Research results and expertise | Teaching | Organisation of teaching | Organisation of research | Superordinate or other organisational matters | Non-academic matters |
|---|---|---|---|---|---|---|
| National media reports (n = 2192) | 53.4 | 2.1 | 7.7 | 9.2 | 11.8 | 17.5 |

target groups, the low attention the media pays to teaching automatically limits the potential of teaching for raising the public profile.

In contrast to teaching, that is, holding a seminar, decision-making on teaching programmes may provide for some novelty value to the media. Correspondingly, organisational matters of teaching receive a three-times-greater share of media attention, compared to teaching as such. In contrast, coverage on research and scientific expertise has a greater share than reporting on organisational matters related to research. Thus, the relation of media attention given to organisational and content related issues differs. Teaching is primarily covered on organisational issues. In contrast, research and research based expertise[9] attract significant levels of media attention besides organisational matters. Essentially no risk of public blame is attached to reports on research findings or teaching as such. At the same time, media attention to organisational matters of the universities relies to some degree on the news value of conflict. Accordingly, the coverage of organisational issues is accompanied by most of the public criticism and negativity a university may encounter in the national media. The figures in Table 6.2 give clear support for the presumption. Media reports stating a non-optimal functioning of a research organisation have a considerably smaller share than coverage on a non-optimal functioning of teaching organisation.

Coverage of problematic organisation of research is for the most part confined to plagiarism in doctoral research studies, and most often refers to former and not current university staff or students. At the same time, the likelihood of being criticised in a report on research organisation is only half of a report on teaching organisation.

**Table 6.2: Content analysis of media reports on problematic organisation (%)**

| | Organisation of teaching (n = 178) | Organisation of research (n = 217) | Superordinate or other organisational matters (n = 269) |
|---|---|---|---|
| Share of reports stating a problematic or non-optimal functioning of organisation | 35.4 | 20.3 | 34.2 |
| For comparison: share of reports on non-optimal functioning (n = 199) that deal with this matter | 31.7 | 22.1 | 46.2 |

Altogether, the total number of reports that refer to problematic or non-optimal organisation at the universities is well below 6 per cent, but most of this blame is placed on teaching organisation. At the same time, teaching does not attract considerable media attention. Combining reports on teaching and on teaching organisation, the chances of organisational blame are as high as a share of 25 per cent. In comparison, when looking at organisational blame in media reports on research and research organisation, the share is below 2 per cent. Thus, the high tendency towards positive visibility in the media fosters decision-makers' willingness to promote research activities and, furthermore, to allow for considerable self-initiative of personnel in research matters. By contrast, decision-makers who are interested in public affairs are inclined to blame-avoidance strategies when it comes to teaching and teaching organisation, which results in the aforementioned shortcomings of the respective policy measures.

Semi-structured interviews conducted in 2014 with collegial executives, deans and full professors of the same HEI we selected for the content analysis (compare above) clearly underscore that academics are aware of different chances of teaching and research to attract positive recognition or blame. However, most academics do not perceive themselves as actively pursuing blame avoidance strategies. While providing some indication of such behaviour, they find it hard to distinguish a reasonable decentralisation of teaching-quality management from blame-avoidance behaviour. To illustrate, a dean of a department of economic science rejects

> the idea that we conceal something [in teaching management], if so, I had not told you about these matters in the first place. I incessantly have to report how I put things into use. One can report oneself to death. I believe that we eventually need to establish procedures that are based on trust. Currently, I face nothing but distrust regarding those matters…while actually only managing penury. (Interview AE2)

A dean of a department of pedagogy backs our interpretation of low chances of a positive recognition of teaching efforts in comparison to teaching, as the media is disinterested

> in systematic processes, how we improve teaching modules, how we improve study regulations and conditions. I think those issues are too detailed, too complex as well, and insufficiently transparent to the general public. Well then, the research cluster and the graduate school are the flagships that are highlighted

at every opportunity. This illustrates the political implications. (Interview CP1)

Overall, most interviewees do not perceive the media as investigative and critical in the first place. More often, media scrutiny and negative media coverage are observed as triggered by protests of students passed on to the media and subsequently motivates critical inquiries by pending authorities (HEI executives and state).

### Overstretching the information value of rankings

Rankings today are considerably relevant to HEI reputation, especially when published in the media (Pallas and Wedlin, 2013). In Germany, a strong connection between rankings and the media integrated into basic knowledge: 'It has become established in the academic field to only refer to the term 'rankings' when dealing with instruments whose effect is based largely on the publication of their results' (Lange, 2010, 322).

The German brain trust CHE produces rankings of study programmes with a handy winners list (which is singled out for its quality and importance in Sadlak, 2014, 143). Additionally, CHE introduced the use of a colourful traffic light icon to highlight average (yellow light), above (green light) or below average evaluations of a study programme (red light). These rankings compare evaluations of study programmes in a specific field of study, for example, chemistry at Humboldt University versus chemistry at University of Cologne. The results are published with a wide circulation in cooperation with the weekly high-quality newspaper *Die Zeit*. Search-term reviews of national media coverage of the 100 largest universities (sample as described above, >50,000 media reports) find an average portion of 2.5 per cent of media reports covering ranking results.

Differently from the focus of most of academic debate on rankings, potential side effects do not only arise from 'data-collection challenges', such as 'how to define quality' (Sadlak, 2014, 152). Instead, we are interested in unwanted consequences that derive from off-topic usage. More precisely, we focus on effects that could be caused by the perception of HEI-executives on how rankings are evaluated by others.

Our empirical expectation is that rankings are used strategically for purposes they are not designed for, thus unduly overstretching their informative value. Given their enormous media visibility, rankings are applied as 'a shared basis for evaluation' for 'multitudes of stakeholders' at the same time (Sadlak, 2014, 140). The EU Commission enumerates 11 target groups of rankings (European Commission, 2011), so it is reasonable to expect that not all have a 'sufficient capacity (or interest) to undertake fully-fledged analysis of the complexity of internal workings of a particular institution' (Sadlak, 2014, 140).

The methodological basis and 'primary intent' of the German CHE rankings is 'providing an orientation for prospective students', and it should be added that the CHE itself expects a side effect, which is an 'impact on university policies' (CHE Ranking, 2012, 10). However, these rankings neither evaluate different courses at the same university at the same time or with the same criteria, nor are they capable of comparing achievements in different fields of study, for example, of a chemistry programme and a biology programme. Most notably, they are not laid out so as to inform policy-makers. In line with Sadlak, who ignores associated risks of side effects, we expect that the rankings are used as an 'additional rationale for selection of partners. They represent a convincing tool for marketing, policy debates, and public relations' (Sadlak, 2014, 145).

In order to test this expectation, we interviewed HEI decision-makers in Germany (full professors in the collegial boards and executives, whole population survey, N = 1,620, response rate 56 per cent) about the effects of study rankings they observe in their specific field. The results displayed in Figure 6.2 strongly support our expectation. Remarkably, the effect most often reported by the decision-makers is *not* on the original target group of the rankings (that is, prospective students).

**Figure 6.2: Reported effects of study rankings at own university (means)**

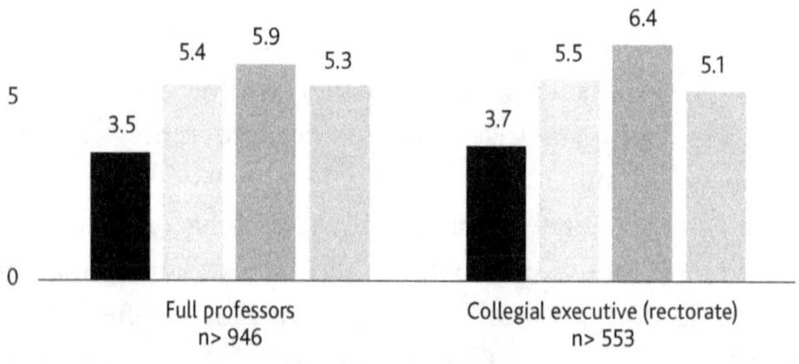

On a scale of 0 ('no effect') to 10 ('very strong effect'), decision-makers report a moderate use of rankings for decision-making on issues between the disciplines, even though the rankings do not contain information that allows for a comparison between different disciplines and fields of study. While the ranking results seem to have a rather small effect on the perceived chances of acquiring external funding, the decision-makers report a high interest in ranking results among politicians and potential partners in private business. Even though the rankings are not designed to deliver relevant information to these groups, they do have a strong impact on decision-making. As presented elsewhere in more detail (Marcinkowski et al, 2013), decision-makers think so all the more, as they are oriented towards positive media coverage. Bivariate correlations of the decision-makers' perception of ranking effects on politicians and of their rating of the susceptibility of politicians to mass media coverage is r = 0.149 (p <0.001). This provides evidence supporting the assumption that broad media visibility of the rankings accounts for the effect. The underlying mechanism is properly depicted by agenda-setting theory (Walgrave et al, 2008), namely a transfer of salience between the media arena and the decision-making arena. The notion of salience transfer refers to the capacity of the media to influence the political importance decision-makers within and outside the university attach to rather simplistically crafted rankings.

## Conclusions

Most of the arguments made in this chapter are related to typical constellations of higher education governance in central European countries with low tuition fees and a long tradition of central governmental control. Empirical findings relate exclusively to the German situation. The effects discussed in this chapter are mostly indirect and inconclusive in terms of causality. Essentially, empirical data is used to underscore concerns about potential negative effects. Investigating a full range of potential side effects, including positive effects, is still pending. The most important follow-up question, which is whether mediatisation actually causes a prevalence of 'looking good' over 'being good' in HEI governance, needs to be put on the agenda of future research. Preferably, further discussion should cover the applicability of the investigated mechanisms on other branches of public sector governance.

The theoretical outline of news media influence in higher education governance (Figure 6.1) depicted actor relationships in a decentralised governance as being bundled in a media arena. All of the actor relationships identified were mediated with the same arena,[10] which made it likely that acting upon one of these actor relationships could affect the others. By addressing case-related expectations derived from this model empirically, potential effects of HEI media orientation could be substantiated. Survey data on perceived effects of public rankings revealed that the rankings' original target group only took third place, so there is clear potential for unwanted repercussions on decision-making. Our first empirical expectation of HEI reacting on opportunities in credit claiming and blame in media coverage could be connected with findings on teaching management and corresponding media coverage. In both cases, we suggested that an analysis of the news frames involved may contribute to the overall understanding of unintended effects.

Politicians presumably play a direct role. They seek media recognition in order to win elections, support and loyalty and are therefore likely to rely on media publicity when it comes to evaluating individual organisations. Instead of basing their appraisal of a public organisation merely on its conformity to political demands (such as to upvalue teaching), they might be lured to think highly of a university that is visible in the media precisely because it puts little effort in teaching.

Decentralisation of HEI governance took place with an intention to be rationalised and de-politicised, though still with the intention of ultimately serving the public interest (Mayntz, 2006). So political issues are still at hand. The subsequent effect, which is that depoliticising in one policy field leads to politicisation in another, is referred to as the 'mirror-image hypothesis' (Hood and Scott, 2004, 83). As investigated in this chapter, efforts to rationalise university governance have the mirror effect of an intensified influence by the media which is indirect and out of focus. Given that policy-makers geared to rationalisation have hesitated so far to fully acknowledge media influence, the potential to thwart intentional governance strategies is present.

When investigating perceived effects of rankings, we found that doing what the media likes in making a piece of information newsworthy is associated with a loss of control on the use of the information. But a lack of precision may not prevent actors in the field from intentionally pursuing media-related political strategies. A growing responsiveness of public organisations to news media might enable vested interests to intentionally exploit this responsiveness. If one speculates on the situation, some actors in German HEI governance might have already resorted to media-related governance strategies, namely the brain trust CHE, which issues the most important study rankings in Germany. Future research should therefore consider to what extent news media have become an integral player in the field of public sector governance.

**Notes**

[1] In 2014, 59 semi-structured interviews (average length 73 of minutes) were conducted at ten HEI with collegial executives, deans, and full professors of chemistry, business sciences, and pedagogy.

[2] Decentralising HEI-reforms started in as early as the 1980s or in as late as the 2000s in some countries. More revealing than a number of differences identified in the literature are close similarities between countries (for example, De Boer et al, 2010). German HEI governance ranks in the middle in terms of progress of reforms, when a greater number of countries is considered.

[3] This view is expressed in interviews with state ministries governing the universities in Germany (Friedrichsmeier and Gohr, 2013, 19–20).

[4] Reported in interviews with the competent state authorities in Germany (Friedrichsmeier and Gohr, 2013, 8–11).

[5] HEI-visibility in the media is brought to bear by competent authorities when negotiating their share of the state budget (Friedrichsmeier and Gohr, 2013, 32–4).

[6] Visibility in the media can be used as an indicator of competitive success (Laukötter, 2014).

[7] Respondents named up to four media titles they personally use to track public opinion on HEI-issues. Selected titles are *DIE ZEIT*, *Frankfurter Allgemeine*, *Süddeutsche Zeitung*, *Tagesspiegel*, *Frankfurter Rundschau*, *taz*, *Der Spiegel*, *Focus* and *Die Welt*, including online sites.

[8] A second criterion was the share of media reports on a given university covering organisational as compared to academic news. This share was calculated by means of automated search-term analysis.

[9] Reports that named a specific academic publication or a specific recent finding were coded as coverage on 'research' (28.5 per cent of all reports). Media references to more general elucidations and scientific explanations by academic staff were coded 'expertise' (29.6 per cent).

[10] Consisting of news media, in contrast to at least some segments of new social media that fail to address more than a particular segment of consumers at a time.

**References**

Blümel, A, Kloke, K, Krücken, G, 2011, Professionalisierungsprozesse im hochschulmanagement in Deutschland, in A Langer, A Schröer (eds) *Professionalisierung im nonprofit management*, Wiesbaden: VS

BMBF (ed), 2012, *Bekanntmachung des bundesministeriums für bildung und forschung von richtlinien zur förderung von forschungsvorhaben zum themenfeld 'Leistungsbewertung in der wissenschaft'*, Berlin: BMBF

Bogumil, J, Burgi, M, Heinze, G, Gerber, S, Gräf, I-D, Jochheim, L, Schickentanz, M, Wannöffel, M, 2012, *Modernisierung der universitäten oder formwandel der staatlichkeit im deutschen universitätssystem*, Bochum: Hans Böckler Stiftung

Bovens, M, 2007, Analysing and assessing accountability: A conceptual framework, *European Law Journal* 13, 4, 447–68

Brunsson, N, Sahlin-Andersson, K, 2000, Constructing organizations: The example of public sector reform, *Organization Studies* 21, 4, 721–46

Capano, G, 2011, Government continues to do its job: A comparative study of governance shifts in the higher education sector, *Public Administration* 89, 4, 1622–42

Carvalho, L (ed), 2007, Knowledge, policy-making and public action in education, *Sísifo: Educational Sciences Journal* 4, 3–4

CHE Ranking (ed), 2012, *Methodische genauigkeit und öffentlicher nutzen des che hochschulrankings*, Gütersloh: CHE

Clark, B, 1983, *The higher education system: Academic organization in cross-national perspective*, Berkeley, CA: University of California Press

Davenport, T, Beck, J, 2001, *The attention economy: Understanding the new currency of business*, Boston, MA: Harvard Business School Press

De Boer, H, Enders, J, Schimank, U, 2010, *Progress in higher education reform across Europe: Governance reform*, Brussels: Directorate General for Education and Culture

European Commission, 2011, *Implementation of a user-driven, multi-dimensional and international ranking for higher education institutions*, Open call for tender EAC/42/2011

Friedrichsmeier, A, Geils, M, Kohring, M, Laukötter, E, Marcinkowski, F, 2013, *Organisation und öffentlichkeit von hochschulen*, Münster: IfK

Friedrichsmeier, A, Gohr, M, 2013, *Wie wissenschaftsministerien ihre hochschulen über die medien beobachten*, Münster: IfK

Fuchs, D, Pfetsch, B, 1996, Die beobachtung der öffentlichen meinung durch das regierungssystem, in WVD Daele, F Neidhardt (eds) *Kommunikation und entscheidung*, pp 103–38, Berlin: Sigma

Hasler, K, Kübler, D, Cchristmann, A, Marcinkowski, F, 2015 Over-responsibilised and over-blamed, *Policy & Politics*, 44, 1, 135–52.

HEA, GENIE, 2009, *Reward and recognition in higher education: Institutional policies and their implementation*, York: HEA

Hood, C, 2011, *The blame game: Spin, bureaucracy, and self-preservation in government*, Princeton, NJ: Princeton University Press

Hood, C, Heald, D, 2006, *Transparency: The key to better governance?*, Oxford: Oxford University Press

Hood, C, Scott, C, 2004, Higher education and university research, in C Hood, O James, B Peters, C Scott (eds) *Controlling modern government*, pp 75–84, Cheltenham: Edward Elgar

Huber, M, 2011, The risk university: Risk identification at higher education institutions in England, *CARR Discussion Chapter* 69, London: London School of Economics

Jacobs, S, Schillemans, T, 2015, Media and public accountability, *Policy & Politics*, 44.1. 23–40.

Kepplinger, H, 2008, News values, in W Donsbach (ed) *The international encyclopedia of communication, Vol VII*, Oxford: Blackwell, 3281–86

Klijn, E, 2015, Managing commercialised media attention in complex governance networks, *Policy & Politics,* 44, 1, 115–33.

Kloke, K, 2014, *Qualitätsentwicklung an deutschen hochschulen: Professionstheoretische untersuchung eines neuen tätigkeitsfeldes*, Wiesbaden: Springer

Lange, R, 2010, Benchmarking, rankings und ratings, in D Simon, A Knie, S Hornbostel (eds) *Handbuch wissenschaftspolitik*, pp 322–33, Wiesbaden: VS

Laukötter, E, 2014, *Die sichtbarkeit deutscher hochschulen in print- und online-medien*, Münster: IfK

Leggett, W, 2014, The politics of behaviour change: Nudge, neoliberalism and the state, *Policy & Politics* 42, 1, 3–19

Luhmann, N, 1992, *Die wissenschaft der gesellschaft*, Frankfurt: Suhrkamp

McCombs, M, Weaver, D, 1973, Voters' need for orientation and use of mass communication, *Annual conference of the International Communication Association*, Montreal, Canada

Magalhães, A, Veiga, A, Ribeiro, F, Sousa, S, Santiago, R, 2013, Creating a common grammar for European higher education governance, *Higher Education* 65, 1, 95–112

Marcinkowski, F, Kohring, M, Friedrichsmeier, A, Fürst, S, 2013, Neue Governance und die Öffentlichkeit der Hochschulen, in E Grande, D Jansen, O Jarren, A Rip, U Schimank, P Weingart (eds) *Neue Governance der Wissenschaft*, Bielefeld: Transcript-Verlag

Marcinkowski, F, Friedrichsmeier, A, Geils, M, 2014a, Transparenz oder PR?, in R Krempkow, A Lottmann, T Möller (eds) *Völlig losgelöst? iFQ-Working Chapter No15*, Berlin: iFQ

Marcinkowski, F, Kohring, M, Fürst, S, Friedrichsmeier, A, 2014b, Organizational Influence on Scientists' Efforts to Go Public, *Science Communication* 36, 1, 56–80

Marginson, S, 2007, Five somersaults in Enschede: Rethinking public/private in higher education for the global era, in J Enders, B Jongbloed (eds) *Public–private dynamics in higher education: Expectations, developments and outcomes*, pp 187–220, Bielefeld: Transcript Verlag

Mayntz, R, 2006, From government to governance: Political steering in modern societies, in D Scheer, F Rubik (eds) *Governance of integrated product policy*, pp 18–25, Aizlewood Mill: Greenleaf

Mazzoleni, G, Schulz, W, 1999, 'Mediatization' of politics: A challenge for democracy?, *Political Communication* 16, 3, 247–61

Meijer, A, Schillemans, T, 2009, Fictional citizens and real effects: Accountability to citizens in competitive and monopolistic markets, *Public Administration, Management* 14, 2, 254–91

Merton, R, 1973, *The sociology of science: Theoretical and empirical investigations*, Chicago, IL: University of Chicago Press

Meyer, J, 1992, Conclusion: Institutionalization and the rationality of formal organizational structure, in J Meyer, W Scott (eds) *Organizational environments: Ritual and rationality*, pp 261–82, Newbury Park: Sage

Mouritsen, J, 2000, Valuing expressive organizations: Intellectual capital and the visualization of value creation, in M Schultz, M Hatch, M Larsen (eds) *The expressive organization: Linking identity, reputation, and the corporate brand*, pp 208–29, Oxford: Oxford University Press

Nickel, S, 2012, Engere kopplung von wissenschaft und verwaltung und ihre folgen für die ausübung professioneller rollen in hochschulen, in U Willkesmann, C Schmid (eds) *Hochschule als organisation*, pp 279–92, Wiesbaden: VS

O'Donnell, G, 1998, Horizontal accountability in new democracies, *Journal of Democracy* 9, 3, 112–26

OECD (ed), 2008, *Tertiary education for the knowledge society, volume 1: Special features: Governance, fundings, quality*, Paris: OECD Publishing

OECD (ed), 2013, *Education at a glance 2013: OECD indicators*, Paris: OECD Publishing

Pallas, J, Wedlin, L, 2013, Governance of science in mediatized society: Media rankings and the translation of global governance models for universities, in G Drori, M Llerer, P Walgenbach (eds) *Global themes and local variations in organization and management*, pp 295–308, New York: Routledge

Paradeise, C, Thoenig, J, 2013, Academic institutions in search of quality: Local orders and global standards, *Organization Studies* 34, 2, 189–218

Patterson, T, 1993, *Out of order*, New York: Knopf

Peters, H, Heinrichs, H, Jung, A, Kallfass, M, Petersen, I, 2008, Medialization of science as a prerequisite of its legitimization and political relevance, in D Cheng, M Claessens, T Gascoigne, J Metcalfe, B Schiele, S Shunke (eds) *Communicating science in social contexts: New models, new practices*, pp 71–92, Dordrecht: Springer

Rifkin, J, 2014, *The zero marginal cost society*, New York: Palgrave

Rödder, S, Franzen, M, Weingart, P (eds), 2012, *The sciences' media connection: Public communication and its repercussions*, Dordrecht: Springer

Sadlak, J, 2014, University rankings: The manifestation and driver of competition for excellence within the new higher-education landscape, in P Mattei (ed) *University adaptation in difficult economic times*, pp 137–56, Oxford: Oxford University Press

Schneijderberg, C, Teichler, U, 2013, Hochschulprofessionelle als prototyp der veränderten verwaltung an universitäten, in C Schneijderberg, N Merkator, U Teichler, B Kehm (eds) *Verwaltung war gestern? Neue hochschulprofessionen und die gestaltung von studium und lehre*, pp 389–414, Frankfurt: Campus

Schultz, M, Hatch, M, Larsen, M, 2000, Why the expressive organization?, in M Schultz, M Hatch, M Larsen (eds) *The expressive organization: Linking identity, reputation, and the corporate brand*, pp 1–7, Oxford: Oxford University Press

Seeber, M, Lepori, B, Montauti, M, Enders, J, De Boer, H, Weyer, E, Bleiklie, I, Hope, K, Michelsen, S, Nyhagen Mathisen, G, Frølich, N, Scordato, L, Stensaker, B, Waagene, E, Dragsic, Z, Kretek, P, Krücken, G, Magalhãe, A, Ribeiro, FM, Sousa, S, Veiga, A, Santiago, R, Marini, G, Reale, E, 2014, European universities as complete organizations? Understanding identity, hierarchy and rationality in public organizations, *Public Management Review*, DOI: 10.1080/14719037.2014.943268

Strøm, K, 2000, Delegation and accountability in parliamentary democracies, *European Journal of Political Research* 37, 3, 261–89

Turner, R, 2012, Rewarding excellent teaching: The translation of a policy initiative in the United Kingdom, *Higher Education Quarterly* 66, 4, 415–30

UNESCO (ed), 2005, *Towards knowledge societies: UNESCO world report*, Paris: UNESCO

Vällima, J, Hoffman, D, 2008, Knowledge society discourse and higher education, *Higher Education* 56, 3, 265–85

Walgrave, S, Soroka, S, Nuytemans, M, 2008, The mass media's political agenda-setting power, *Comparative Political Studies* 41, 6, 814–36

Weaver, K, 1986, The politics of blame avoidance, *Journal of Public Policy* 6, 4, 371–98

Weick, K, 1976, Educational organizations as loosely coupled systems, *Administrative Science Quarterly* 21, 1, 1–19

Whitchurch, C, 2009, The rise of the blended professional in higher education: A comparison between the United Kingdom, Australia and the United States, *Higher Education* 58, 3, 407–18

Wilkesmann, U, Schmid, C, 2011, The impacts of new governance on teaching at German universities, *Higher Education* 62, 1, 33–52

Wissenschaftsrat, 2008, *Empfehlungen zur Qualitätsverbesserung von Lehre und Studium*, Drs 8639-08, Berlin: Wissenschaftsrat

Wissenschaftsrat, 2013, *Perspektiven des deutschen wissenschaftssystems*, Drs 3228-13, Braunschweig: Wissenschaftsrat

Young, P, 2006, Out of balance: Lecturers' perceptions of differential status and rewards in relation to teaching and research, *Teaching in Higher Education* 11, 2, 191–202

# Managing commercialised media attention in complex governance networks: positive and negative effects on network performance

Erik Hans Klijn

## Introduction: public managers coping with commercialised media

Society and governance processes have become very complex, and many authors argue that most service delivery and public decision-making takes place within networks of interdependent actors, characterised by complex decision and interaction processes and requiring collaborative leadership (Mandell, 2001; Koppenjan and Klijn, 2004; Ansell and Gash, 2008). This literature emphasises that, to be successful in these networks, political leaders and administrators must engage in interactions with various stakeholders to be effective and actively manage their network (Koppenjan and Klijn, 2004; Huxham and Vangen, 2005).

The growing literature on mediatisation and media attention on political and administrative events gives a different impression, however. Although some of the literature emphasises the positive functions of the media as a democratic forum where information is provided, where citizens can judge political events and media act as critical watchdog of politics (see Schudson, 1998; Graber, 2004), another branch of the literature adopts a more critical stance. This literature (Cook, 2005; Bennett, 2009) emphasises that it is very hard to avoid media attention and that media attention follows its own (media) logic with an emphasis on drama, storytelling, and focusing on conflict and personal stories in the news.

Although there is a strong tradition of research on agenda forming that also looks at media attention on these processes (Cobb and Elder, 1983; Baumgartner and Jones, 2009), the subject of the attention paid by the media to complex governance processes has so far largely been ignored. The governance literature has predominantly focused on the complexity of decision-making processes and the way that they are managed. Thus, from the perspective of this literature, an examination of how media attention affects that decision process, and the relation of media attention and network management, seems both very interesting and a new research area for the governance literature.

The literature on mediatisation has been focusing more on political leaders and on (national) issues that are salient and that catch the attention of many media. From that perspective, more attention on (other) governance processes might generate interesting new findings and bring new insights to the literature on media attention. Thus, the purpose of this chapter is to connect the media and the governance literature to each other and extend the research questions of both branches of literature. The research question at the starting point of this chapter is therefore: *what is the influence of commercialised media attention on network performance and how is this affected by (network) managerial strategies?* This chapter addresses the question of whether managerial strategies mitigate the impact of perceptions of commercialised media attention on network performance.

The research question is addressed by exploring empirically how much commercialised media attention is directed at governance processes around urban spatial planning projects according to managers of these projects and what the effects are on network performance. To approach this question and test the hypotheses developed in the following section, a survey is used among managers involved in urban projects in The Netherlands to measure their perceptions.

The theoretical framework of the chapter is first elaborated and then the hypotheses to be tested. The section after that deals with the operationalization of the key variables. The main findings are then given. The chapter ends with conclusions and reflections.[1]

## Front-stage and backstage: commercialised media attention and network management in networks

Public managers who want to initiate governance processes or arrange service delivery often find themselves in networks of interdependent actors (Hanf and Scharpf, 1978; Rhodes, 1997). Dependency relations between actors are crucial to the emergence and existence of networks (Hanf and Scharpf, 1978). The resource dependencies around policy problems or policy programmes require actors to interact with one another and to create more intensive and enduring interactions (Hanf and Scharpf, 1978). Governance networks can roughly be defined as 'more or less stable patterns of social relations between mutual[ly] dependent actors, which form around policy problems and/or cluster of means and which are formed, maintained and changed through series of games' (Koppenjan and Klijn, 2004, 69–70).

Because actors have their own perceptions of the nature of the problem and the solution, and because each actor acts strategically from his/her own perceptive, networks are often characterised by complex interaction and decision-making processes. This means that it is not easy to achieve socially relevant outcomes in these networks. The literature on networks thus deals extensively with leadership and/or managerial strategies and roles to stimulate and facilitate complex processes in networks, mostly called network management. The basic argument is usually that without adequate network management strategies it is very difficult – or even impossible – to achieve appealing outcomes in these complex interaction processes in networks (see Klijn et al, 2010b; McGuire and Agranoff, 2011).

## The front-stage: media logic as institutional rules

Public managers have to deal not only with multiple actors with divergent perceptions of problems and solutions, but also with possible attention from the media.

There is no doubt that the media have become very important in both understanding our world and getting information on what is happening (Bennett, 2009). The media have many functions. For a long time, they have been attributed an important role as a democratic forum, providing information to citizens, without which the latter would not be able to discuss political issues (Schudson, 1998). The media also have an important role in setting the political agenda (see Cobb and Elder, 1983; Walgrave and Van Aelst, 2006; Baumgartner and Jones, 2009). Last but not least, the media function as an instrument whereby actors convey their messages. The literature on public relations and branding strongly emphasises this aspect (see Hankinson, 2004; Strömbäck and Kiousis, 2011; Eshuis and Klijn, 2012).

Besides these different media functions, however, various authors argue that society is increasingly submitted to, or becoming dependent on, news media and their logic in a process known as the *mediatisation of society* (Mazzoleni and Schulz, 1999; Hjarvard, 2008; Strömbäck and Esser, 2009; Reunanen et al, 2010). This media logic refers both to the process of news-making led by the media's rules, aims, production routines and constraints (Altheide and Snow, 1979; Brants and Van Praag, 2006; Hjarvard, 2008; Strömbäck and Esser, 2009) and to the content of news reporting (Patterson, 2000; Bennet, 2009). Before the argument is progressed, a closer look must be taken at the concept of media logic and how it is used in this chapter.

The media form a separate institution with their own rules and modus operandi (Cook, 2005; Hjarvard, 2008; Strömbäck and Esser, 2014).

This means that media logic can be seen as an institutional practice; as a set of rules regulating actors' behaviour (see Scharpf, 1997; Cook, 2005; Asp, 2014). Media logic thus provides a set of rules for journalists and others involved in the media that both enables sensible actions and constrains actions. Media logic is not static however, but changes over time in processes of institutionalisation (Cook, 2005). Many different rules are mentioned when it comes to media logic (see Altheide and Snow, 1979; Bennett, 2009; Landerer, 2013; Asp, 2014). Strömbäck and Esser (2014, 17–18; see also Esser and Matthes, 2013) identify three distinctive dimensions that could be used to categorise the various rules and norms of media logic:

1. *Professionalism* (see also Bennett, 2009; Asp, 2014): journalistic norms and values prescribe journalists to be independent; to maintain standards of newsworthiness in news selection; and to serve the public interest. Scholars stress that rules about objectivity, being unbiased, and the separation of facts and figures gradually emerged at the beginning of the twentieth century (see Cook, 2005).
2. *Commercialism*: because all media have commercial interests, the question of how to maximise publics relevant for advertisers is very relevant. Rules inspired by commercialism are related to the logics of running a business and have implications for processes of news production, news selection and news presentation. Consequences for the news production process have to do with the efficient use of scarce resources. For instance, when news media allocate reporters to a specific event, news has to be generated even if there is none. Furthermore, growing competition can harm the watchdog role of journalism when commercial interests overrule professional standards (Patterson, 2000). In addition, rules relating to commercialism have a strong content dimension, in terms of news selection and news presentation. News has to be attractive for an audience, and this often results in dramatising and personalising news (see Bennett, 2009) and an emphasis on negative news and a critical attitude towards officeholders (see Patterson, 2000; Bennett, 2009).
3. *Media technology*: each communication platform has its own format criteria in which news has to be presented. Media technology shapes the production process and content (the 7 am news, the 8 pm news and so forth) and the way messages have to be communicated (in a news format, in images, sound and/or text).

As in all institutions, the rules generally do not form a naturally coherent and unambiguous set. Clear tension exists between the rules of professionalism and those of commercialism. The latter rules tend to push journalists to a more sensational, dramatic framing of the news, whereas the former tend to stimulate fact finding and the separation of news from opinion. The first set of rules is connected to the more positive functions of media as a democratic forum and watchdog. Even so, the institutional rules of media logic change gradually over time.

Various authors emphasise that commercialism has become a stronger element of media logic in the last decades (see Patterson, 2000; Bennett, 2009). Moreover, commercialism and its consequences seem to be one of the most significant motives behind studies on mediatisation (Landerer, 2013). Mediatisation studies generally focus on consequences of the interference of the commercial news media logic with logics of other societal institutions; studies on the mediatisation of politics report the extent to which and how adaption to the commercial news media logic has been changing politics and other spheres (Mazzoleni and Schulz, 1999; Hjarvard, 2008; Landerer, 2013; Strömbäck and Esser, 2014).[2]

Thus, this chapter focuses on the commercialised rules and their effects on governance processes. It investigates whether news reporting on complex governance networks in environmental projects has – as it is called in this chapter – a commercialised character, that is, whether it has a strong negative, sensational character. However, this chapter does not examine whether macro sociological theories about mediatisation are correct or not, simply looking at:

1. whether there is commercialised media attention in the perception of managers involved in complex governance networks;
2. whether this has any significant effect on (perceived) performance of the networks involved in these projects;
3. whether network management strategies may effectively mediate this effect.

## The effect of commercialised news on network performance

Before commercialised news can be operationalised, it is necessary to assess what influence it is expected to have on network performance. In general, commercialised news would be expected to have a negative impact on network performance. This expectation is rooted in several causal mechanisms.

The first causal mechanism has to do with the biased character of media attention. If the news has a more commercialised character, it is more negative and dramatised. This will mean that it is more difficult to bring the complex character of issues in networks to the stage and the issue will on average feature more negatively than positively in the news; this in itself is not helpful for performance. It is also known that negative attention has stronger effects on people than positive attention, and this effect will have a tendency to be self-reinforcing. Moreover, many authors (see Cook, 2005; Bennett, 2009) stress that journalists tend to reproduce every story and follow one another. This view is supported by Baumgartner and Jones' (2009) work on the dynamics in agendas and policy subsystems in the US over the longer term. These authors emphasised the positive feedback often provided by media attention.

More commercialised news, however, also has effects on actors' relations within the network through two causal mechanisms. The first is through the strategies of separate actors in the network and the second is through their trust relations. Actors might change their strategies as a result of commercialised media attention. When media attention tends to emphasise negative and conflicting aspects, there might be a need for actors to profile themselves more strongly. As a result, more conflicting strategies might be expected within networks because of commercialised media attention. This will reduce possibilities to compromise and explore new options in the bargaining process (see also Spörer-Wagner and Marcinkowski, 2010).

Commercialised media attention will also influence actors' trust relations within the network. Trust is often mentioned as an important characteristic that enables the achievement of good network performance (see Provan et al, 2009; Klijn et al, 2010a). Trust relations among actors mitigate, or even enable actors to overcome, some of the problems in networks: conflicts, lack of coordination, and actors' unwillingness to exchange resources and work on joint solutions (see Nooteboom, 2002; Provan et al, 2009). As argued widely in the network literature, trust especially stimulates information exchange among actors in networks and fosters cooperation and long-term investment in relations among actors (see Lane and Bachman, 1998; Nooteboom, 2002). When actors trust one another, they tend to act less opportunistically (as implied by the definition of trust); this in turn reduces uncertainty about behaviour and facilitates interaction and cooperation. Empirically, several authors have shown the positive relation between the level of trust in networks and good network performance (see Provan et al, 2009; Klijn et al, 2010a).

Commercialised media attention can lead in particular to more conflicting strategies that can damage the trust level between actors. Thus, media attention has not only a direct effect on conflicting strategies (and thus a negative effect on performance) but also an indirect effect through the possible decline of trust. Thus, the first hypotheses is:

> Hypothesis 1: Perceptions of more commercialised news reports
> on a project have a negative effect on network performance.

### Managing media attention: network management

There is broad consensus in the literature that the type of leadership and/or management required in networks differs significantly from the classical leadership image of leaders of organisations. Ansell and Gash (2008) talk about 'facilitating leadership'; by which they signify that the task of a leader is to mediate between actors and empower the process of collaboration (see also Gage and Mandell, 1990; Agranoff and McGuire, 2001; Huxham and Vangen, 2005).

In the literature on network management, frequently mentioned management and leadership strategies include initiating and facilitating interaction processes between actors (Friend et al, 1974), for instance by activating (or de-activating) actors and resources; creating and changing network arrangements for better coordination (Scharpf, 1978; Rogers and Whetten, 1982); creating new content and win–win situations (Mandell, 2001), for example by exploring new ideas, working with scenarios, organising joint research (and joint fact finding) (Koppenjan and Klijn, 2004); and guiding interactions (Gage and Mandell, 1990). The literature on collaborative governance and collaborative advantages mentions similar activities. Huxham and Vangen (2005) mention activities like mobilising member organisations, dealing with power relations, empowering actors that can deliver collaborative aims, and trust building. Ansell and Gash (2008) mention elements such as committing to the process, creating shared understanding, aiming for participatory inclusiveness.

This chapter focuses on two types of network management strategies that seem to have the most impact: exploring and connecting (see Klijn et al, 2010b). Connecting strategies are aimed at activating actors and resources, linking actors together, nurturing inter-organisational relations and dealing with conflicts. Exploring strategies are aimed at creating and looking at new solutions, collecting (joint) information, organising research, combining conflicting points of view and so on.

It can be assumed that network management strategies lead to better network performance (see Meier and O'Toole, 2007; Klijn et al, 2010b); but what is the influence of network management on commercialised news? According to the literature, network management can bind actors and solidify cooperation. From earlier research (see Korthagen, 2015), it is known that media attention on spatial planning projects focuses on neglected societal actors who oppose the projects. When network management is performed properly, these groups can be expected to be more connected to the project and less inclined to actively seek media attention, because they have more influence on the content of proposals. There will also be less conflict, because stakeholders are more connected to the process and therefore the project is less attractive for commercialised news reporting. This leads to the second hypothesis:

> Hypothesis 2: When more network management strategies are employed in networks, these projects will generate less commercialised news media attention.

## Methodology: operationalising the concepts

The data used in this study come from a web-based survey conducted in 2011 (April–July) among project managers in the four largest cities of the Netherlands (Amsterdam, Rotterdam, The Hague and Utrecht) and managers within two private firms (P2 and DHV) who manage urban spatial planning projects. No significant statistical differences exist between respondents from the four different municipalities or consultancy firms in ANOVA tests comparing the six groups.

Three preparation sessions were held with eight project managers from the four participating cities and the two organisations to discuss the clarity and relevance of the questions, and to validate our survey. Surveys were sent (with one reminder and a phone reminder) with the consent of their organisations to all project leaders of urban projects in implementation. In total, 288 project leaders from the four municipalities and 57 project leaders from the two consulting firms were approached. Respondents were asked to fill in the survey for the specific urban project (and the network around that project!) of which they were project leader. This means that finally data were collected for 141 projects, as 141 managers answered the survey. Table 7.1 describes the population and the response rate (40.9 per cent).

Managers of urban projects operate in complex networks. They are the persons with the most intensive knowledge of the projects and thus are in the best position to answer the questions about the project (and especially about the media attention on the project). The managers are involved in a

**Table 7.1: Response to the survey**

| | Population | Response (absolute) | Response (%) |
|---|---|---|---|
| Municipalities (4) | 288 | 117 | 40.6 |
| Private organisations of project managers (2) | 57 | 24 | 42.1 |
| Total | 345 | 141 | 40.9 |

wide variety of projects, but most of the projects involve the restructuring of parts of a city. Some of the projects concern restructuring/building dwellings in a neighbourhood; others concern business functions and/ or commercial functions (shopping malls and so forth). As these projects usually involve the implementation of local political decisions, the project managers generally have connections to an alderman, to whom they report their project's progress.

The study considers the group of interdependent actors around the urban projects as the network; this is also how it was presented to the survey respondents. Some characteristics of these networks (number of actors, involved actors, policy problems and so on) are now discussed.

### Characteristics of the networks around urban projects included in this study

Networks are characterised, as most authors argue, by 1) a significant number of interdependent actors, 2) being involved in policymaking or service delivery, and 3) policy issues that mostly have a wicked character (see Agranoff and McGuire, 2001; Koppenjan and Klijn, 2004; Ansell and Gash, 2008).

In 66 per cent of the projects, more than ten different organisations were involved in the surrounding networks, as reported by the managers. A significant number of the managers (27.0 per cent) worked in networks consisting of at least 20 organisations. It can therefore be concluded that they are dealing with policy problems that are addressed through collective actions of a set of interdependent actors: one of the main characteristics of networks. Most of the networks included societal interest groups (94.3 per cent), private developers (78.6 per cent), architectural firms (79.4 per cent) and various governmental organisations (national government 60.3 per cent; province 58.9 per cent; other municipalities 47.5 per cent).

These network actors work on projects encompassing multiple activities. On average, more than three tasks (M=3.76) play a medium to large part in the project. These activities include environmental development (public parks), houses, business/shopping areas, water storage, infrastructure (rail and public highways) and social issues (schools, sport facilities, other social facilities). So it may safely be concluded that these urban projects concern wicked problems since they concern complex policy problems.

### Methodology: operationalising the main variables

First, the main variables have to be operationalised: network performance, commercialised news, network management and the moderating variable trust. As a survey was used, all variables are perceived variables.

*Perceived network performance:* It is difficult to measure network performance. One reason for this is that actors have different goals and it is thus difficult to pick a single goal by which to measure outcomes. Measuring network performance is also problematic because policy processes in governance networks are lengthy and actors' goals are likely to change over time (see Koppenjan and Klijn, 2004). This problem is addressed in this chapter by using perceived network performance as a proxy for these outcomes and by using more than one criterion to measure them. Respondents were asked to rank their project's performance at the moment of the survey. From earlier research and the literature, five different dimensions to measure performance were distinguished (see Klijn et al, 2010b): 1) the innovative character of the outcome; 2) the integrative aspect of the solution, that is, the way in which the plan represents different environmental functions (housing, recreation and so on); 3) the problem-solving capacity of results, that is, the extent to which the solutions really address the problem; 4) the robustness of the results, that is, the future robustness (time frame) of the results; 5) the relationship between the costs and benefits of results from governance networks: the costs of the plan should not overrun the benefits of a project. Table 7.2 presents the items used.

**Table 7.2: Measurement of perceived network performance**

| Dimension | | Items | Literature |
|---|---|---|---|
| 1 Innovative character | INN | Do you think that innovative ideas have been developed during the project? | Nooteboom, 2002 |
| 2 Integral nature of solution | INT | Do you think that different environmental functions have been connected sufficiently? | Klijn, Steijn and Edelenbos, 2010 |
| 3 Effectiveness solutions | EFF | Do you think that the solutions that have been developed really deal with the problems at hand? | Fischer, 2003; McGuire and Agranoff, 2011 |
| 4 Effectiveness in the future | FUT | Do you think that the developed solutions are durable solutions for the future? | Koppenjan and Klijn, 2004 |
| 5 Relation costs and benefits | RCB | Do you think that – in general – the benefits exceed the costs of the cooperation process? | Mantel, 2005 |

Note: One item was deleted from Klijn et al's scale because of its low loading on performance: 'Do you think that in general the involved actors have delivered a recognisable contribution to the development of the results?'

Cronbach's alpha for these items is 0.76. The mean score for perceived network performance is 3.71 (SD=0.61) on a 5-point Likert scale, indicating a quite high evaluation of performance.

*Commercialised news:* No measurement scale exists for the degree to which media attention can be qualified as commercialised news in a survey. Therefore, a new scale had to be developed. It uses horizontal rating scales, providing respondents with opposite attitude positions and asking them to show where on the 10-point scale – in between two opposites – their own view falls (see De Vaus, 2002, 102). In this manner, excluding answers – which are not provided by a Likert scale – were extracted.

What is most important here is that commercialised news gives less substantive information and has more sensational content (Patterson, 2000). Moreover, this more sensational framing relates to a trend of critical, negative news reporting (Bennett, 2009; Esser and Matthes, 2013) and inaccurate news reporting (Witschge and Nygren, 2009; Schillemans, 2012). Personalisation bias was not included; such bias is often mentioned in the literature, but only limited support can actually be found for it in recent studies (Esser and Matthes, 2013). Respondents were asked to rate media attention on the three (10-point) scales presented in Table 7.3. This again entails a perceived scale for commercialised news. Thus, what is measured is the way managers perceive commercialised news. Since managers act on their perception of media attention, this does not seem a huge disadvantage, but of course it does create a limitation for the research.[3] In the rest of the chapter, the phrase *perceived commercialised news* is used to indicate that the measurement is managers' perception of commercialised media attention.

Cronbach's alpha for these items is 0.84. The mean score on commercialised news is 5.03 on the 10-point scale, indicating a moderate degree of commercialisation. However, the standard deviation of 1.85 shows quite some variance between responses. This actually provides a first interesting conclusion. Although the degree of commercialised news

**Table 7.3: Measurement of perceived commercialised news**

| Dimension | | Items | Literature |
|---|---|---|---|
| 1 Sensationalism in news reports | SEN | From informing to sensational | Patterson, 2000; Bennett, 2009; Esser and Matthes, 2013 |
| 2 Negativity in news reports | NEG | From positive to negative | Patterson, 2000; Bennett, 2009 |
| 3 Mistakes in news reports | MIS | From accurate to full of mistakes | Witschge and Nygren, 2009; Schillemans, 2012 |

differs significantly per project, not all projects are mainly negatively, sensationally and inaccurately reported. This also nuances the extensive literature on negativity bias in the news.

*Network management:* This study looked at two types of network management strategies: exploring and connecting. These strategies were found to be most influential in earlier research (see Klijn et al, 2010b). For each type of strategy, three items were used (see Table 7.4). Cronbach's alpha for each of these sets of items is satisfactory (exploring 0.675 and connecting 0.704).

**Table 7.4: Items for measuring network management strategies**

| Network management strategy | Items |
|---|---|
| Exploring (looking for solutions and available information) | In this project, special attention has been paid to the sharing of diverse points of view (E1)<br>During the collection of information, emphasis was placed on establishing starting points and common information needs (E2)<br>Sufficient attention is paid in this project to the involvement of external organisations that can bring in new ideas and solutions (E3) |
| Cronbach's alpha | 0.675 |
| Connecting (binding and connecting actors to one another and enhancing interactions) | The leaders of the project consulted with the people who carried it out. Decisions were made collectively (C1)<br>The project leaders took into account existing interpersonal relationships, their basis, and how they were generated and developed (C2)<br>When deadlocks were reached or problems arose in the project, the management tried to find common ground between the positions of the conflicting interests (C3) |
| Cronbach's alpha | 0.704 |

*Trust between network actors:* Klijn, Edelenbos and Steijn's (2010) scale, consisting of five dimensions derived from the business management literature, was used to measure trust within the network. In this research, a sixth item (feeling a good connection) was added to improve the overall scale. The six items are listed in Table 7.5. Cronbach's alpha of the six items is 0.80. The mean score on trust is 3.31 (SD=0.60) on a 5-point Likert scale, indicating a moderate degree of trust between the actors in the networks.

*Control variables:* Three control variables were used: task complexity (measured by the number of tasks [already discussed] included in the environmental project); the project phase (measured by an indication of completed activities); and the size of the network. The last was included because there are indications in network research that it is more difficult to achieve good results in larger networks. The last item was measured by a simple item that asked managers how many actors were involved in the network around their project (on a 5-point scale: 5, 5–10, 10–15, 15–20, >20).

**Table 7.5: Measurement of trust**

| Dimension | | Items | Literature |
|---|---|---|---|
| 1 Agreement trust | AGR | The parties in this project generally live up to the agreements made with one another | Sako, 1998 |
| 2 Benefit of the doubt | BEN | The parties in this project give one another the benefit of the doubt | Lane and Bachman, 1998 |
| 3 Reliability | REL | The parties in this project keep in mind the intentions of the other parties | McEvily and Zaheer, 2006 |
| 4 Absence of opportunistic behaviour | ABS | Parties do not use the contributions of other actors for their own advantage | Sako, 1998; Nooteboom, 2002 |
| 5 Goodwill trust | GDW | Parties in this project can assume that the intentions of the other parties are good in principle | Sako, 1998; Nooteboom, 2002 |
| 6 Good connection | CON | Parties in this project feel a good personal connection with one another | Lane and Bachman, 1998 |

## *Common method source bias*

Because in this research the independent and dependent variables were collected from the same respondents, a problem of common source bias could exist. To explore this, the Lindell and Whitney (2001) test was performed. In this model, a theoretically unrelated construct (marker variable) is used to adjust the correlations between the principal constructs. Any high correlation between any of the items of the study's principal constructs and the marker variable would be an indicator of common method bias. A variable used in the survey, but not used in this study, was used as a marker (the amount of attention the project received from politicians measured with a 10-point scale from high to low). Table 7.6 presents the correlation of the marker variable with our variables.

Table 7.6 shows that there are no high correlations (some authors consider 0.3 the starting point to be worried about a common method bias). The analysis suggests that common method bias (in terms of common source) is not a problem in our study. An unrotated factor analysis was also performed with all the items of the dependent and independent variables to see whether a single factor existed (Podsakoff et al, 2003), but the first factor explains only 27 per cent of the variance. This is another indication that common method bias is not a problem here.

**Table 7.6: Correlation and R2 between variables and marker**

| Variables in the model | Pearson Coefficient | R2 |
| --- | --- | --- |
| Media attention | -0.205 | 0.042 |
| Trust | 0.107 | 0.011 |
| Perceived network performance | -0.004 | 0.000 |
| Network management strategies | 0.278 | 0.07248 |
| Conflict | 0.148 | 0.022 |

## Results: the impact of (network) management strategies

A two-step analysis was performed to test the hypotheses. The first step was an exploration of the relations between perceived commercialised news, network performance and network management by using simple regression analysis. The second step was an attempt to analyse the combined effects with a structural equation analysis to get more information about the relations between various variables.

### Media logic and network performance: a first look at possible relations

First of all, the effect is explored of perceived commercialised news on perceived performance: hypothesis 1. As can be seen in Table 7.7, commercialised news has a significant effect on network performance and a relatively high Beta (-0.408). It is also clear that the control variable *network size* does matter (Beta 0.190) and is significant. The other two control variables are not significant. The total explained variance of this model is 0.215 (adjusted $R^2$).

**Table 7.7: Effects of commercialised news on perceived network performance[a]**

| Model | Unstandardised coefficients | | Standardised coefficients | | | Collinearity statistics | |
|---|---|---|---|---|---|---|---|
| | B | Std. Error | Beta | t | Sig. | Tolerance | VIF |
| (Constant) | 3.925 | 0.246 | | 15.958 | 0.000 | | |
| Commercial-ised news | -0.134 | 0.026 | -0.408 | -5.179 | 0.000 | 0.971 | 1.030 |
| Task complexity | -0.004 | 0.033 | -0.010 | -0.124 | 0.902 | 0.882 | 1.133 |
| Project phase | 0.053 | 0.036 | 0.116 | 1.461 | 0.146 | 0.962 | 1.040 |
| Size of the network | 0.092 | 0.040 | 0.190 | 2.316 | 0.022 | 0.896 | 1.116 |

Note: [a] Dependent variable: Network performance, $R^2$ 0.239; adjusted $R^2$ 0.215

### *The influence of managerial strategies on commercialised news*

It can now be investigated whether network management strategies do affect the degree of perceived commercialised news: hypothesis 2. A regression analysis was performed with perceived commercialised news as dependent variable and network management as independent variable, using the same control variables as in the previous analysis. The results are shown in Table 7.8. As can be seen, the control variables have very little effect on the degree of commercialised news. Obviously, media attention, and especially commercialised news, is generated by mechanisms unrelated to either the complexity or the size of the network.

The network management strategy of exploring is the only variable that has significant impact on commercialised news. The more exploring strategies are employed, the less negative media attention occurs. Thus, if more different views on the project content are made visible and care is taken to include different external organisations with new ideas and to establish joint points of view and shared information, there is a lower degree of commercialised news on the project. The overall explained variance is not very high however. This leads to the conclusion that the source of media attention and commercialised news is found largely in factors other than those considered in this chapter. Media attention might also come from factors like coincidence or factors strongly associated with the media system itself (newsworthiness, the attractiveness of the story and so forth; see for instance Cook, 2005).

**Table 7.8: The impact of network management on commercialised news**

| Model | Unstandardised coefficients | | Standardised coefficients | | |
|---|---|---|---|---|---|
| | B | Std. Error | Beta | t | Sig. |
| (Constant) | 9.252 | 1.058 | | 8.744 | 0.000 |
| exploring | -0.344 | 0.094 | -0.376 | -3.641 | 0.000 |
| connecting | 0.009 | 0.105 | 0.009 | 0.088 | 0.930 |
| Project phase | -0.192 | 0.124 | -0.138 | -1.543 | 0.125 |
| Task complexity | -0.022 | 0.105 | -0.018 | -0.210 | 0.834 |
| Size of the network | -0.014 | 0.129 | -0.010 | -0.110 | 0.912 |

Note: [a] Dependent variable: Media logic scale. $R^2$ 160; adjusted $R^2$ 0.126

### *The intermediate effects of network management: the full model*

In order to further explore the relationship between network management, (perceived) commercialised news and (perceived) network performance, another analysis was performed: a structural equation modelling (SEM) analysis with an additional variable: the level of conflict in the network. This was done to assess whether the level of conflict might add to the explanation of the amount of commercialised news, thereby including a possible effect of network characteristics (the level of conflict) on commercialised news. One horizontal rating scale was used to indicate the perceived conflicts between the organisations in the network. Respondents were asked to rate the amount of conflict on a 10-point scale from no conflict between organisations to much conflict between organisations. The mean score of 4.85 and the standard deviation of 2.0 show that networks can generally be characterised by some conflicts, but that the amount of conflict differs per project.

The AMOS (20.0) SEM programme was used (Byrne, 2010). SEM has two advantages compared to regression analysis. First, path analysis can be performed in SEM, testing more statistical relations at the same time. In this study, it is hypothesised for instance that commercialised news has a negative effect on trust relations and that it is consequently harder to reach good collaborative outcomes. In addition, it is assumed that commercialised news is influenced by network management strategies. In the SEM analysis, both strategies of network management are collated into one coherent variable, thereby drawing both direct relations between commercialised news and network performance, and indirect relations, through trust. This can be better executed in SEM than in regression analysis. The second advantage of SEM is the exact calculation of the latent factors, using separate factor loadings for the different items. In regression analysis, the different items are summed, and the average mean is used in the analysis. Figure 7.1 shows the hypothesised relations and the correlations that were found.

Before the results are discussed, a few remarks have to be made about causality and the hypothesised relations. SEM is especially suited to test theoretical models. In this case, a model was tested that included trust and the level of conflict and the indirect relations between these and the main variables. Given the theoretical framework, the model presented in Figure 7.1 is the most logical model. Of course, it is also possible to look at other causal models, for instance where the causal relations are drawn the other way (from performance to commercialised news) and this also leads to a good, although lower, fit. This study was interested in the effects of commercialised news on network performance.

This study looked only at relations that were significant in the earlier analysis and consequently did not look at the relation between conflict and performance, since this relation was not significant (see correlation matrix in the appendix). In reality, of course, the relations are more complex than

**Figure 7.1: Results of SEM analysis**

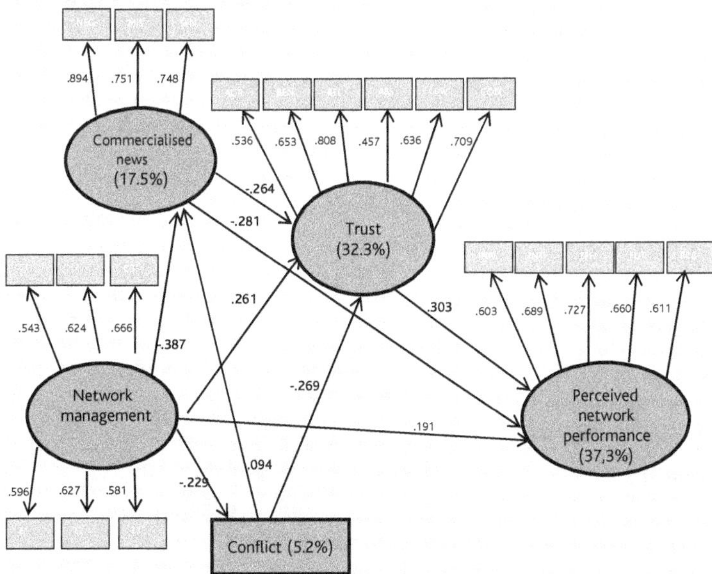

visualised in Figure 7.1 as there will be feedback mechanisms (negative media attention leading to less performance which in its turn leads to more negative media attention). Because the survey was conducted at one point in time, these time effects cannot be measured, but the model fits most adequately with how the items were measured.[4]

The model again reveals a strong correlation between perceived commercialised news and (perceived) network performance. Commercialised news also has a negative effect on the level of trust (-0.264), but the model also shows the various indirect ways in which, for instance, network management strategies influence network performance. Although the direct influence is not that large (0.191) (but significant at a 0.1 level), network management also strongly mitigates commercialised news (-0.387) and improves trust (0.261). Through these effects, network management has an indirect effect on network performance which is almost as strong as the direct effect (0.186). The effect of conflict is limited. The effect on commercialised news is very small (and not significant) but it does have a significant effect on trust (-0.269).

The model presented above has a good fit. Normally, several indices are used to evaluate the fit of the model. The CMIN/DF has a score between 1 and 3; CFI above 0.95; and RMSEA under 0.5 by which the PCLOSE is above 0.5; these indices indicate a good fit (Byrne, 2010); see Table 7.9.

**Table 7.9: Fit indices for the model**

| Model | N | df | CMIN/DF | CFI | RMSEA | PCLOSE |
|---|---|---|---|---|---|---|
| Full sample | 141 | 181 | 1.223 | 0.952 | 0.040 | 0.8242 |

## Conclusion: the importance of network management for reducing commercialised news

This study has revealed that media attention – and then especially perceptions of media attention that shows strong media bias (tendency to focus on conflict, sensation and negative news) characterised here as commercialised news – has a strong impact on network performance and is influenced itself by network management.

Exploring strategies in particular seem to be most effective. This is not surprising, because this means that more different solutions and interests are taken into account. Commercialised news stories, defined as sensational, negative *and* inaccurate, are more likely to occur when exploration strategies, tuned towards the various interests in the network, are absent. Furthermore, as Korthagen (2015) shows, media attention in environmental issues is fairly strongly connected with oppositional actors in the network, thus societal interest groups and oppositional politicians. This is of course related to the fact that the media look for confrontational storylines in which 'good guys' and 'bad guys' can be identified. The explanation for the success of the exploration strategy might lie in the fact that more different opinions are brought into the process, thereby securing the inclusion of more different interests and views and providing fewer reasons for less involved actors to actively seek out media attention in order to publicise their views.

### Limitations of the study

There are of course limitations to the analysis in this chapter. In the first place, the study involves managers' perceptions about both performance and media attention. Although they are the most knowledgeable about their project, they might also be biased. On the other hand, it is especially their perception of media attention that is relevant for their actions in the project. Another limitation is that it is not possible to analyse dynamics because the data were collected at one point in time. The causality imposed on the data is theoretically motivated, although the model tested against the data did have the best fit.

### A last reflection: where does (negative) media attention come from?

Interestingly enough, the data in this study also nuance the negative image of some of the negativity-bias literature where the media are always negative and ubiquitous. The managers' scores show that managers perceive only moderately negative media attention, and there is quite some variation between the projects. Thus, the idea that managers perceive mainly negative media attention on their project is not confirmed by our empirical data. And the analysis of the causes of commercialised news shows only a relatively low explained variance, meaning that additional factors must be sought to explain why media pay attention to particular projects. This may very well be found within the media system itself in the judgements and criteria of news reporters; but it may also very likely be found in simple coincidence. Journalists report on events and incidents that are central to political life: constant reactions to events (see Rhodes, 2011). This goes back to the distinction between front-stage and backstage made at the beginning of the chapter. Both the front-stage and the backstage have increased in complexity, but it is a different form of complexity. Whereas the complexity backstage can at least be somehow analysed in terms of actors, positions and interests (although processes can be very erratic: see Koppenjan and Klijn, 2004), front-stage processes seem to be even more erratic. The fact that 'good old-fashioned network management' seems to help front-stage is at least somewhat reassuring for public managers: their actions do seem to matter; although they do not guarantee success of course.

## Notes

[1] The author would like to thank Iris Korthagen for her assistance with the AMOS analysis.

[2] See for empirical evidence: Patterson, 2000; Kleinnijenhuis et al, 2006; Reunanen et al, 2010).

[3] Coding actual media attention would be an enormous amount of work since over 120 projects would have to be coded – a very laborious task (see Korthagen, 2015, who did this for only six projects).

[4] The respondents were asked to rate the outcomes of the projects at the time they filled in the survey. So, in terms of time sequence, that variable should be at the end as dependent variable. Trust is something that is developed gradually most of the time, so that variable in the time sequence should be before performance. And two important questions were asked about media attention. The first asked how much attention several media had for the project. In the second question, the respondents were asked to characterise that attention (the questions used for the commercialised scale). Thus, attention in the past period was elicited. Consequently, it is more logical to draw the causal arrows from media attention to performance since chronologically that is how they are positioned.

## References

Agranoff, R, McGuire, M, 2001, Big questions in public network management research, *Journal of Public Administration Research and Theory* 11, 3, 295–326

Altheide, DL, Snow, RP, 1979, *Media logic*, Beverly Hills, CA: Sage

Ansell, C, Gash, A, 2008, Collaborative governance in theory and practice, *Journal of Public Administration Research and Theory* 18, 4, 543–72

Asp, K, 2014, News media logic in a new institutional perspective, *Journalism Studies* 15, 3, 256–70

Baumgartner, FR, Jones, B, 2009, *Agendas and instability in American politics* (2nd edn), Chicago, IL: University of Chicago Press

Bennett, WL, 2009, *News: The politics of illusion* (8th edn), New York: Pearson Longman

Brants, K, Van Praag, P, 2006, Signs of media logic: Half a century of political communication in the Netherlands, *Javnost – The Public* 13, 1, 25–40

Byrne, BM, 2010, *Structural equation modeling with AMOS: Basic concepts, applications, and programming*, New York: Routledge

Cobb, RW, Elder, CD, 1983, *Participation in American politics: The dynamics of agenda-building*, Baltimore, MD: Johns Hopkins University Press

Cook, TE, 2005, *Governing with the news: The news media as a political institution*, Chicago, IL: The University of Chicago Press

De Vaus, D, 2002, *Surveys in social research*, London: Routledge

Eshuis, J, Klijn, EH, 2012, *Branding in governance and public management*, London: Routledge

Esser, F, Matthes, J, 2013, Mediatization effect on political news, political actors, political decisions, and political audiences, in H Kriesi, S Lavenex, F Esser, J Matthes, M Bülmann, D Bochsler (eds) *Democracy in the age of globalization and mediatization*, pp 177–201, Hampshire: Palgrave Macmillan

Fischer, F, 2003, *Reframing public policy: Discursive politics and deliberative practices*, Oxford: Oxford University Press

Friend, JK, Power, JM, Yewlett, CJL, 1974, *Public planning: The inter-corporate dimension*, London: Tavistock

Gage, RW, Mandell, MP (eds), 1990, *Strategies for managing intergovernmental policies and networks*, New York/London: Preager

Graber, D, 2004, Mediated politics and citizenship in the twenty-first century, *Annual Review of Psychology* 55, 545–71

Hanf, K, Scharpf, FW (eds), 1978, *Inter-organizational policy making*, London: Sage

Hankinson, G, 2004, Relational network brands: Towards a conceptual model of place brands, *Journal of Vacation Marketing* 10, 2, 109–21

Hjarvard, S, 2008, The mediatization of society: A theory of the media as agents of social and cultural change, *Nordicom Review* 29, 2, 105–34

Huxham, C, Vangen, S, 2005, *Managing to collaborate: The theory and practice of collaborative advantage*, London: Routledge

Kleinnijenhuis, J, Van Hoof, AMJ, Oegema, D, 2006, Negative news and the sleeper effect of distrust, *The Harvard International Journal of Press/Politics* 11, 2, 86–104

Klijn, EH, Edelenbos, J, Steijn, B, 2010a, Trust in governance networks: Its impact and outcomes, *Administration and Society* 42, 2, 193–221

Klijn, EH, Steijn, B, Edelenbos, J, 2010b, The impact of network management strategies on the outcomes in governance networks, *Public Administration* 88, 4, 1063–82

Koppenjan, JFM, Klijn, EH, 2004, *Managing uncertainty in networks*, London: Routledge

Korthagen, I, 2015, Who gets on the news? The relation between media biases and different actors in the news reporting on complex policy processes, *Public Management Review* 17, 5, 617–642

Landerer, N, 2013, Rethinking the logics: A conceptual framework for the mediatization of politics, *Communication Theory* 22, 3, 239–58

Lane, C, Bachman, R (eds), 1998, *Trust within and between organizations: Conceptual issues and empirical applications*, Oxford: Oxford University Press

Lindell, MK, Whitney, DJ, 2001, Accounting for common method variance in cross-sectional designs, *Journal of Applied Psychology* 86, 114–24

McEvily, B, Zaheer, A, 2006, Does trust still matter? Research on the role of trust in interorganizational exchange, in R Bachmann, A Zaheer (eds) *The handbook of trust research*, pp 280–300, Cheltenham: Edward Elgar

McGuire, M, Agranoff, R, 2011, The limitations of public management networks, *Public Administration* 98, 2, 265–84

Mandell, MP (ed), 2001, *Getting results through collaboration*, Westport, CT: Quorum Books

Mantel, SJ, 2005, *Core concepts of project management*, 2nd edn, New York: Wiley

Mazzoleni, G, Schulz, W, 1999, 'Mediatization' of politics: A challenge for democracy?, *Political Communication* 16, 3, 247–61

Meier, KJ, O'Toole, LJ, 2007, Modeling public management: Empirical analysis of the management–performance nexus, *Public Management Review* 9, 4, 503–27

Nooteboom, B, 2002, *Trust: Forms, foundations, functions, failures and figures*, Cheltenham: Edward Elgar

Patterson, TE, 2000, *Doing well and doing good: How soft news and critical journalism are shrinking the news audience and weakening democracy – and what news outlets can do about it*, Cambridge, MA: Joan Shorenstein Center on the Press, Politics and Public Policy, Kennedy School of Government, Harvard University

Podsakoff, PM, MacKenzie, SB, Lee, J-Y, Podsakoff, NP, 2003, Common method bias in behavioral research: A critical review of the literature and recommended remedies, *Journal of Applied Psychology* 8, 5, 879–903

Provan, KG, Huang, K, Milward, BH, 2009, The evolution of structural embeddedness and organizational social outcomes in a centrally governed health and human service network, *Journal of Public Administration Research and Theory* 19, 873–93

Reunanen, E, Kunelis, R, Noppari, E, 2010, Mediatization in context: Consensus culture, media and decision making in the 21st century: The case of Finland, *Communications* 35, 3, 287–307

Rhodes, RAW, 1997, *Understanding governance*, Buckingham: Open University Press

Rhodes, RAW, 2011, *Everyday life in British government*, Oxford: Oxford University Press

Rogers, DL, Whetten, DA (eds), 1982, *Interorganizational coordination: Theory, research and implementation*, Iowa City, IA: Iowa State University Press

Sako, M, 1998, Does trust improve business performance?, in C Lane, R Bachmann (eds) *Trust within and between organizations*, pp 88–117, Oxford: Oxford University Press

Scharpf, FW, 1978, Interorganizational policy studies: Issues, concepts and perspectives, in KI Hanf, FW Scharpf (eds) *Interorganizational policy making: Limits to coordination and central control*, pp 345–70, London: Sage

Scharpf, FW, 1997, *Games real actors play*, Boulder, CO: Westview Press

Schillemans, T, 2012, *Mediatization of public services: How organizations adapt to news media*, Frankfurt: Peter Lang

Schudson, M, 1998, *The good citizen: A history of American civic life*, New York: Martin Kessler Books

Spörer-Wagner, D, Marcinkowski, F, 2010, Is talk always silver and silence golden? The mediatisation of political bargaining, *Javnost – The Public* 17, 2, 5–26

Strömbäck, J, Esser, F, 2009, Shaping politics: Mediatization and media interventionism, in K Lundby (ed) *Mediatization: Concept, changes, consequences*, pp 205–24, New York: Peter Lang

Strömbäck, J, Esser, F, 2014, Introduction: Making sense of the mediatization of politics, *Journalism Studies* 14, 2, 243–55

Strömbäck, J, Kiousis, S, 2011, *Political public relations: Principles and applications*, Abington: Routledge

Walgrave, S, Van Aelst, P, 2006, The contingency of the mass media's political agenda setting power: Toward a preliminary theory, *Journal of Communication* 56, 88–109

Witschge, T, Nygren, G, 2009, Journalism: A profession under pressure?, *Journal of Media Business Studies* 6, 1, 37–59

# Over-responsibilised and over-blamed: elected actors in media reporting on network governance. A comparative analysis in eight European metropolitan areas

Karin Hasler, Daniel Kübler, Anna Christmann and
Frank Marcinkowksi

## Introduction[1]

Since the mid-1990s, scholars in the field of public administration have increasingly focused on processes of public-policy making in which the traditional state authorities do not play the central role. Such 'governing without government', as Rhodes (1996, 65) has called it, is based on self-organising, inter-organisational networks as a mode of coordination distinct from state and market. Later on, the term of network governance was coined to define 'public policy-making and implementation through a web of relationships between government, business and civil society actors' (Klijn, 2008, 511). Empirically, governance networks have been studied in a wide range of fields (see Pierre, 2000), ranging from local and urban policy, over public sector reform, to international relations. Research on governance networks has also focused on a broad array of theoretical topics. At the outset, it was mainly concerned with the novelty of governance networks, exploring their formation, their distinctive characteristics compared to states and markets, as well as their potential contribution to policy effectiveness and efficiency. More recently however, a 'second generation of governance network research' (Torfing, 2005, 311) has enlarged the agenda to include more general and overarching questions. This notably entails a growing interest in normative issues, that is, the 'democratic problems and potential of governance networks' (Sørensen, 2005) related to the tensions that exist between governance networks and the 'workings of the traditional institutions of representational democracy' (Klijn, 2008, 520). In this respect the democratic quality of governance networks is often criticised as problematic with respect to democratic accountability (Papadopoulos, 2003). They involve corporate, private or civil society actors who make a substantial contribution to policy-making, but cannot be held accountable by citizens via mechanisms of electoral control. The upshot of empirical research on this question, however, is that there is no general rule. Indeed, the democratic accountability of governance networks is seen to depend on their 'anchorage' in representative institutions and democratic practice (Sørensen and Torfing, 2005).

This chapter aims to contribute to this debate on the democratic accountability of governance networks. In doing so, we will shed light on a dimension that has been overlooked in this debate so far: the public sphere. Indeed, analyses of the democratic implications of governance networks have been characterised by a somewhat narrow institutional perspective, neglecting the processes of political communication that are crucial, in mass democracies, for the accountability of policy actors to the public. More precisely, we will show that the media play an important and independent role in ensuring democratic accountability in governance networks, and that specificities related to the workings of the media system provides a crucial key to understanding the democratic implications of governance networks more generally. We will do so by focusing on area-wide governance in eight European metropolitan areas which, as we will show, provide exemplary laboratory cases for the study of governance networks. We proceed in four steps. The second section develops the theoretical perspective and lays out the main research question and hypotheses. The section after that gives an overview of the cases, research design and data. This is followed by a section presenting results on the involvement of different types of policy actors in decision-making about metropolitan policies, their visibility in media reports on these policies, as well as the public attribution of responsibility for policy failures and successes. The final section wraps up the main findings and discusses their implications.

## The role of the media in (metropolitan) governance networks

The organisation of governance in metropolitan areas is at the core of a long running scientific debate (see Kübler, 2003; Feiock, 2004; Savitch and Vogel, 2009; Lefèvre and Weir, 2012). The basic problem is that metropolitan areas are very fragmented spaces. They have grown by spatial extension, independently from institutional boundaries, and therefore span over large numbers of local jurisdictions. For a long time, territorial institutional reforms have been viewed as the privileged way to overcome the challenges to effective policy-making resulting from the 'geopolitical fragmentation' (Zeigler and Brunn, 1980) of metropolitan areas. Since the 1990s, however, research on metropolitan governance has increasingly emphasised the role of policy networks in ensuring area-wide governance at the metropolitan scale (see Van den Berg et al, 1993;

Lefèvre, 1998; Savitch and Vogel, 2000; Heinelt and Kübler, 2005). Indeed, many metropolitan areas across the world have seen a strengthening of area-wide governance capacity by relying on governance networks, that is, non-hierarchical forms of coordination and cooperation, where policy-relevant actors act on the basis of agreements reached by negotiation. Some observers argue that these governance networks have led to a 'new regionalism' (Savitch and Vogel, 2000) in metropolitan areas.

Similarly to other instances of governance networks, the workings of new regionalism in metropolitan areas have raised the question of its democratic quality (Heinelt and Kübler, 2005). Case studies examining institutional mechanisms of democratic control over metropolitan policy-making (Kübler and Schwab, 2007; Zimmermann, 2014) suggest that, while network governance increases inclusiveness of metropolitan policy-making by involving civil society actors, it results in blurred democratic accountability and reduced citizen control, as policy responsibility is diluted among a large variety of policy-actors not all of whom are electorally accountable. When area-wide governance relies on governance networks, democratically elected local councillors lose grip, and input-legitimacy is reduced (Plüss, 2015). Koch's historical study on the change of mechanisms of institutionalised democratic control indeed shows that functional cooperation in metropolitan policy-making was often paralleled by a retreat of electoral (and/or direct democratic) politics due to 'depoliticisation and technocratisation' (Koch, 2011, 224). The main problem with governance networks in metropolitan areas thus seems to be that it reduces democratic accountability of policy actors, as decision-making increasingly involves actors from outside the 'democratic chain of delegation' (Bergman et al, 2000) that goes from citizens to public administration via parliament and government. New regionalism, thus, seems to have an in-built democratic deficit.

## The information function of the media in democracies

The focus on the institutional mechanisms of democratic control in governance networks, however, overlooks the non-institutional dimension of public accountability. Democratic accountability not only depends on the existence of institutional procedures of citizen control by which voters can hold decision-makers accountable – renew their mandate or remove them from office. Democratic accountability is also conditional to voters' ability to express satisfaction (or dissatisfaction) with policy performance, identify decision-makers and attribute responsibility for policy success or failure to political actors. Hence, democratic accountability is constructed in processes of communication that help citizens form their opinion about policy performance and connect their appreciation of those whom they consider responsible. In mass democracies, these communication processes are not of an immediate and inter-individual nature, but are mediated by the mass media. Citizens can hold decision-makers accountable for their actions only when mass media provide information about policy decisions and their outcomes. Thus, besides the institutional dimension, there is also a 'communicational dimension' of democratic accountability, relating to the public sphere as one of the foundations for democratic legitimacy (Habermas, 1992).

According to Bovens '[a]ccountability is a relationship between an actor and a forum, in which the actor has an obligation to explain and to justify his or her conduct, the forum can pose questions and pass judgement, and the actor may face consequences' (2007, 450). In this regard, the link between representatives and the electorate involves a communicational relationship. But because representatives cannot directly communicate to the electorate, the mass media are the forum where candidates can conduct a dialogue with the electorate. This not only happens in the run-up to elections, but also between them. While elections are held on a regular basis (for example, every four years), communication on policy performance and/or responsibility of decision-makers is not limited to any particular period. Although there might be peaks of communicational activity at the time of elections, the media can and do inform on policy failures or successes continuously and independently of elections. Even though such information is politically relevant only in relation to some more or less distant moments of electoral control, the media are largely independent from electoral cycles and can thereby play the role of holding decision-makers accountable for their acts in periods between elections.

Moreover, accountability of decision-makers also implies an evaluation against norms of conduct or standards defined by legal, administrative or professional forums (Bovens, 2007, 456). In the media any actor of public interest can be held accountable with regard to a broad range of standards, triggering sanctions by the relevant forum – or influencing actor behaviour in anticipation of these sanctions. Decision-makers, be they elected politicians, appointed officials or independent agencies, can be held accountable for the violation of legal norms, malpractice or incompetence – independently from elections. The media contribute to the legal, administrative or professional accountability of decision-makers by revealing violations of norms to a wider audience (for example, through investigative journalism). They 'serve as citizens' eyes and ears to survey the political scene and the performance of politicians', as well as to 'act as a public watchdog that barks loudly when it encounters misbehaviour, corruption, and abuses of power in the halls of government' (Graber, 2003,

143). The unwritten laws of political culture can force decision-makers to resign following 'public pressure' – even long before a violation of norms or standards has been legally established. Although the media do not have formal sanctioning power, they can 'name and shame' political actors: clarify who is responsible for what and foster public opinion about adequate sanctions.

The media, on the one hand, take up a role of an autonomous 'accountability forum' (Bovens, 2007) that have the potential to hold actors accountable to the public independently from electoral processes. On the other hand, the media also serve as a platform that make actors' behaviour and their responsibilities visible and thereby help other forums to hold them to account. This means that the media provide an additional – communicational – channel by which public accountability of governance networks can be ensured beyond their 'democratic anchorage' (Sørensen and Torfing, 2005) in mechanisms of electoral control. From a functionalist perspective (Gurevitch and Blumler, 1990), we can argue that the media have the function to inform the public adequately about (metropolitan) politics and policy-making. This assumption is plausible, in that the public is interested in knowing who is in charge of metropolitan policy-making and who is responsible for policy success and failure. Media reporting will thus be driven by the quest to provide the audience with an accurate picture of the policy-making reality, and therefore seek to adequately cover those actors who are effectively relevant in policy-making. The media will make those actors visible to the public, and provide the information necessary to evaluate their performance. Given the often complex nature of governance networks, this will be no simple task. But provided with adequate means, the media will eventually fulfil their democratic function to provide the public with information about who is responsible for what, irrespective of policy actors' anchorage in formal democratic institutions and practice. Based on this functionalist perspective, we can formulate the hypothesis that the media adequately mirror decision-making and policy responsibilities in network governance. In other words: the media can reduce the formal democratic deficit of network governance, if they play their role appropriately.

## Media logic and media bias

This is, however, quite a normative perspective about the role of the media in processes of political communication. The media are far from being neutral reporters of reality. As Mazzoleni and Schulz (1999) have argued, the media are not simply a mediating or intermediary agent whose function is to bridge the relation between a communicator and an audience as a substitute for interpersonal exchange. In reality, the media is a system composed of a multiplicity of competing actors who have their own preferences and (commercial) interests. The media thereby add a specific bias to the information they process and to the political content they communicate (Mazzoleni and Schulz, 1999, 250–53).

Communication scientists have captured this bias through the concept of 'media logic' (Altheide and Snow, 1979) focusing on the conditions that shape the process of news production. Given that not only their resources but also public attention is limited, mass media have to be selective on the events they report. Only 'newsworthy' events are covered, according to 'news value' criteria (for example, proximity, conflict, drama, personalisation), determined by journalists' worldviews and media production routines. With respect to politics, journalists can therefore be expected to have an attention bias towards decision-makers who are directly elected or who are under the control of elected politicians who bear the responsibility for their acts. Elections are institutionalised moments of power struggle and of public attention. Individuals standing for election are therefore of higher news value to journalists compared with actors who are not elected or who operate outside the democratic chain of delegation. As a consequence elected actors are likely to receive more media attention than non-elected actors, independently from their actual importance in policy-making processes.

Moreover, media logic can also be expected to influence the tone in which news is reported. Journalists and editors assume 'good news is no news' and tend to report on problems rather than on solutions, on conflict rather than cooperation, and on scandals and failure rather than on success and performance (Lengauer et al, 2012). Media bias can mean that media actors 'exaggerate their control functions and focus excessively on the negative aspects of politics' (Mazzoleni and Schulz, 1999, 252). The ways in which media logic plays out differs across types of media outlets, mainly depending on their sensitivity to commercial success. The more news organisations are financially dependent on large audience figures, the stronger the media logic will bias the content of the news they report as they seek to maximise audience shares. This is the reason for the 'tabloidisation of news' (Esser, 1999) observed as a consequence of commercialisation.

In sum, we can hypothesise that media reporting about metropolitan policy-making will be biased in specific ways. Assuming an attention bias of the media towards 'newsworthy' elected actors, we would expect that policy actors operating outside the democratic chain of delegation will be less often the subject of media coverage on metropolitan policy-making, even if they play crucial roles in governance networks. In addition, we can expect that negativism will prevail in media coverage on metropolitan policy-making, that is, that actors are more often blamed for failures than praised for success. This is particularly likely with media outlets that are under commercial pressure, that is, large audience media such as tabloid newspapers. The media bias hypothesis therefore suggests a more tainted picture of democratic accountability of network governance in metropolitan policy-making. Not only does it mean that, due to media bias, media reports on metropolitan policy-making will be far from an accurate portrait of the actors involved, or of their responsibilities and merits. It also links the bias in this picture to the formal institutional arrangements, and notably the democratic anchorage of policy actors. Media attention bias towards elected actors will make non-elected policy actors even less visible, and reduce the public's ability to hold them accountable for their acts. If there is media bias, the media cannot be expected to compensate the institutional democratic deficits of governance networks.

## Media system effects

The ways in which the media report on politics varies across national contexts, however. In their seminal comparative study Hallin and Mancini (2004) argue that national media systems can be classified into three broad types. One of the core differences between the types relates to 'political parallelism', that is, the extent to which the media are integrated into party politics. In the so-called Polarised Pluralist Model, found in Mediterranean countries, the media are closely tied to factional politics and are often used by parties to communicate and debate their positions. The so-called Democratic-Corporatist Model is found in North and Central European countries, and is characterised by professional journalism rooted not so much in political parties, but rather in various segments of the civil society. The Liberal Model, which is found in the USA as well as in Great Britain, has the strongest tradition of non-partisan, professional journalism portending an ethos of political objectivity. An additional distinction between the three models relates to the degree of commercialisation, which is particularly high in the Liberal Model – especially in the print media sector.

The distinction between the three types of media systems is important with respect to the media bias hypothesis that we have formulated, as different media systems can be expected to foster different kinds of media bias. Due to high political parallelism, we can expect the media in Polarised Pluralist systems to portend a strong attention bias towards elected actors who, in most cases, pertain more clearly to party elites than non-elected actors. And due to stronger commercial pressures, we can expect the media in Liberal systems to be particularly biased by media logic, resulting most notably in stronger negativism in the coverage of policy-making processes.

### Summary of hypotheses

Two rivalling hypotheses have thus been formulated. The first, functionalist hypothesis argues that media reports on governance networks will make policy actors visible to the public, and report about their responsibility according to these actors' effective involvement in policy-making, and independently of the institutional status of these actors. The second hypothesis assumes that media logic leads to biases in the content of media reports on governance networks, resulting in an attention bias towards elected (rather than non-elected) actors, as well as in negativism in news reports on these actors. Additionally, we have qualified the media bias hypothesis in two ways. On the one hand, we expect media bias to be stronger in media outlets that are under high commercial pressure. On the other hand, we expect the media system context to play a role, in the sense that we expect a stronger attention bias towards elected actors in Polarised Pluralist media systems, and negativism to be stronger in Liberal systems.

## Research design and data

The aim of the analysis presented in this chapter is to measure variations in media reporting on metropolitan policy-making, and explore to what extent these variations are related to differences in the institutional 'democratic anchorage' (Sørensen and Torfing, 2005) of governance networks. The core question here is whether media reports on policy actors differ depending on these actors' location inside or outside the democratic chain of delegation, that is, whether or not a policy actor can ultimately be held accountable by the citizens in elections. More precisely, we distinguish between three different types of actors: elected actors, non-elected actors as well as an intermediary category of mixed actors. The term 'elected' is understood rather broadly: the category of 'elected actors' includes actors who are either directly elected by voters or accountable to an elected actor and therefore part of the democratic chain of delegation. Non-elected actors are those who are appointed to their position by other mechanisms than democratic election, and who are not accountable to any elected actor. The mixed category represents collective actors (for example, organisations or firms), in which both elected and non-elected actors exercise some form of control. Actors that do not fit any of these three categories (for example, parties, experts, citizens) are subsumed under the residual category of 'others'.

*Case selection: public transport and economic promotion policies in eight European metropolitan areas*

Two fields of metropolitan policy-making were selected for the empirical analysis: public transport and economy promotion. Both are paramount to the development of metropolitan areas and can be seen as exemplary fields for metropolitan policy-making more generally (see Brenner, 2003). Public transport is a key infrastructure for urban regional development, as it secures territorial connectivity and accessibility. Activities in economic promotion are equally important to metropolitan development, as their goal is to attract new businesses to a metropolitan area, and/or strengthening existing economic clusters.

The empirical investigation was conducted in eight large metropolitan areas in western Europe (Bern, Zurich, Berlin, Stuttgart, Paris, Lyon, London and Birmingham), selected with the objective to maximise variance on the main two independent variables of interest (Table 8.2).

First, this is the mix between elected and non-elected actors involved in metropolitan policy-making. As the precise nature of this mix is difficult to establish ex ante, the more general institutional set-up of metropolitan governance arrangements was used as a proxy. At present, metropolitan areas across the world have followed mainly two distinct institutional models: metropolitan government or new regionalism (see Kübler and Pagano, 2012). The metropolitan government model focuses on hierarchical decision-making, centralised planning and public bureaucracies: elected actors can be expected to play a crucial role here. The new regionalist model emphasises flexible coordination based on governance networks: non-elected actors can be expected to be more important in these settings. The eight metropolitan areas under scrutiny therefore represent these two main institutional models (see Heinelt and Kübler, 2005; Lefèvre, 2009). While new regionalism prevails in Bern, Berlin, Paris and Birmingham, consolidated metropolitan governments operate in Stuttgart (Verband Region Stuttgart), Lyon (Grandlyon), London (Greater London Authority) and Zurich (the canton).[2]

Second, the eight metropolitan areas under scrutiny were drawn from national contexts representing the three different media system types identified by Hallin and Mancini (2004): the United Kingdom (Liberal media system), France (Polarised Pluralist media system), as well as Germany and Switzerland (Democratic Corporatist media system).

### Variables, method and data

The empirical study entailed the investigation of three variables: the involvement of elected, non-elected and mixed actors in decision-making processes, the visibility of these actors in media reports, the attribution of responsibility to these actors as well as the tonality of these attributions of responsibility. The first variable was investigated via case study evidence, the remaining two draw on standardised media content data.

### Involvement of actors in decision-making processes

In order to identify the mix of actors involved in metropolitan policy-making, we examined strategically significant decision-making processes in the two policy fields in each metropolitan area. In the field of public transport, we focused on the formulation of the most recent (in the year 2010) metropolitan transport strategies. In the field of economic promotion, we investigated the setting up of economic promotion agencies operational in the year 2010. Qualitative documentary evidence on these decision-making processes drawn from publications, newspapers and websites was standardised using the Actor Process Event Scheme (APES) software tool (Widmer et al, 2008). The APES tool systematises information on decision-events and the actors involved in these on a time scale extending over the whole decision-making process. On this basis, the number of actor participations in decision events can be computed, and then further analysed to determine the involvement of different types of actors for the decision-making processes under scrutiny. Overall, the 16 decision-making processes that were investigated (one for each policy field in the eight metropolitan areas) yielded a total number of 611 actor participations in decision events.[3]

### Standardised media content analysis

Our analysis of media reporting uses content data from locally relevant newspapers. For each metropolitan area, three newspapers with high circulation figures, as well as a head office located in the metropolitan area were selected. Among those, two quality newspapers were selected, as well as one large audience newspaper, ideally a tabloid – the exception is Lyon, where only one locally relevant newspaper was found (see Table 8.2 ).[4] The distinction between quality and large audience newspapers is important as quality newspapers are less exposed to commercial pressure than are tabloids, in which we expect a stronger media bias as they 'produce all news and information with an eye towards its "saleability"' (Esser, 1999, 292).

For the collection of newspaper content data we followed the research strategy and coding scheme developed by Gerhards et al (2007). In a first step, the digital archives of the selected newspapers were used to identify articles reporting on the fields of metropolitan policy-making (that is, public transport and economic promotion) in the year 2010. The large sample of articles thus identified was then reduced via stratified randomisation to 200 articles for each metropolitan area (100 per policy field). The content of these 1,600 articles was coded in their original languages (German, French and English) by a team of five student assistants, according to a standard coding procedure. Tests of inter–coder reliability yielded results comparable to other studies working with similar coding schemes.[5]

Visibility of an actor in media reports is measured on the basis of his or her mentions in the media articles (on the whole, 9,062 different actors were mentioned at least once in the whole sample of articles). Attributions of responsibility to actors, were captured on the basis of statements in which someone (the attribution addressee) was made responsible by someone (the attribution sender) for a given policy decision or outcome (the attribution subject) in a positive or negative assessment (the attribution type) (see Table 8.1). Overall, 1,224 attributions of responsibility to identifiable addressees were found, of which 688 were classified as negative and 536 as positive.

The subsequent analysis is based on contingency tables and bivariate statistics. Unless otherwise stated, the threshold for statistical significance is defined at p <0.05. Table 8.2 presents an overview of cases and data.

**Table 8.1: Public attributions of responsibility: coding examples**

| Text example attribution subject | Attribution sender | Attribution addressee | Type of attribution |
|---|---|---|---|
| 'The Mayor's policy successfully contributed to the quality of local transport in our city.' | Journalist | Mayor | Positive attribution of responsibility |
| 'The Mayor accused the Parliament of undermining his efforts to promote the local transport of the city by holding back money.' | Mayor | Parliament | Negative attribution of responsibility |

**Table 8.2: Summary of cases and data**

| | Switzerland | | Germany | | United Kingdom | | France | |
|---|---|---|---|---|---|---|---|---|
| | Bern | Zürich | Berlin | Stutt-gart | Birming-ham | London | Paris | Lyon |
| Metropolitan area | Bern | Zürich | Berlin | Stutt-gart | Birming-ham | London | Paris | Lyon |
| Institutional setting* | NR | MG | NR | MG | NR | MG | NR | MG |
| Media System** | DC | DC | DC | DC | LIB | LIB | PP | PP |
| Actors in decision-events | 64 | 36 | 36 | 126 | 114 | 130 | 59 | 46 |
| Newspapers *** | Bund BZ 20m BE | TA ZSZ 20m ZH | BMp BerlZ MAZ | StZ StN NürZ | BEM BP SN | Guard Indep LES | Paris Figaro Croix | Progrès |
| News Chapters | 200 | 200 | 200 | 200 | 200 | 200 | 200 | 200 |
| Actors mentioned in news articles | 1376 | 1014 | 1085 | 1546 | 838 | 1222 | 1186 | 804 |
| Attributions of responsibility in news articles | 121 | 99 | 151 | 167 | 155 | 225 | 233 | 73 |

* Governance Type: NR = New Regionalism, MG = Metropolitan Government
** National Media System: DC = Democratic Corporatist, LIB = Liberal, PP = Polarized-Pluralist
*** Newspapers: Bund = 'Der Bund'; BZ = 'Berner Zeitung'; 20m BE/ZH = '20Minuten Bern / Zürich'; TA = 'Tages-Anzeiger'; ZSZ = 'Zürichsee Zeitung'; BMp =' Berliner Morgenpost'; BerlZ ='Berliner Zeitung'; MAZ = 'Märkische Allgemeine Zeitung'; BEM = 'Birmingham Evening Mail'; BP = ' Birmingham Post'; SN = 'Solihull News'; Guard = 'The Guardian'; Indep =' The Independent'; LES = 'London Evening Standard'; Paris = 'Le Parisien'; Figaro = 'Le Figaro'; Croix = 'La Croix'; Progrès = 'Le Progrès'.

## Empirical findings

### Involvement, visibility and accountability of elected and non-elected actors: overall results

In spite of the differences in the institutional set-up, elected actors prevail in all eight metropolitan areas (Table 8.3). They are the dominant actors in decision-making processes, they are the actors whom the media make most publicly visible, and they are the ones to whom most attributions of responsibility are addressed. Nevertheless, non-elected actors are clearly present in all three domains; roughly a quarter of the actors involved in policy-decisions, visible in media reports, and adressees of public attributions of responsibility are non-elected actors. This seems largely commensurate with the functionalist hypothesis: media reports seem to provide quite an accurate picture about the policy actors and their responsibilities in metropolitan policy-making.

**Table 8.3: Frequencies of actor types involved in policy-decisions, mentioned in media reports, and as addressees of responsibility attributions (all eight metropolitan areas)**

| Actor types | Involvement (in decision-making) | Visibility (actor mentions in media reports) | Responsibility (Addressees of responsibility attributions) |
|---|---|---|---|
| Other | 50 (8.2%) | 1260 (13.9%) | 90 (7.4%) |
| Non-elected* | 151 (24.7%) | 2403 (26.5%) | 249 (20.3%) |
| Mixed | 47 (7.7%) | 592 (6.5%) | 131 (10.7%) |
| Elected** | 363 (59.4%) | 4807 (53.0%) | 754 (61.6%) |
| N = | 611 (100%) | 9062 (100%) | 1224 (100%) |

Chi-square test for homogeneity of proportions (overall): $X^2 = 111.04$, $p < 0.001$
* Chi-square test for goodness of fit (non-elected actors): $X^2 = 16.24$, $p < 0.001$
** Chi-square test for goodness of fit (elected actors): $X^2 = 17.55$, $p < 0.001$

We also see, however, significant differences between the distributions of the types of actors across the three domains. Elected actors are more present in decision-making, and they are more often addressees of public attributions of accountability than they are made visible in media reports. The opposite is true for non-elected actors. While their presence in decision-making is comparable to their visibility in media reports, they are less often addressees of responsibility attributions. This suggests that media reporting on metropolitan policies, although it does make non-elected actors and their roles in decision-making publicly visible, focuses on elected actors when it comes to qualifying the role of different policy actors, that is, praise for what went well or blame for what went wrong. Non-elected actors are not generally less exposed to media attention than elected actors, compared to their involvement in decision-making processes. But non-elected actors are less often addressees of attributions of responsibility, unlike elected actors who appear as the media's preferred targets when it comes to assess the ways in which policy issues are dealt with.

Looking at the tone of media reports, Table 8.4 shows that negative attributions of responsibility are more frequent (56.2 per cent) than positive attributions of responsibility (43.8 per cent). Actors to whom responsibility is attributed in media reports are more often blamed for policy failures than praised for policy success. Interestingly, the ratio between blame and praise is reversed between non-elected actors and elected actors. Non-elected actors receive more praise than blame, while elected actors receive more blame than praise.

**Table 8.4: Positive and negative public attributions of responsibility according to types of addressee**

| Adressee actor types | 'Praise' (positive attr. of resp.) | 'Blame' (negative attr. of resp.) | Total |
|---|---|---|---|
| Other | 40 (44.4%) | 50 (55.6%) | 90 (100%) |
| Non-elected* | 144 (57.8%) | 105 (42.2%) | 249 (100%) |
| Mixed | 49 (37.4%) | 82 (62.6%) | 131 (100%) |
| Elected** | 303 (40.2%) | 451 (59.8%) | 754 (100%) |
| N = | 536 (43.8%) | 688 (56.2%) | 1224 (100%) |

Chi-square test for homogeneity of proportions (overall): $X^2 = 26.110$, $p < 0.001$
* Chi-square test for goodness of fit (non-elected actors): $X^2 = 19.82$, $p < 0.001$
** Chi-square test for goodness of fit (elected actors): $X^2 = 3.98$, $p < 0.001$

This indicates a media bias in reporting about elected and non-elected actors. Indeed, elected actors appear twice as often as non-elected actors in newspaper articles, but are made responsible three times as often. Moreover, elected actors are blamed more often than are non-elected or mixed actors. However, in the absence of detailed case study evidence on the exact role of the various actors in decision-making processes, we cannot be sure that this is a result of media bias in reporting. It could well be that, although non-elected actors are present in decision-making processes, elected actors were decisive and that the media thus reported adequately on their role and distributed blame and praise in an accurate way. But if we differentiate according to the type of newspaper (quality versus large audience newspapers) we see that both the responsibilisation of elected actors and the predominantly negative tone of media reports on them is a result of media logic related to commercial pressure in the media market. Indeed, there is a difference in both the visibility/responsibility ratio and the blame/praise ratio of elected actors across the two types of newspapers: these ratios are more unbalanced in large audience newspapers than in quality newspapers (Table 8.5).

**Table 8.5: Visibility/responsibility and praise/blame ratios of addressees according to types of newspaper**

| | Large audience newspapers | | Quality newspapers | |
|---|---|---|---|---|
| Addressee actor types | Visibility/ responsibility ratio | Praise/blame ratio | Visibility/ responsibility ratio | Praise/ blame ratio |
| Other | 15:6 | 58:42 | 14:8 | 41:59 |
| Non-elected | 28:17 | 52:48 | 6:7 | 60:40 |
| Mixed | 7:14 | 37:63 | 26:22 | 38:62 |
| Elected | 50:63 | 37:63 | 54:61 | 41:59 |

## Effects of national media systems

Comparing the importance of the different types of actors in each of the three domains across the different media systems, Table 8.6 confirms the general pattern previously identified. In all three media systems, elected actors are the dominant actors in decision-making, are those that the media make most visible in their reports, and are those that are most frequently attributed responsibility for policy failure or success. Similarly, in all media systems, non-elected and mixed actors are made visible in media reports to an extent that is commensurate with their involvement in decision-making processes. Finally, in all three media systems, the level of responsibility attributions to elected actors is higher than their involvement in decision-making or their visibility in media reports would suggest. The results of the Chi-square test for homogeneity of proportions within each media system show that these findings are statistically significant.

There are nevertheless two important variations of this general pattern between the three media systems. First, media visibility of the four actor types is significantly different across the three media systems. More precisely, the media visibility of non-elected and mixed actors is more pronounced in the democratic-corporatist and the liberal media systems, than in the polarised-pluralised media system, where the media focus on elected actors is much stronger. The media in the polarised-pluralist

**Table 8.6: Frequencies of actor types involved in policy decisions, mentioned in media reports, and as addresses of responsibility attributions, according to media systems**

| | Democratic corporatist | | | Polarised pluralist | | | Liberal | | |
|---|---|---|---|---|---|---|---|---|---|
| Actor types | Involvement | Visibility | Responsibility | Involvement | Visibility | Responsibility | Involvement | Visibility | Responsibility |
| Other | 23 (8.8%) | 691 (13.8%) | 58 (10.8%) | 5 (4.8%) | 175 (8.8%) | 9 (2.9%) | 22 (9.0%) | 394 (19.1%) | 23 (6.1%) |
| Non-elected | 45 (17.2%) | 1219 (24.3%) | 101 (18.8%) | 30 (28.6%) | 536 (26.9%) | 50 (16.3%) | 76 (31.1%) | 648 (31.5%) | 98 (25.8%) |
| Mixed | 15 (5.7%) | 424 (8.5%) | 86 (16.0%) | 13 (12.4%) | 79 (4.0%) | 36 (11.8%) | 19 (7.8%) | 89 (4.3%) | 9 (2.4%) |
| Elected | 179 (68.3%) | 2678 (53.4%) | 293 (54.5%) | 57 (54.3%) | 1200 (60.3%) | 211 (69.0%) | 127 (52.0%) | 929 (45.1%) | 250 (65.8%) |
| N = | 262 (100%) | 5012 (100%) | 538 (100%) | 105 (100%) | 1990 (100%) | 306 (100%) | 244 (100%) | 2060 (100%) | 380 (100%) |

Chi-square test for homogeneity of proportions (within democratic corporatist media system): $X^2 = 109.275$, p <0.001
Chi-square test for homogeneity of proportions (within polarised pluralist media system): $X^2 = 126.270$, p <0.001
Chi-square test for homogeneity of proportions (within liberal media system): $X^2 = 198.716$, p <0.001
Chi-square test of independence (involvement across media systems): $X^2 = 45.560$, p <0.001
Chi-square test of independence (visibility across media systems): $X^2 = 214.377$, p <0.001
Chi-square test of independence (responsibility across media systems): $X^2 = 73.406$, p <0.001

media system therefore do have a stronger attention bias towards elected actors, compared to their counterparts in the other two media systems. Second, the attributions of responsibility to the different types of actors differ significantly across the three media systems. Indeed, the tendency of media reports to attribute responsibility predominantly to elected actors is clearly less pronounced in the democratic-corporatist media system, than in the other two. It is particularly strong in the liberal media system, where elected actors are much more frequently attributed responsibility for metropolitan policies compared with their involvement in decision-making or with their visibility in media reports.

Looking at the tone of responsibility attributions, the general pattern is confirmed for each of the three media systems: negative attributions of responsibility are more frequent than positive ones, and the praise vs blame ratio is particularly unfavourable for elected actors. However, this pattern varies significantly between the three media systems ($X^2 = 26.110$, $p = 0.000$). This is nicely shown in Figure 8.1, giving a sense of 'over-blaming' of elected actors, that is, their likeliness to be more often blamed for policy failures than other actors.[6] The values in the figure represent the difference between the blame/praise ratio of each actor category from the overall blame/praise ratio found in the cases under scrutiny. A positive value means that an actor is more often blamed than the mean, a negative value means that he/she is more often praised than the mean. While elected actors are generally over-blamed and non-elected and mixed actors are somewhat over-praised, over-blaming of elected actor is less pronounced in the polarised-pluralist media system, and over-praising of non-elected and mixed actors is less pronounced in the liberal media system.

**Figure 8.1: Blaming of policy actors in media reports compared to the mean blame ratio, according to types of media system (across the 16 cases)**

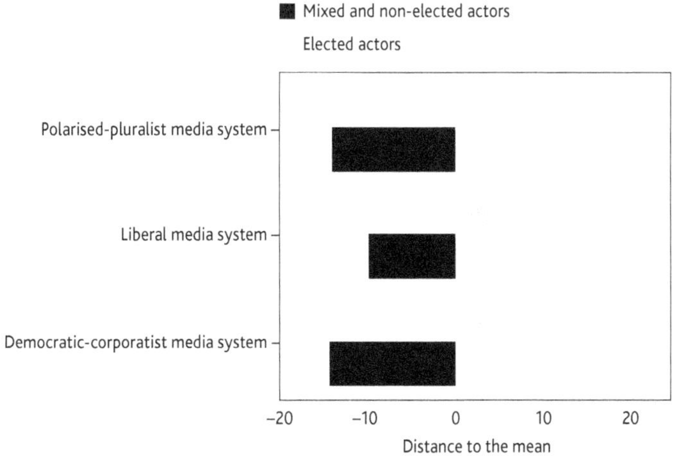

## Conclusion

The goal of this chapter was to explore the role of the media in relation to the democratic implications of governance networks. In order to do this, two main rivalling hypotheses – a functionalist and a media-bias hypothesis – were formulated and tested on the basis of empirical data on the involvement of different types of policy actors in decision-making processes in eight European metropolitan areas, their visibility in media reports, as well as the responsibility attributed to them in these reports for policy success or failure.

The overall findings show that the neither of the two hypotheses can be rejected in globo. The functionalist hypothesis postulates that, in democracies, the media fulfil a basic information function which will lead to a public coverage of policy actors and an assessment of their responsibility that adequately mirrors their effective role in policy-making, independently from their anchorage in institutional mechanisms of democratic control. The findings do not contradict this hypothesis. Indeed, non-elected actors and mixed actors, as well as elected actors are made publicly visible in the media reports in a way that is commensurate with their effective involvement in policy-making. It appears that the media can keep up with the complexity of network governance to a remarkable extent. The media therefore seem to play a somewhat compensating role with respect to institutional deficits of democratic control in network governance. However, while no media bias towards a particular type of policy-actor could be detected with respect to their visibilisation in media report, a bias was found with respect to the attribution of responsibility to different types of policy actors. Unlike non-elected actors or mixed actors, elected actors are clearly in the focus of the media when it comes to attributing responsibility for policy success or failure. We have shown that this is linked to the degree of commercialisation of news outlets, therefore suggesting that a bias due to media logic is at work here. Elected actors are clearly 'over-responsiblised' in the media, compared to their real involvement in decision-making processes, or compared to their visibility in media reports. And elected actors are also 'over-blamed': responsibility for policy failures or problems is more often attributed to them than to other types of actors. It seems that it is mainly in combination with blame for policy failure that elected actors appear to be more newsworthy to the media than non-elected or mixed actors. In this respect, the media do not play a compensating role with respect to institutional democratic deficits of network governance. Very much to the contrary: they can be seen to reinforce these deficits.

This general pattern, however, was found to vary across different media systems. Over-responsibilisation of elected actors is particularly pronounced in the polarised pluralist media system, while over-blaming is particularly noticeable in the liberal media system. In media outlets drawn from countries with a democratic-corporatist media system, both over-responsibilisation and over-blaming is less manifest. This suggests that the aptitude of the media to compensate institutional democratic deficits of network governance differs across media systems. In polarised-pluralist media systems, journalists and media organisations seem to have less experience in understanding or scrutinising the role of hybrid or private policy actors in metropolitan policy-making, hence their focus on elected actors as the main target for accountability claims. In the democratic-corporatist systems, the media seem to have a better understanding of the variety of actors involved in policy-making, scrutinise their role and also assign accountability to them. Finally, in the liberal system, the traditional watchdog journalism, combined with commercial pressure on media outlets, leads to an exacerbated negativism.

Our findings have implications for the debate on the democratic quality of governance networks more generally. Indeed, we have shown the relevance of the communicational dimension of democratic legitimacy in this debate. But the role of the media in democratic accountability of network governance seems to be a sword that cuts both ways. On the one hand, the media do contribute to making policy actors visible to the public, independently from their anchorage in democratic institutions. On the other hand, a media logic is at work when it comes to assessing and qualifying the responsibility of these policy actors, biasing the reports in a way that makes electorally controlled actors the primary target of accountability and blame – particularly so in polarised-pluralist and liberal media systems. This could exacerbate the challenges that governance networks pose for the legitimacy of the democratic political system more generally. Whether this is the case, however, depends on the role that media reporting on actors of policy-making plays for assessment by the citizens and for their electoral decisions. Hence, the results of the research reported in this chapter suggests that, in order to deepen our understanding of democratic implications of network governance, the next logical step consists in exploring the effect that exposure to different media reports on network-based policy-making has on citizens' assessment.

## Notes

[1] This chapter is based on research conducted in the project 'Cleavages, governance and the media in European metropolitan areas', funded by NCCR 'Challenges to Democracy in the 21st Century' of the Swiss National Science

Foundations. The authors acknowledge research assistance by Christopher Goodman, Christian Schalch, Su Yun Woo, Nina Astfalck and Nadja Hauser in the coding of media content data, as well as by Sarah Ott for the analysis of decisiön-making processes. Special thanks go to Jon Pierre, Monika Djerf Pierre, Thomas Schillemans, as well as to the two anonymous reviewers for their comments and constructive criticism on earlier drafts.

[2] In the case of Zurich, the spatial extension of the metropolitan area coincides more or less with the boundaries of the canton, that is, the second tier subnational authority, which has thereby become a functional equivalent to a metropolitan policy fields studied here (Jouve, 2003; Kübler, 2004).

[3] A detailed description of the method as well as the results of a more fine-grained analysis on the actors involved in these decision-making processes can be found in Christmann (2014).

[4] In the absence of existing typologies for regional newspapers, our distinction draws mainly on circulation figures. 'Large audience newspapers' are those with the highest circulation figures in their metropolitan area. Clear tabloids could thus be identified and were retained for the analysis: *20 Minuten (Bern and Zurich)*, *Le Parisien*, the *London Evening Standard*, *Solihull News*. In Berlin and Stuttgart, the archives of the regional tabloids *Berliner Tageszeitung (BZ)* and *Bild Stuttgart* were not accessible for digital analysis. Hence, the next largest regional newspapers *Berliner Zeitung* (for Berlin) and *Nürtinger Zeitung* (for Stuttgart) were chosen for the category 'large audience' newspapers.

[5] Full details of the method used for the media content analysis (in particular: on the selection of articles, coding procedures and reliability checks) are published in Hasler (2014).

[6] For the sake of graphic representation, the two actor categories of mixed as well as non-elected actors were collapsed, and the categories of 'other actors' was omitted.

## References


Altheide, DL, Snow, RP, 1979, *Media logic*, Beverly Hills, CA: Sage

Bergman, T, Müller, WC, Strom, K, 2000, Introduction: Parliamentary democracy and the chain of delegation, *European Journal of Political Research* 37, 3, 255–60

Bovens, M, 2007, Analysing and assessing accountability: A conceptual framework, *European Law Journal* 13, 4, 447–68

Brenner, N, 2003, Standortpolitik, state rescaling and the new metropolitan governance in Western Europe, *DISP* 152, 15–25

Christmann, A, 2014, Von government zu governance? Acht europäische metropolregionen im vergleich, *Zeitschrift für Vergleichende Politikwissenschaft* 8, 141–67

Esser, F, 1999, 'Tabloidization' of news: A comparative analysis of Anglo-American and German press journalism, *Eurpean Journal of Communication* 14, 3, 291–324

Feiock, R (ed), 2004, *Metropolitan governance*, Washington, DC: Georgetown University Press

Gerhards, J, Offerhaus, A, Roose, J, 2007, Die öffentliche zuschreibung von verantwortung, *Kölner Zeitschrift für Soziologie und Sozialpsychologie* 59, 105–24

Graber, D, 2003, The media and democracy: Beyond myths and stereotypes, *Annual Review of Political Science* 6, 139–60

Gurevitch, M, Blumler, JG, 1990, Political communication systems and democratic values, in J Lichtenberg (ed) *Democracy and the mass media,* Cambridge: Cambridge University Press, 269–89

Habermas, J, 1992, *Faktizität und geltung: Diskurstheorie des rechts und des demokratischen rechststaats,* Frankfurt: Suhrkamp

Hallin, DC, Mancini, P, 2004, *Comparing media systems: Three models of media and politics,* New York: Cambridge University Press

Hasler, K, 2014, *Accountability in the metropolis,* Baden-Baden: Nomos

Heinelt, H, Kübler, D (eds), 2005, *Metropolitan governance: Capacity, democracy and the dynamics of place,* London: Routledge

Jouve, B, 2003, Les formes du gouvernement urbain en Europe, *DISP* 39, 152, 37–42

Klijn, E-H, 2008, Governance and governance networks in Europe: An assessment of ten years of research on the theme, *Public Management Review* 10, 4, 505–25

Koch, P, 2011, *Governancewandel und demokratie in schweizer agglomerationen,* Baden-Baden: Nomos

Kübler, D, 2003, 'Metropolitan governance' oder: Die unendliche geschichte der institutionenbildung in stadtregionen, *Informationen zur Raumentwicklung* 9, 535–41

Kübler, D, 2004, Métropolisation à la zurichoise: Tertiarisation, fragmentation et démocratie directe, in B Jouve, C Lefèvre (eds) *Horizons métropolitains,* Lausanne: Presses polytechniques et universitaires romandes

Kübler, D, Pagano, MA, 2012, Urban politics as multi-level analysis, in K Mossberger, SE Clarke, P John (eds) *The Oxford Handbook of Urban Politics,* Oxford: Oxford University Press, 114–32

Kübler, D, Schwab, B, 2007, New regionalism in five Swiss metropolitan areas: An assessment of inclusiveness, deliberation and democratic accountability, *European Journal of Political Research* 46, 4, 473–502

Lefèvre, C, 1998, Metropolitan government and governance in western countries: A critical review, *International Journal of Urban and Regional Research* 22, 1, 9–25

Lefèvre, C, 2009, *Gouverner les métropoles*, Paris: LGDJ – lextenso éditions

Lefèvre, C, Weir, M, 2012, Building metropolitan institutions, in K Mossberger, SE Clarke, P John (eds) The Oxford handbook of urban politics, pp 624–41, Oxford: Oxford University Press

Lengauer, G, Esser, F, Berganza, R, 2012, Negativity in political news: An assessment of inclusiveness, deliberation and democratic accountability, *Journalism* 13, 2, 179–202

Mazzoleni, G, Schulz, W, 1999, 'Mediatization' of politics: A challenge for democracy?, *Political Communication* 16, 3, 247–61

Papadopoulos, Y, 2003, Cooperative forms of governance: Problems of democratic accountability in complex environments, *European Journal of Political Research* 42, 4, 473–501

Pierre, J (ed), 2000, Debating governance: Authority, steering and democracy, Oxford: Oxford University Press

Plüss, L, 2015, Municipal councillors in metropolitan governance: Assessing the democratic deficit of new regionalism in Switzerland, *European Urban and Regional Studies,* 22, 3, 261-284.

Rhodes, RAW, 1996, The new governance: Governing without government, *Political Studies* 44, 4, 652–67

Savitch, H, Vogel, RK, 2000, Paths to new regionalism, *State and Local Government Review* 32, 3, 158–68

Savitch, H, Vogel, RK, 2009, Regionalism and urban politics, in JS Davies, DL Imbroscio (eds) *Theories of urban politics* (2nd edn), pp 106–24, London: Sage

Sørensen, E, 2005, The democratic problems and potentials of network governance, *European Political Science* 4, 3, 348–57

Sørensen, E, Torfing, J, 2005, The democratic anchorage of governance networks, *Scandinavian Political Studies* 28, 3, 195–218

Torfing, J, 2005, Governance network theory: Towards a second generation, *European Political Science* 4, 3, 305–15

Van Den Berg, L, Van Klink, A, Van Der Meer, J (eds), 1993, *Governing metropolitan regions*, Avebury: Aldershot

Widmer, T, Hirschi, C, Serdült, U, Vögeli, C, 2008, Analysis with APES, the Actor Process Event Scheme, in MM Bergmann (ed) A*dvances in mixed-methods research: Theories and applications*, pp 150–71, London: Sage

Zeigler, DJ, Brunn, SD, 1980, Geopolitical fragmentation and the pattern of growth and need, in SD Brunn, JO Wheeler (eds) *The American metropolitan system: Present and future*, pp 77–92, New York: John Wiley

Zimmermann, K, 2014, Democratic metropolitan governance: Experiences in five German metropolitan regions, *Urban Research and Practice* 7, 182–99

191

# Index

References to figures and tables are in *italics*

CPSIA information can be obtained
at www.ICGtesting.com
Printed in the USA
BVHW040208080219
539770BV00006B/44/P